A Reference Grammar of Egyptian Arabic

Georgetown University Classics in Arabic Language and Linguistics

Karin C. Ryding and Margaret Nydell, series editors

This series makes available seminal publications in Arabic language and linguistics that have gone out of print. Chosen for their quality of research and scholarship, these books will serve the growing national and international need for reference works on Arabic language and culture, as well as provide access to quality textbooks and audiovisual resources for teaching Arabic language in its written and spoken forms.

The Acquisition of Egyptian Arabic as a Native Language
Margaret K. (Omar) Nydell

Arabic Language Handbook
Mary Catherine Bateson

The Arabic Language Today
A. F. L. Beeston

The Arabic Linguistic Tradition
Georges Bohas, Jean-Patrick Guillaume, and Djamel Kouloughli

A Basic Course in Iraqi Arabic with MP3 Audio Files
Wallace M. Erwin

A Basic Course in Moroccan Arabic with MP3 Files
Richard S. Harrell with Mohammed Abu-Talib and William S. Carroll

A Dictionary of Iraqi Arabic: English-Arabic, Arabic-English
English-Arabic edited by B. E. Clarity, Karl Stowasser, Ronald G. Wolfe
Arabic-English edited by D. R. Woodhead and Wayne Beene

A Dictionary of Moroccan Arabic: Moroccan-English/English-Moroccan
Richard S. Harrell and Harvey Sobelman, Editors

A Dictionary of Syrian Arabic: English-Arabic
Karl Stowasser and Moukhtar Ani, Editors

Eastern Arabic with MP3 Files
Frank A. Rice and Majed F. Sa'id

Formal Spoken Arabic Basic Course with MP3 Files, Second Edition
Karin C. Ryding and David J. Mehall

Formal Spoken Arabic FAST Course with MP3 Files
Karin C. Ryding and Abdelnour Zaiback

Modern Arabic: Structures, Functions, and Varieties, Revised Edition
Clive Holes

The Modern Arabic Literary Language: Lexical and Stylistic Developments
Jaroslav Stetkevych

A Reference Grammar of Egyptian Arabic
Ernest T. Abdel-Massih, Zaki N. Abdel-Malek, and El-Said M. Badawi

A Reference Grammar of Syrian Arabic with Audio CD
Mark W. Cowell

A Short Reference Grammar of Iraqi Arabic
Wallace M. Erwin

A Short Reference Grammar of Moroccan Arabic with Audio CD
Richard S. Harrell

A Reference Grammar of Egyptian Arabic

Ernest T. Abdel-Massih

Zaki N. Abdel-Malek

El-Said M. Badawi

with Ernest N. McCarus

Georgetown University Press
Washington, DC

Georgetown University Press, Washington, D.C. www.press.georgetown.edu

Library of Congress Cataloging-in-Publication Data

Abdel-Massih, Ernest T.
A reference grammar of Egyptian Arabic / Ernest T. Abdel-Massih, Zaki N. Abdel-Malek, El-Said M. Badawi.
p. cm.—(Georgetown University classics in Arabic language and linguistics)
Includes bibliographical references and index.
ISBN 978-1-58901-260-8 (pbk. : alk. paper)
1. Arabic language—Dialects—Egypt—Grammar. I. Abdel-Malek, Zaki N. II. Badawi, El-Said M. III. Title.
PJ6777.A234 2009
492'.770962—dc22 2008046574

∞ This book is printed on acid-free paper meeting the requirements of the American National Standard for Permanence in Paper for Printed Library Materials.

15 14 13 12 11 10 09 08 9 8 7 6 5 4 3 2

First printing

Printed in the United States of America

This work was developed under a grant from the U.S. Office of Education, Department of Health, Education and Welfare. However, the content does not necessarily reflect the position or policy of that agency, and no official endorsement of these materials should be inferred.

الإهداء

إلى مصر

مهد الحضارة والمدنيّة

A Study Dedicated to Egypt,

the Cradle of Civilization

Contents

Foreword from the Original Edition

The preparation of this volume was facilitated by the University of Michigan Center for Near Eastern and North African Studies as part of its general program of research and training on the languages and cultures of the area. We are indebted to the United States Office of Education for grants to the Center that have made this work possible.

W. D. Schorger
Director

Foreword to the Georgetown Classics Edition

The addition of *A Reference Grammar of Egyptian Arabic* by Abdel-Massih, Abdel-Malek, and Badawi to the Georgetown Classics in Arabic Language and Linguistics series is a significant contribution to the literature on spoken Arabic. Since well before Egyptian independence, spoken Egyptian Arabic has played a major role in the Arab world. The Egyptian educational system, the media, and the entertainment industries, as well as the individual in literature, the arts, and areas of intellectual life—all of these combined with economic and political developments to disseminate knowledge of spoken Egyptian Arabic far beyond the country's geographical boundaries. Egypt has also long been an international center for students and scholars of Arabic and Middle Eastern studies. The tragedies of September 11, 2001 have only added to the interest in spoken Egyptian Arabic in the United States and elsewhere.

One result of the importance of and interest in spoken Egyptian Arabic is an enormous body of linguistic research on this variety of Arabic. Works include textbooks, dictionaries, collections of folkloric and other texts, and book-length analyses of various aspects of spoken Egyptian Arabic, as well as monographs, scholarly articles, and reviews. To date, however, reference grammars of spoken Egyptian Arabic are surprisingly few. Woidich's *Das Kairenisch-Arabische Eine Grammatik* (2006) is, unfortunately, currently published only in German. *A Reference Grammar of Egyptian Arabic* is the single reference available in English.

At a length of over 300 pages, *A Reference Grammar of Egyptian Arabic* is deceptively slim but surprisingly comprehensive. It treats topics in dictionary order. The detailed index will save readers from paging through the work as they look for a specific grammatical feature. In keeping with the conventions of the day, *A Reference Grammar of Egyptian Arabic* transcribes spoken Egyptian Arabic in Latin script to reflect pronunciation. To anyone who is used to reading spoken Arabic in Arabic script, he or she may find this disconcerting at first, but will soon grow accustomed to Latin script.

A Reference Grammar of Egyptian Arabic was originally planned to be in a book series by Richard Slade Harrell of works on spoken Arabic. The Harrell series had planned to produce reference works and teaching materials for four varieties of spoken Arabic: Egyptian, Iraqi, Moroccan, and Syrian. Harrell was, in fact, conducting field research in Egypt in 1964 when the project was cut short by his untimely death. It is with pride that Georgetown University Press adds this important reference grammar on spoken Egyptian Arabic to the Georgetown Classics in Arabic Language and Linguistics series.

Elizabeth M. Bergman
Miami University

Introduction from the Original Edition

A Comprehensive Study of Egyptian Arabic, volumes I–IV, is designed for the Intermediate-Advanced student of Egyptian Arabic to serve as a course in the language, culture, customs and traditions of Egypt. The study presupposes knowledge of Egyptian Arabic on the elementary level. *A Comprehensive Study of Egyptian Arabic* consists of four volumes, of which the present study is volume three.

Volume One. *Conversations, Cultural Texts and Sociolinguistic Notes*, 1978 (Second Edition) aims at acquainting the student with the people of Egypt–how they live, act and react on happy and unhappy occasions, how they relate to each other in their daily lives, how they spend their leisure time, etc.–through conversations and cultural notes. It also presents glimpses of the history of Egypt and its role in the evolution of human civilization. The 50 cultural texts of volume one also shed some light on the Egyptian personality: humor, folk literature, craftsmanship, etc.

Volume Two. *Proverbs and Metaphoric Expressions*, A Preliminary Edition, 1978, includes 695 proverbs and 276 metaphoric expressions. It aims at acquainting the American student with the important roles these expressions play in everyday speech in Egyptian society.

Volume Three. The main emphasis of this volume is on grammatical and linguistic terms in a dictionary form with definitions and illustrations of all the grammatical features of Egyptian Arabic conveniently arranged in alphabetical order.

Volume Four. *Lexicon.* Part I: Egyptian Arabic-English
(34 cultural categories)
Part II: English-Egyptian Arabic
(34 cultural categories)

Includes basic, high-frequency words in such categories as Animals and Insects, Colors, Food and Kitchen Utensils, Greetings and Etiquette, etc.

We would like to express our thanks to those who have helped us in the preparation of this edition. We are indebted to the U.S. Office of Education of the Department of Health, Education and Welfare for the financial support which enabled us to complete this study; to the Center for Near Eastern and North African Studies at the University of Michigan and to its director, William D. Schorger, for all the help and support extended during the work on the study. Thanks are due to Wallace M. Erwin for giving freely of his time, for his valuable suggestions and his great interest in the study. To Amy Van Voorhis, who helped in proofreading the entire manuscript, we owe a special debt of gratitude. Her devotion, conscientiousness, constructive remarks and creativity throughout the work on the study are deeply appreciated. Thanks are extended also to Amy Van Voorhis and Nancy Adams for an excellent job in typing the English and phonetic sections of the study. Their dependability and dedication are deeply appreciated.

Ernest T. Abdel-Massih
Ann Arbor, Michigan
June 1979

Key to Transcription

Arabic Script	Transcription	
ا	aa	
ب	b	
ت	t	
ث	t s	Pronounced /t/ or /s/ in Egyptian Arabic.
ج	g	
ح	ɦ	
خ	x	
د	d	
ذ	-	
ر	r ṛ	A dot below indicates an emphatic (or pharyngealized) pronunciation.
ز	z	
س	S	
ش	Š	
ص	ṣ	
ض	ḍ	
ط	ṭ	
ظ	ẓ	
ع	ʕ	
غ	ɣ	
ف	f	
ق	ʔ q	Usually pronounced as a glottal stop or *hamza* in Egyptian Arabic.
ك	k	
ل	l ḷ	A dot below indicates an emphatic (or pharyngealized) pronunciation.
م	m	
ن	n	
ه	h	

Key to Transcription

Arabic Script	Transcription	
و	w	
	uu	
ي	Y	
	yii	
ء	ʔ	
ة	a	
	t	
	it	
پ	p	in foreign borrowings
ڤ	v	in foreign borrowings
ج	ž	in foreign borrowings
ـِ	i	‘bit’
ي	ii	‘beet’
	e	‘bet’
ـَي	ee	‘bait’
ـَ	a	Similar to ’bat’but shorter.
ا	aa	‘bat’ ‘bot’
	o	Like ‘soap’ but shorter
ـَو	oo	‘boat’
ـُ	u	‘pull’
و	uu	‘pool’

Based on Abdel-Massih, Ernest T. and A. Fathy Bahig, *A Comprehensive Study of Egyptian Arabic, Volume One: Conversations, Cultural Texts, Sociolinguistic Notes*, Ann Arbor, MI: Center for Near Eastern and North African Arabic, The University of Michigan, p. 397.

Egyption Arabic Consonants and Semi-Vowels

		Bilabial	Labiodental	Dental	Alveolar	Alveopalatal	Palatal	Velar	Back-Velar	Uvular	Pharyngeal	Glottal
Stop	Voiceless	p		t	ṭ			k		q		ʔ
	Voiced	b		d	ḍ			g				
Fricative	Voiceless		f	s	ṣ	š			x		ɦ	h
	Voiced		v	z	ẓ	ž			ɣ		ʕ	
Nasal	Voiced	m		n								
Lateral	Voiced			l	ḷ							
Flap	Voiced				r							
					ṛ							
Semi-Vowel	Voiced	w					y					

Abdel-Massih, Ernest T. and A. Fathy Bahig, *A Comprehensive Study of Egyptian Arabic, Volume One: Conversations, Cultural Texts, Sociolinguistic Notes*, Ann Arbor, MI: Center for Near Eastern and North African Arabic, The University of Michigan, p. 397.

A

REFERENCE GRAMMAR

OF

EGYPTIAN ARABIC :

GRAMMATICAL AND LINGUISTIC TERMS

- A -

ACTIVE PARTICIPLES : DEFINITENESS

If an active participle (AP) denotes a semantic extension (see "Active Participles : Meaning"), it is made definite by the addition of il-

Indefinite		Definite	
kaatib	'an author'	ilkaatib	'the author
muxrig	'a producer'	ilmuxrig	'the producer'

If it denotes the basic designation (see: Active Participles: Meaning), an active participle is made definite by placing illi or il- before it (il- and illi being interchangeable when the participle constitutes the entire modifier, and illi being the favored choice when the participle is the first word of an adjectival phrase) :

Indefinite	Definite
ṛaagil naayim 'a sleeping man'	iṛṛaagil illi naayim or iṛṛaagil innaayim 'the sleeping man'
ṛaagil miṭallaʔ miṛaatu 'a man who has divorced his wife	iṛṛaagil illi mṭallaʔ miṛaatu 'the man who has divorced his wife'

*** *** ***

ACTIVE PARTICIPLES : DERIVATION

For Measure I of triliteral verbs the active participle is of the measure FaaʕiL. For doubled verbs the variant of FaaʕiL is Faaʕiʕ; for hollow verbs, FaayiL; and for defective verbs, Faaʕi. The following are examples :

Measure	Verb		AP
FaaʕiL	daxal	'to enter'	daaxil
	ʕirif	'to find out'	ʕaarif
Faaʕiʕ	ħaṭṭ	'to put'	ħaaṭiṭ
FaayiL	naam	'to sleep'	naayim
	ɣaab	'to be absent'	ɣaayib
Faaʕi	šawa	'to roast'	šaawi
	baka	'to cry'	baaki
	giri	'to run'	gaari

For all other active verbs (i.e., verbs which co-occur with a a form designating the agent) the active participle is derived from the imperfect huwwa form by substituting mi- for the initial yi-. If the huwwa form of the verb ends in /a/, that /a/ is replaced by /i/. Examples :

huwwa form		AP
yinawwim	'he puts to sleep'	minawwim
yiħaddid	'he sets (time)'	miħaddid
yiʕayyin	'he appoints'	miʕayyin
yikaatib	'he corresponds with'	mikaatib
yiʕaayin	'he inspects'	miʕaayin
yitsallim	'he receives'	mitsallim
yitħayyin	'he takes advantage of an opportunity'	mitħayyin
yitfaahim	'he reaches an under-standing with'	mitfaahim

huwwa form		AP
yitʕaawin	'he cooperates with'	mitʕaawin
yiħtimil	'he bears'	miħtimil
yiħtaaṛ	'he becomes perplexed'	miħtaaṛ
yiħmaṛṛ	'he becomes red'	miħmiṛṛ
yistaʕmil	'he uses'	mistaʕmil
yitniʔil	'he moves(intransitive)'	mitniʔil
yistalaʔʔaf	'he catches(a ball,etc.)'	mistalaʔʔif
yidaħṛag	'he rolls(something)'	midaħṛig
yitbargil	'he becomes confused'	mitbargil
yiṭmaʔinn	'he becomes reassured'	miṭmaʔinn
yiṛabbi	'he rears'	miṛabbi
yidaawi	'he administers medical treatment'	midaawi
yitbanna	'he adopts'	mitbanni
yistaɣla	'he considers(something) expensive'	mistaɣli
yistamanna	'he longs for'	mistamanni

Under the influence of Standard Arabic, educated Egyptians sometimes substitute mu- (rather than mi-) for the initial yi- of imperfect derived verbs. When this takes place, /a/ is also inserted before the F of Measure V and Measure VI of the triliteral as well as Measure II of the quadriliteral (in Standard Arabic, Measures V and VI have /a/ before F).
Examples : yitsabbib 'to become the cause of' : mutasabbib , yitraagiʕ 'to retreat' : mutaraagiʕ , yitzabzib 'to be unstable' : mutazabzib.

As may be expected, such "classicisms" occur only when the EA participle corresponds to a Standard Arabic participle.

Verbs of Measure IV and those of Measure VII are usually borrowings from Standard Arabic; it is therefore not surprising to find that the active participle of Measure IV is usually muFʕiL (rather than miFʕiL) and that the active participle of Measure VII is usually munFaʕiL (rather than minFiʕiL). Examples : aʕdam 'to execute' : muʕdim , aʕṛab 'to express' : muʕṛib , inʕaqad 'to convene (intransitive)' : munʕaqid , insaħab 'to withdraw (intransitive)' : munasaħib.

Passive verbs (q.v.) do not usually yield the active participle. This is because the active participle is agentive (it usually means 'doer' or 'is doing'), and passive verbs belong to a construction whose agent is not specified (the grammatical subject of the passive construction designates the recipient). Thus the form itnaʔal yields an active participle if it is used with reflexive meaning but not when it is passive.

Sentence with itnaʔal	Sentence with mitniʔil
fariid itnaʔal min makaanu wʔaʕad fi makaan taani. 'Farid moved from his place and sat in another place.'	lamma rgiʕt, laʔeet fariid mitniʔil min makaanu wʔaaʕid fi makaan taani. 'When I returned I found that Farid had moved from his place and sat in another place.'
aʕṛaf inn fariid itnaʔal laakin maʕṛafš miin naʔalu. 'I know that Farid has been transferred, but I do not know who transferred him.'	Uncommon

*** *** ***

ACTIVE PARTICIPLES : GENDER OF SINGULAR

A singular active participle (whether it denotes the basic designation or a semantic extension) can be inflected for gender. The feminine singular form usually results from adding /-a/ to the corresponding masculine form :

Masculine		Feminine
kaatib	'having written, writer'	katba
naayim	'sleeping'	nayma
mitkallim	'having spoken'	mitkallima
maaši	'walking'	mašya
mistanni	'waiting'	mistanniyya

Notice that the masculine singular form undergoes certain changes upon the addition of -a ; those changes are as follows :

1. If the masculine singular form is of the shape Faaʕi , /y/ is added after /i/.

   maaši + -a ---> maašiy + -a ---> mašya (after Vowel Elision and Vowel Shortening)

2. The /i/ of the sequence -ʕiL is elided (see: Vowels : Elision at Word Boundaries).

   kaatib + -a ---> katba

3. If the masculine singular form ends in /i/ but is not of the shape Faaʕi , /yy/ is added after the /i/:

   mistanni + -a ---> mistanniyya

*** *** ***

ACTIVE PARTICIPLES : MEANING

A. "Basic" Designation or Meaning

EA verbs may be divided into the following types (see "Verbs : Aspect") :

1. Verbs with which bi- does not indicate continuity ("continuity" being viewed as the feature of an act or an event in progress). Two major groups belong to this type :

   (a) Stative verbs (i.e., verbs which designate a state rather than an act or event); e.g.,

biyifham	'he catches on'
biyiʕṛaf	'he (usually) knows'

   (b) Verbs which designate change of, or fixation of, location; e.g.,

biyṛuuħ	'he goes'
biyirgaʕ	'he returns'
biyuskun	'he (usually) resides'
biyibʔa	'he remains'

2. Verbs with which bi- indicates continuity (as well as repetitiveness, i.e., repeated action); e.g.,

biyiktib	'he is writing'
biyidris	'he is studying'
biyitkallim	'he is speaking'

The active participle from verbs of Type 1(a) expresses a current state.

Examples :

faahim	'understands'
ʕaarif	'knows'

ana faahim illi hiyya bitʔuulu
'I understand what she is saying.'

The active participle from verbs of Type 1(b) means 'is performing what the verb designates'.

Examples :

ṛaayiħ	'(is) going'
saakin	'(is) residing'
raagiʕ	'(is) returning'
ana ṛaayiħ maṣṛ.	'I am on my way to Egypt.'

The active participle from verbs of Type 2 means '(in a state of) having performed what the verb designates'.

Examples :

daaris	'having studied'
kaatib	'having written'
mitkallim	'having spoken'
fariida darsa	'Farida has studied (literally 'is in a state of having studied').'

The above statements point out an interesting observation : when bi- does not express continuity, the active participle does; when bi- expresses continuity, the active participle expresses something else.

To obtain the correct English translation, one must make sure that the Arabic participle and the English equivalent occur with comparable temporal and aspectual reference.

ilmayya garya.	'The water is running.'
ilmayya ggarya	'The running water'
iṛṛaagil naazil.	'The man is coming down.'
iṛṛaagil innaazil	'The man who is coming down'

In some contexts, certain active participles designate futurity; such contexts often include adverbials referring to the future :

ana ṛaayiɦ maṣṛ bukṛa.	'I am going to Egypt tomorrow.'
ana miš mitnaazil ʕan ɦaʔʔi ɦatta law iṭṭaṛṛeet astaʔiil.	'I will not relinquish my rights even if I find it necessary to resign.'

B. Semantic Extension

Some active participles can be used in either of the following ways :

1. With the basic designation
2. With a meaning which is related to, but which is not precisely the same as, the basic designation; this meaning will be called

the "extension". For example, kaatib can mean 'having written' but it also can mean 'an author':

miin minkum kaatib ilwaagib ?
'Who among you has written the homework?
issibaaʕi kaatib mašhuuṛ.
'Al-Siba'i is a famous author.'

Likewise, ɦaakim can mean 'is ruling' but it can also mean 'governor, ruler'.

Difference in aspect is part of what distinguishes the basic designation from the extension: while the basic designation includes aspect, the extension does not. Compare, for example, the participles in each of the following pairs. (Basic designation = Verbal adjective; Extension = Noun):

liɣaayit dilwaʔti ʕali kaatib ʕišriin maqaala.	'As of this moment, Ali has written twenty articles.'
ʕali kaatib maʕṛuuf.	'Ali is a well-known author.'
iṛṛaʔiis ɦaakim iddawla byadd min ɦadiid	'The president is ruling the country with an iron hand.'
mafiiš ɦaakim aɦsan min da.	'There is no better ruler than this one.'

C. Absence of Person Designation

Unlike verbs, active participles do not denote person. Thus in isolation the form faahim does not indicate whether reference is to first, second, or third person; the same is true of fahma and fahmiin.

*** *** ***

ACTIVE PARTICIPLES : NUMBER

A. Active participles which denote a semantic extension (typically nominal)

If it denotes a semantic extension (see; Active Participles : Meaning), an active participle may be singular, dual, or plural. The dual is formed by addition of -een to the singular form :

Singular		Dual	
kaatib	'an author (m)'	katbeen	'two authors (m)'
ʔaaḍi	'a judge (m)'	ʔaḍiyeen	'two judges (m)'
muṛabbi	'an educator (m)'	muṛabbiyyeen	'two educators (m)'
katba	'an author (f)'	katbiteen	'two authors (f)'
ʔaḍya	'a judge (f)'	ʔaḍyiteen	'two judges (f)'
muṛabbiyya	'an educator (f)'	muṛabbiyyiteen	'two educators (f)'

Notice that certain masculine singular forms undergo specifiable changes upon the addition of -een ; those changes are as follows :

1. If the masculine singular form is of the shape Faaʕi, /y/ is added after /i/.
   ʔaaḍi + -een ----> ʔaaḍiy + -een ----> ʔaḍyeen
2. The /i/ of the sequence -ʕiL is elided (see "Vowels : Elision at Word Boundaries") :
   kaatib + -een ----> katbeen (after Vowel Shortening)
3. If the masculine singular form ends in /i/ but is not of the shape Faaʕi , /yy/ is added after the /i/ :
   muṛabbi + -een ----> muṛabbiyyeen

Provided it is derived from a verb other than a Measure I triliteral, and provided it denotes a human being, each of the active participles being discussed typically has two plural forms : the sound masculine, and the sound feminine; the former results from adding -iin to the masculine singular, while the latter results from adding -aat to the feminine singular.

Singular		Plural
muṛabbi	'an educator (m)'	muṛabbiyyiin
muṛabbiyya	'an educator (f)'	muṛabbiyyaat

Notice that the addition of -iin is governed by the same rules which govern the addition of -een.

Provided it is derived from a verb other than a Measure I triliteral, and provided it designates a non-human referent, each of the active participles in question typically has a sound feminine plural form :

Singular		Plural
musakkin	'a tranquilizer'	musakkinaat
muxaddir	'a narcotic'	muxaddiṛaat
muqaatila	'combat plane'	muqaatilaat
muɦarrik	'a propeller'	muɦarrikaat

If derived from Measure I triliteral verbs, the active participles in question typically have broken plurals; the following measures are among the most common for these plurals :

1. FuʕʕaaL , from hollow roots when the referents are human.
2. Fuʕaah , from defective roots when the referents are human.
3. FawaaʕiL , when the referents are nonhuman.

Educated Egyptians sometimes use a Standard Arabic sound feminine plural, instead of the broken plural, to designate human referents which are exclusively female. However, the majority of speakers use the broken plurals below:

Singular		Plural
zaaʔir ~ zaayir	'a guest, visitor'	zuwwaaṛ
naaʔib ~ naayib	'a delegate'	nuwwaab
taagir	'a merchant'	tuggaaṛ
ʔaaḍi	'a judge'	ʔuḍaah
ṛaawi	'a narrator'	ṛuwaah
daafiʕ	'an incentive'	dawaafiʕ
ṭaaṛiʔ	'an emergency'	ṭawaaṛiʔ
daaʕi	'a necessity'	dawaaʕi
ɦadsa	'an accident'	ɦawaadis
saʔya	'a water wheel'	sawaaʔi

B. Active Participles which denote the basic designation (i.e., = adjectival)

If it denotes the basic designation, an active participle may be made singular or plural (the dual is rarely used). The plural is typically a sound form which results from adding -iin to the masculine singular, and which may modify a masculine or a feminine plural noun.

Certain masculine singular forms undergo specifiable changes upon the addition of -iin. The changes in question are the same as those which take place upon adding -iin to a masculine singular participle with a semantic extension.

Masculine Singular		Feminine Singular	Plural
waaʔif	'standing'	waʔfa	waʔfiin
faahim	'understands'	fahma	fahmiin
maaši	'walking'	mašya	mašyiin
mistanni	'waiting'	mistanniyya	mistanniyyiin
mitʕaadi	'to be enemies (with)'	mitʕadiyya	mitʕadiyyiin

irraagil illi waaʔif	'the man who is standing'
irraagleen illi waʔfiin	'the two men who are standing'
irriggaala lli waʔfiin	'the men who are standing'
issitt illi waʔfa	'the lady who is standing'
issittiteen illi waʔfiin	'the two ladies who are standing'
issittaat illi waʔfiin	'the ladies who are standing'

Combining number and gender contrasts, we get the following forms :

1. For participles with a semantic extension (i.e., = nominal)
   - (a) Masculine singular; e.g., murabbi 'an educator', kaatib 'an author'.
   - (b) Feminine singular; e.g., murabbiyya , katba.
   - (c) Masculine dual; e.g., murabbiyyeen , katbeen.
   - (d) Feminine dual; e.g., murabbiyyiteen , katbiteen.
   - (e) Plural
     - (i) Sound masculine; e.g., murabbiyyiin.
     - (ii) Sound feminine; e.g., murabbiyyaat.

(iii) Broken; e.g., kuttaab.

2. For participles with the basic designation (i.e., = adjectival)

(a) Masculine singular; e.g., waa?if 'standing'.

(b) Feminine singular; e.g., wa?fa.

(c) Plural; e.g., wa?fiin.

*** *** ***

ACTIVE PARTICIPLES : SYNTACTIC USAGE

1. When they denote the "basic designation" (see: Active Participles : Meaning), active participles usually occur in adjectival slots :

irṛaagil illi waa?if miš biyiʕṛaf ʕaṛabi.

'The man who is standing does not know Arabic.'

When used adjectivally, active participles agree with the modified noun in number, gender, and definiteness (see: Adjectival Use of Participles)

Active participles with the basic designation also occur in nominal slots :

ilħaḍṛiin yixabbaṛu lɣaybiin.

'Those who are present should inform those who are not.'

Notice however that, when used nominally, an active participle with the basic designation is actually a contraction of an attributive construction; thus ilħaḍṛiin and ilɣaybiin in the above sentence are contractions of il?ašxaaṣ ilħaḍṛiin 'the persons who are present' and il?ašxaaṣ ilɣaybiin 'the persons who are absent' respectively.

2. An active participle of a transitive verb, when it denotes the basic designation, may be used with verbal force, i.e., it can have a direct object :

(a) inta fakirni ?

'Do you remember me ?'

(b) ilbint illi fahma ddars ismaha eeh ?

'What is the name of the girl who understands the lesson ?

In sentence (a), the pronominal suffix attached to the active participle is -ni (the direct object suffix which is attached to verbs, e.g., kallimitni 'she talked to me') rather than -i (the possessive suffix which is attached to nouns, e.g., kitaabi 'my book'). In sentence (b), iddars is a direct object of the participle; were iddars in construct with the participle, the latter would have assumed the form fahmit (compare maktabit gamʕitna 'the library of our university').

3. When used as a semantic extension (see "Active Participles : Meaning"), active participles usually occur in nominal slots :

    ilħaakim ṛaagil ʕandu zimma.
    'The governor is a man of integrity.'
    waẓẓafna ʕaamil gidiid.
    'We employed a new laborer.'
    itkallimt maʕa ṭṭaalib.
    'I spoke with the student.'

*** *** ***

ADJECTIVAL PHRASE INTRODUCED BY bitaaʕ

The word bitaaʕ (feminine : bitaaʕa, plural : bituuʕ) usually occurs as the first term of a definite construct phrase which modifies a preceding definite noun, and agrees in gender and number with the noun modified :

    ilkitaab bitaaʕ ilʔustaaz feen ?
    'Where is the professor's book ?'
    iššanṭa btaʕtak feen ?
    'Where is your suitcase ?'
    dool ilkitabeen bituuʕi.
    'These are my two books.'

Occasionally, the bitaaʕ construct is indefinite and modifies a preceding indefinite noun :

    di ʕaṛabiyya btaaʕit waziir.
    'This is a (cabinet) minister's car.'

As the above examples show, bitaaʕ usually indicates a relationship of possession or belonging : the referent of the preceding form is possessed by or belongs to the referent of the following form. Another common meaning is 'having to do with, used for, dealing in, etc.' :

išširka btaʕt il?aflaam

'the film (-producing) company'

iddukkaan bitaaʕ issagaayir

'the cigarette shop'

ilʕaṛabiyyaat bitaʕt ijjilaati

'the ice cream (-vending) cars'

ilfingaan bitaaʕ il?ahwa

'the coffee cup'

iṛṛaagil bitaaʕ ilfigl

'the radish seller'

When it designates possession or belonging, the construct with bitaaʕ often corresponds to a semantically equivalent noun construct, for example,

iššanṭa bitaaʕit ilwaziir = šanṭit ilwaziir

'the minister's suitcase'

Many bitaaʕ constructions meaning "having to do with, used for, etc.' also have semantically equivalent noun constructs, for example,

išširka bitaaʕit il?aflaam = širkit il?aflaam

'the film company'

Some bitaaʕ constructions meaning "used for, dealing in, etc." can drop the modified noun, e.g.,

bitaaʕ ilfigl = iṛṛaagil bitaaʕ ilfigl

'the radish seller'

Many noun constructs do not designate possession or belonging, and for most of these there are no synonymous bitaaʕ constructs. The following noun constructs have no corresponding bitaaʕ constructs :

aʕḍaa? ilfir?a (where the second noun

'the members of the team' comprises the first)

madiinit ṭanṭa
'the city of Tanta';
kilmit kitaab
'the word kitaab'
(where the sequence is a naming construction)

ʕaṛabiyyaat iddiizil
'Diesel (-driven) cars'
(where the second noun drives the first)

ɦayaat ilmaṛaɦ
'the life of merriment'
(where the second noun is semantically a qualifier of the first)

umm ilwalad
'the boys mother ;
diraaʕi
'my arm'
(where the possession designated is inalienable)

fingaal ʔahwa
'a cup of coffee'
(where the first noun is a container and the second is the contents)

The following comments deal with the choice between the bitaaʕ construct and the noun construct :

1. The choice between the bitaaʕ construct and the equivalent noun construct may be stylistic : if the speaker for some reason prefers to make the "possessed" noun definite, he selects the bitaaʕ construct; consider, for example, the following sentence :

xadt talat kutub : ilkitaab illi kaan ʕala ṭṭaṛabeeza, wilkitaab illi kaan fi maktabak, wilkitaab bitaaʕi (instead of wi ktaabi).
'I took three books : the book which was on the table, the book which was in your office, and my book (literally : "and the book which belongs to me").'

Having used a definite noun in referring to the first book and a definite noun in referring to the second, the speaker chooses (but is not forced) to use a definite noun in referring to the third book; this choice forces him to use the bitaaʕ construct since a definite noun cannot be used as the first member of a noun construct.

2. When the "possessed" noun is to be modified by an adjective, the noun construct may result in ambiguity; to avoid such ambiguity, the bitaaʕ construct is used. For example, kitaab ittilmiiz iggidiid may mean 'the new student's book' or 'the student's new book'; to avoid the ambiguity, one would usually say ilkitaab iggidiid bitaaʕ ittilmiiz 'the student's new book' or ilkitaab bitaaʕ ittilmiiz iggidiid 'the new student's book'.

3. An attributive construction may constitute a compound word or a stereotyped expression whose noun cannot be separated from the adjective. To express a relationship of possession between the noun of such a construction and some other noun, speakers commonly use the bitaaʕ construct rather than the noun construct. For example, 'your university city (i.e. the complex where students reside)' is expressed in EA by ilmadiina ggaamiʕiyya btaʕitkum rather than madinitkum iggaamiʕiyya.

The attributive constructions under discussion include expressions of measurement where the modifier is muṛabbaʕ 'square' or mukaʕʕab 'cube'. Thus ilmitr ilmuṛabbaʕ bitaaʕak 'your square meter' is common while miṭrak ilmuṛabbaʕ is hardly used.

4. Some loan words -- mostly ones which end in a vowel -- seldom take pronominal suffixes (e.g., kiilu 'kilogram', radyu 'radio', banyu 'bathtub', antinna 'antenna'); instead, those words are modified by the bitaaʕ construct.

5. "Inalienable possession" (which applies to kinship and parts of the body) is expressed by a noun construct but not by the bitaaʕ construct :

uxti 'my sister'

rigli 'my leg'

An exception to this rule is :

issitt bitaʕti 'my wife'

6. Dual nouns and sound masculine plural ones do not enter into construct with a following pronominal suffix; possession of such nouns is indicated through use of the bitaaʕ construct :

ilkitabeen bituuʕi

'my two books'

ilmuʕallimiin bituuʕi

'my teachers'

7. In certain idiomatic expressions, the occurrence of bitaaʕ is governed by no general rule; the following sentences contain some of the expressions in question :

da ṛaagil bitaaʕ niswaan.

'He is a skirt-chaser.'

ana miš bitaaʕ kalaam zayy da.

'I don't go for that kind of thing.'

dool naas bituuʕ ṛabbina.

'These are godly people.'

issitt btaʕti lubnaniyya.

'My wife is Lebanese.'

da lbeeh bitaaʕi.

'This is my husband.'

Idioms such as these must be learned as items.

*** *** ***

ADJECTIVAL USE OF PARTICIPLES

A participle may fill an adjectival slot. In this case the participle is governed by the rules of agreement stated under "Adjectives : Attributive Construction".

If it constitutes the entire modifier, the participle is made definite by placing either il- or illi before it. Although both alternatives are possible in this context, il- is favored with passive participles while illi is favored with active participles.

bint wa?fa 'a girl standing'

ilbint illi wa?fa or (less commonly)

ilbint ilwa?fa 'the girl who is standing'

ilbanaat illi naymiin or (less commonly)

ilbanaat innaymiin 'the sleeping girls'

ilkutub ilmanšuuṛa hina or (less commonly)

ilkutub illi manšuuṛa hina 'the books published here'

When it is the first word of an adjectival construction, an active participle occurs with illi much more commonly than it does with il- (this is especially true when the active participle has an object), while a passive participle occurs more commonly with il- than it does with illi.

issitt illi wa?fa hnaak or (rarely)

issitt ilwa?fa hnaak 'the lady who is standing over there'

iṛṛaagil illi raakib gamal or (rarely)

iṛṛaagil irraakib gamal 'the man who is riding a camel'

ilmaqaala lmanšuuṛa fgaridt il?ahṛaam or (less commonly)

ilmaqaala lli manšuuṛa fgaridt il?ahṛaam 'the article published in the newspaper Al-Ahram'

Adjectival participles have three forms : the masculine singular, the feminine singular, and the plural; the first modifies a masculine singular noun, the second modifies a feminine singular noun, and the third modifies a dual or a plural noun :

iṛṛaagil illi waa?if hinaak

'the man who is standing over there'

issitt illi wa?fa hnaak

'the lady who is standing over there'

iṛṛagleen / issitteen illi wa?fiin hinaak

'the two men / ladies who are standing over there'

irriggaala / issittaat illi wa?fiin hinaak

'the men / ladies who are standing over there'

irṛaagil ilmaʕṛuuf
'the well-known man'
issitt ilmaʕṛuufa
'the well-known lady'
irṛagleen / issitteen ilmaʕṛufiin
'the two well-known men / ladies'
irriggaala / issittaat ilmaʕṛufiin
'the well-known men / ladies'

*** *** ***

ADJECTIVE

A word which limits, qualifies or describes a noun or a pronoun.
Many Egyptian Arabic adjectives have the structure FVʕVVL, e.g.,

kibiir   'big'

However, the patterns vary, e.g.,

FaʕʕaaL   naṣṣaab   'swindler'

It is worth mentioning that /naṣṣaab/ is a noun that serves as a
modifier and therefore is classified as an adjective.

Noun	Adjective	
ṛaagil	naṣṣaab	'a swindler'
		(a swindling man)

*** *** ***

ADJECTIVE : AGREEMENT WITH NOUNS

An adjective (modifier) agrees in gender with the singular noun
it modifies, (n m + adj m) or (n f + adj f), e.g.,

iṭṭaaliba nnabiiha   'the intelligent student'

Singular adjectives must agree in gender with the singular nouns they
modify, e.g.,

walad kibiir 'a big boy'

bint kbiira 'a big girl'

With human plural nouns, adjectives agree in number but not usually in gender :

awlaad kubaaṛ 'big boys'

banaat kubaaṛ 'big girls'

However, with non-human plural nouns, either plural adjectives or feminine singular adjectives may be used :

kutub kubaaṛ 'big books'

kutub kibiira 'big books'

Some speakers of EA use the latter structure even when the modified noun is human plural.

awlaad kutaaṛ 'many boys'

awlaad kitiira 'many boys'

and

banaat kutaaṛ 'many girls'

banaat kitiira 'many girls'

*** *** ***

ADJECTIVE : ATTRIBUTIVE CONSTRUCTIONS (OR NOUN-ADJECTIVE PHRASES)

An adjective follows the noun it modifies. The form of the adjective is determined by the number, gender, definiteness and humanness of the modified noun. The masculine singular form of the adjective follows a masculine singular noun, the feminine singular form follows a feminine singular or a non-human plural noun, and the plural form follows a dual noun (whether human or non-human) or a human plural noun. The adjective is definite when the modified noun is definite, and indefinite when the modified noun is indefinite.

ʔabilt ṛaagil maṣri. 'I met an Egyptian man.'

ʔabilt sitt maṣriyya. 'I met an Egyptian woman.'

ištareet kutub maṣriyya. 'I bought (some) Egyptian books

ʔabilt ṛagleen maṣriyyiin.	'I met two Egyptian men.'
ʔabilt binteen maṣriyyiin.	'I met two Egyptian girls.'
ištareet kitabeen ɣalyiin.	'I bought two expensive books.'
ʔabilt riggaala maṣriyyiin.	'I met (some) Egyptian men.'
ʔabilt sittaat maṣriyyiin.	'I met (some) Egyptian women.'
ʔabilt irrigaala lmaṣriyyiin.	'I met the Egyptian men.'
ʔabilt issittaat ilmaṣriyyiin	'I met the Egyptian women.'

Notice that when a suffix consisting of or beginning with a vowel is added to a form ending in /i/ (provided that form is not of the shape Faaʕi), /yy/ is inserted between the form and the suffix.

As illustrated above, the adjective shows contrast for humanness when the modified noun is plural : if the plural noun designates human referents, the adjective is usually plural; if the plural noun designates non-human referents, the adjective is usually feminine singular.

zuṛt baʕḍ iṭṭullaab ilmaṣriyyiin.
'I visited some Egyptian students (m).'
zuṛt baʕd issittaat ilmaṣriyyiin.
'I visited some Egyptian ladies.'
zuṛt baʕd ilmudun ilmaṣriyya.
'I visited some Egyptian cities.'
ʕandi kutub kibiira.
'I have large books.'

Nisba adjectives denoting color, e.g., ṛamaadi 'ash-grey', bunni 'brown', samaawi 'sky-blue', and those denoting place of origin (when modifying non-human nouns) are usually masculine singular regardless of the form of the modified noun, e.g.,

ʕaṛabiyya gdiida 'a new car'	but	ʕaṛabiyya almaani 'a German car'
siggaada gamiila 'a pretty carpet'	but	siggaada ʕagami 'a Persian carpet'

fasatiin ɣalya 'expensive dresses'	but	fasatiin ṛamaadi 'grey dresses'
buḍaaʕa wiħša 'bad goods'	but	buḍaaʕa baladi 'local (locally manufactured) goods'
naas kwayyisiin 'nice people'	but	naas baladi 'low class people'

Note that the last example is a special case where the rule is extended to a noun with human referent.

Certain structures are made up of a noun followed by another noun where the second noun expresses a 'made of' relationship, e.g.,

saaʕa dahab
'a gold watch'

fustaneen ħariir
'two silk dresses'

riggaala waraʔ
'feeble men'
(literally: 'paper men')

Notes : 1. Although EA usually employs a single sound plural form of the adjective (which form ends in -iin), educated Egyptians occasionally use two sound plural forms : a masculine form ending in -iin, and a feminine one ending in -aat, e.g.,

murabbiyyiin faḍliin 'virtuous educators (m)'
murabbiyyaat faḍilaat 'virtuous educators (f)'

Expressions where sound feminine plural adjectives occur are usually "classicisms".

2. An adjective which modifies a collective noun is masculine singular. The collective form referred to here is that which yields the "unit noun" by acquiring the suffix -a (e.g., tiffaaħ 'apples', from which the unit noun is tiffaaħa 'an apple'). (see: Collective Nouns)

tiffaaħ kibiir	'large apples'
wara? xafiif	'thin paper'

3. Although it was stated that an adjective modifying a plural noun with non-human reference is usually feminine singular in form, the plural form of the adjective is also often used in this instance, especially if the noun is a broken plural, e.g.,

talat kutub gidiida	
or	'three new books'
talat kutub gudaad	

4. Though more commonly followed by the plural form of the adjective, broken plural nouns which designate human beings but are morphologically feminine singular are sometimes followed by the feminine singular form of the adjective, e.g.,

riggaala ħafyiin	'(a group of) inconse-
or	quential men'
riggaala ħafya	

*** *** ***

ADJECTIVE : COMPARATIVE AND SUPERLATIVE

The comparative adjective is invariable in form. For the majority of adjectives the comparative form is of the measure aFʕaL, e.g.,

kibiir	'big'	----->	akbaṛ	'bigger'
gamiil	'pretty'	----->	agmal	'prettier'
ṭawiil	'tall'	----->	aṭwal	'taller'

Adjectives ending in /-i/ or /-w/ have comparative forms of the measure aFʕa, e.g.,

ʕaali	'high'	----->	aʕla	'higher'
ħilw	'sweet'	----->	aħla	'sweeter'

Adjectives with a doubled root have comparative forms on the measure aFaʕL, e.g.,

gidiid	'new'	----->	agadd	'newer'
muhimm	'important'	----->	ahamm	'more important'

In expressions indicating comparison, "than" is expressed by min 'from', e.g.,

ilbint akbaṛ min ilwalad.	'The girl is bigger than the boy.'
hiyya akbaṛ minnu.	'She is bigger than him.'

In Egyptian Arabic there is no separate morphological form for the superlative. It is expressed by one of the following constructions using the comparative form :

Comparative + indefinite form of the noun (s or p)

dool aṭwal banaat.	'These are the tallest girls.'
da aṭwal walad.	'This is the tallest boy.'

Comparative + numeral + indefinite noun

dool aṭwal talat banaat.	'These are the three tallest girls.'

min + comparative + definite plural noun

huwwa min aṭwal il?awlaad.	'He is one of the tallest boys.'

Notice that the comparative adjective is not inflected for gender or number, whereas the following noun is inflected for both.

*** *** ***

ADJECTIVE FUNCTIONING AS PREDICATE

An adjective may function as the predicate of a sentence or clause. In this usage, the subject determines the number and gender of the adjective.

ʕali ṭawiil.	'Ali is tall.'
nadya ṭawiila.	'Nadia is tall.'

iṛṛagleen ṭuwaal.	'The two men are tall.'
ilbinteen ṭuwaal.	'The two girls are tall.'
irriggaala ṭwaal.	'The men are tall.'
issittaat ṭuwaal.	'The women are tall.'
iṭṭarabizaat ṭawiila.	'The tables are long.'

Notice that adjectives in predicate position are normally indefinite.

*** *** ***

ADJECTIVE : GENDER

In Egyptian Arabic (EA), nouns (n) are either masculine (m) or feminine (f) in gender, e.g., walad (m) 'boy' bint (f) 'girl'. Henceforth, gender indicators will not be entered for those nouns where the sex of the referent clearly indicates the grammatical gender.

Adjectives (adj) show two genders, e.g., nabiih (m) 'intelligent' nabiiha (f) 'intelligent'. Compare the following nouns and adjectives:

ṭaalib (m)	ṭaaliba (f)	'student'
nabiih (m)	nabiiha (f)	'intelligent'

Notice that singular (s) feminine nouns and adjectives end in /-a/. Exceptions to this will be indicated by (f). Masculine singular nouns and adjectives will thus be identifiable by the absence of /-a/ or by the insertion of (m). This convention of indicating gender for singular forms will be followed regularly; thus ṭaalib 'student' and ṭaaliba 'student' have no imposed gender indicators, since it is clear that the first word is masculine and the second is feminine. Indicators, however, will be entered next to items such as arḍ (f) 'land' and mabna (m) 'building' since their endings do not follow the rule above.

*** *** ***

ADJECTIVE : INFLECTION FOR NUMBER AND GENDER

In EA, an adjective has three forms : the masculine singular, the feminine singular, and the plural.

The feminine singular form is usually formed by adding the suffix -a to the masculine singular form (which is considered the base). The plural form is "sound" in the case of some adjectives and "broken" in the case of others; the sound plural is formed by adding -iin to the masculine singular form, while the broken plural is formed by "breaking up" the masculine singular through internal change :

kuwayyis	'good'	(ms)
kuwayyisa	'good'	(fs)
kuwayyisiin	'good'	(sound plural)
kibiir	'big'	(ms)
kibiira	'big'	(fs)
kubaaṛ	'big'	(broken plural)

There is no structural device which infallibly forecasts the plural form for each singular adjective; nevertheless, the student will be reasonably safe in assuming that the following adjectives have sound plural forms :

1. Active and passive participles which have the basic designation (see "Active Participles : Meaning" and "Passive Participles : Meaning") :

Singular		Plural
naayim	'sleeping'	naymiin
mitʕallim	'educated'	mitʕallimiin
maʕṛuuf	'known'	maʕṛufiin
muʕaaqab	'punished'	muʕaqbiin

2. Relative (nisba) adjectives :

Singular		Plural
maṣṛi	'Egyptian'	maṣṛiyyiin
azhari	'Azharite'	azhariyyiin

3. Adjectives of the measures FuʕayyaL, FaʕʕaaL, and FaʕLaan :

Singular		Plural
kuwayyis	'good'	kuwayyisiin
ʔuṣayyaṛ	'short'	ʔuṣayyaṛiin
naṣṣaab	'a swindler'	naṣṣabiin
kaslaan	'lazy'	kaslaniin

Exceptions do occur; for example, the plural of turki 'Turkish' is atṛaak .

Broken plural adjectives have numerous measures; in addition, it is not possible to predict with certainty which broken plural measure a given singular adjective will have. The student is therefore advised to learn the broken plural forms as items.

Singular		Plural
ʕabiiṭ	'stupid'	ʕubaṭa
maskiin	'poor'	masakiin

For nisba adjectives designating color or place of origin and for attributive constructions indicating type of product or social status, see Adjectives : Attributive Construction .

*** *** ***

ADJECTIVES JOINED BY COORDINATING CONJUNCTIONS

Two adjectives may be joined by a coordinating conjunction :

samiira nabiiha wšaṭra.
'Samira is intelligent and clever.'
ibnak nabiih laakin kaslaan.
'Your son is intelligent but lazy.'
humma ṭwaal walla ʔṣayyaṛiin ?
'Are they tall or short ?'

In Arabic the coordinating conjunction cannot be dropped when more than two adjectives are conjoined (as it can be in English, e.g., "tall, dark and handsome).

ṭawiil wasmaṛ wi wasiim 'tall, dark, and handsome'

Since they usually refer to the same noun, conjoined adjectives are usually identical in regard to number, gender, and definiteness.

*** *** ***

ADJECTIVE : NUMBER AND DEMONSTRATIVES

Singular adjectives must agree in gender with the singular nouns they modify. With human plural nouns, adjectives agree in number. However, with non-human plural nouns, either plural adjectives or feminine singular adjectives may be used. The same is true of /da, di,dool/ 'this, that, these, those'.

da walad kuwayyis.	'This is a good boy.'
dool awlaad kuwayyisiin.	'These are good boys.'
da ktaab kuwayyis.	'This is a good book.'
dool kutub kuwayyisiin.	'These are good books.'
di kutub kwayyisa.	'These are good books.'

*** *** ***

ADJECTIVE : RELATIVE

(See : Nisba Adjective)

*** *** ***

ADJECTIVE : RELATIVE CLAUSES

A sentence may be embedded (q.v.) in the adjectival slot of another sentence, provided that the two sentences contain an identical noun (the "shared noun").

If the shared noun functions as subject in the sentence to be embedded, that noun is deleted when the two sentences are combined. In the following examples, the second sentence of each set is the one to be embedded; the third sentence results from the embedding transformation.

	iṛṛaagil ṣaħbi.	'The man is my friend.'
+	irraagil gamb ilbaab.	'The man is by the door.'
=	iṛṛaagil illi gamb ilbaab ṣaħbi.	'The man by the door is my friend.'

	ʔabilt ṛaagil.	'I met a man.'
+	iṛṛaagil rigiʕ min maṣr imbaariħ.	'The man returned from Egypt yesterday.'
=	ʔabilt ṛaagil rigiʕ min maṣr imbaariħ.	'I met a man who returned from Egypt yesterday.'

If the shared noun does not function as subject in the sentence to be embedded, that noun is replaced by a pronoun when the two sentences are combined :

issitt mudarrisa.	'The lady is a teacher.'
fariid itkallim ʕan issitt.	'Farid talked about the lady.'
issitt illi fariid itkallim ʕanha mudarrisa.	'The lady about whom Farid talked is a teacher.'

Notice that the relative clause must be preceded by illi when the modified noun is definite, and that illi does not occur when the modified noun is indefinite.

(See also : Relative Clauses with illi)

*** *** ***

ADVERB

A word or phrase used to modify a verb, an adjective, or another adverb. Examples of Egyptian Arabic adverbs are /hina/ 'here', /hinaak/ 'there', /bisuṛʕa/ 'immediately, quickly', /bišweeš/ slowly, softly'.

*** *** ***

ADVERBS

In EA, there is a relatively small set of words -- called adverbs -- which function as modifiers of verbs, adjectives and other adverbs, but which do not have the inflectional properties of adjectives. For example, while kibiir, an adjective, has both a feminine singular form and a plural form, bukra 'tomorrow', an adverb, is invariable in form.

Adverbs may be divided into two large classes: those which usually precede and those which usually follow the modified expression. In the following papagraphs, the most common adverbs of both types are listed. Several sub-classes are given, and each sub-class is followed by illustrative sentences.

1. Adverbs which usually follow the modified expression

(a) Adverbs of place: barra 'outside', guwwa 'inside', foo? 'up, upstairs', taħt 'down, downstairs', ?uddaam 'in the front', wara 'in the back', hina 'here', hinaak 'there'.

ħayzaakir guwwa.	'He will study inside.'
ħanit?aabil hinaak.	'We will meet there.'

(b) Adverbs of time: innaharda 'today', imbaariħ 'yesterday', bukra 'tomorrow', dilwa?ti 'now', baʕdeen 'later on', zamaan 'a long time ago', ?urayyib 'a short time ago, recently, soon', dayman 'always', abadan 'never' (in negative sentences only), badri 'early', waxri 'late', axiiran 'finally', aħyaanan 'sometimes', sabaaħan 'in the morning', masaa?an 'in the evening'.

miš ħaruuħ ?abadan.	'I will never go.'
ħayirgaʕ bukra.	'He will return tomorrow.'

(c) Adverbs indicating degree or quantity: ?awi 'very', xaalis 'very (in affirmative sentences); at all (in negative sentences)', giddan 'very', kitiir 'a lot', kamaan 'more, in addition', ta?riiban 'nearly', šiwayya 'a little, somewhat'.

ziʕil xaaliṣ.	'He became very unhappy.'
maʕṛafuuš xaaliṣ.	'I do not know him at all.'
ʕaawiz talaata kamaan.	'I want three more.'
iddinya bard šwayya.	'It's a bit cold.'

(d) Adverbs of manner : kida 'in this manner', ʔawaam 'quickly, fast', sawa 'together', waħd- or liwaħd- (plus a pronominal suffix) 'alone', duɣri 'straight ahead', ṭawwaali 'straight ahead', ʕamdan 'intentionally'.

ṛuħt l-waħdi.	'I went alone.'
ṛaaħit liwaħdaha.	'She went alone.'
laazim timši duɣri ~ laazim timši ṭawwaali	'You must walk straight ahead.'

2. Adverbs which usually precede the modified expression

(a) Adverbs indicating approximation : ħawaali , yiigi , yitlaʕ , all translatable by 'nearly'.

ištaɣalit hina yiigi ʕašaṛ siniin.	'She worked here for about ten years.'

(b) Intensifiers : lissa 'just', yadoob 'just', ʕumṛ 'ever (used in negative and interrogative sentences, in construct with a following noun or pronoun functioning as subject)'.

lissa ṛayha.	'She has just left.'
ʕumṛ ʕali daras fi gamʕit ilqaahira ?	'Has Ali ever studied at the University of Cairo ?'
ʕumṛi ma šuft maṣr.	'I have never seen Egypt.'
yadoobu gah wana daxla.	'He had just come when I entered.'

Prepositional phrases frequently occur in adverbial slots. Those functioning as time adverbials often begin with fi 'in', baʕd 'after', or ʔabl 'before'. Those functioning as place adverbials are often introduced by fi 'in', ʕala 'on', baṛṛa 'outside', guwwa 'inside', fooʔ 'on top of', taħt 'under, below', ʔuddaam 'in front of', or waṛa 'behind'; and those functioning as manner adverbials are often introduced by bi- 'with, in'.

ʔabiltaha baʕd ʔigtimaaʕ.	'I met her after the meeting.'
binti guwwa lbeet.	'My daughter is inside the house.'
biyaakul bisurʕa.	'He eats fast (literally "with speed").'
mathibbiniiš biššakl da.	'Do not love me in this manner !'

As stated above, some adverbs usually precede while others usually follow the modified expression. This does not mean, however, that every adverb is restricted to one position. Of the ones listed above, the following adverbs are usually restricted to one position, while the rest may occur in either position :

abadan , badri , waxri , ʔawi , xaalis̩ , giddan , yadoob , ʕumr̩ , adverbs of manner, adverbs of probability and doubt, adverbs of approximation.

Placing a given adverb in the non-favored position usually serves the purpose of emphasizing that adverb :

rigiʕ imbaarih.	'He returned yesterday.'
imbaarih rigiʕ.	'It was yesterday that he returned.'

*** *** ***

ADVERBS OF MANNER

Notice that some adverbs of manner are of the form :

bi + Noun

sur̩ʕa	'swiftness'	bisur̩ʕa	'quickly'
suhuula	'ease'	bisuhuula	'easily'
s̩uʕuuba	'difficulty'	bi s̩uʕuuba	'with difficulty'

The adverb bišweeš 'slowly' is of this form but there is no corresponding noun from which it is formed.

*** *** ***

AFFIX

A term used to refer to prefixes (e.g., /bi-/, /mi-/, /yi-, ti-, a-, ni-/), infixes (e.g., gamaʕ 'to collect' and igtamaʕ 'to gather together', where the /-t-/ is an infix), and suffixes (e.g., /-iin/, /-aat/, /-een/ as in fallaħ 'farmer (m)' ---- fallaħiin 'farmers (mp)' and fallaaħa 'farmer (f)' ---- fallaħaat 'farmers (fp)').

*** *** ***

AGREEMENT IN CONSTRUCT PHRASES

Construct Phrases $N_1 + N_2$ = the N_1 of N_2

(a) definite, if N_2 is definite

kitaab ilwalad	'the boy's book'
kitaab ilwalad ilkibiir	'the book of the big boy'
kitaab haani	'Hani's book'

or (b) indefinite, if N_2 is indefinite

kitaab walad	'a boy's book'

In either case the construct phrase consists of two nouns $N_1 + N_2$ in a sequence meaning N_1 of N_2. Note that N_1 is definite in meaning, but cannot be definite in form; N_2 may or may not be definite.

In example (a), N_1 of N_2 + adjective ilkibiir is a modifier of N_2 ilwalad and therefore agrees with it in definiteness, gender, and number.

(See also : Adjective : Agreement with Nouns; Adjective : Gender)

*** *** ***

ALLOMORPH

A positional variant of a morpheme (q.v.) occuring in a specific

environment. English has a noun plural morpheme /-z/ that has the
phonologically conditioned allomorphs /-s ~ -z ~ - z/ as in 'cats',
'dogs', 'kisses'. In Egyptian Arabic the connector wi̲ 'and' has the
allomorphs /w-/ after a vowel and /wi̲-/ after a consonant, e.g.,

daxla wxarga   'Going in and coming out (f)'
daxal wixarag   'He went in and came out'

***   ***   ***

ALLOPHONE

A positional variant of a phoneme (q.v.), occuring in specific
environments and not causing semantic differentiation, e.g., English
initial [kʰ] in "kay" and [k] following /s/ in "ski" are both
members of one and the same phoneme /k/. The only difference between
them is that the first is aspirated whereas the second is unaspirated
(see : Aspiration). In Egyptian Arabic /a/ has the allophones
[æ] as in English 'fa̲t' and [a] as in English 'fa̲ther' in the
environments of non-emphatic (q.v.) and emphatic consonants respectively, e.g., /tab/ = [tæb] 'to repent' and /ṭab/ = [ṭab] 'to
ripen'.

***   ***   ***

ALVEOLAR

The place of articulation at the alveolar ridge, where /ṭ ḍ ṣ ẓ ḷ r ṛ/
are produced.

***   ***   ***

ALVEOLAR RIDGE

The convex portion of the mouth just behind the front teeth; the tooth
ridge.

***   ***   ***

ALVEOPALATAL

A place of articulation consisting of the front part of the palate: / š ž /.

*** *** ***

ANAPTYCTIC VOWEL

(See : Vowels : Extra)

*** *** ***

ANAPTYXIS

The addition of an anaptyctic or helping vowel to break up a sequence of three consonants (CCC), which is inadmissable in Egyptian Arabic.

*** *** ***

ANTECEDENT

A typical relative clause construction contains three elements :

(a) an antecedent

(b) the invariable relative pronoun illi

(c) a clause

Examples :

šuft	ilwilaad	illi	gaabu lgawabaat.
	(a)	(b)	(c)
I saw	the boys	who	(they) brought the letters.
	(a)	(b)	(c)

Note that the relative clause by itself is a complete sentence, i.e. it can stand by itself without the relative pronoun : gaabu lgawabaat

'They brought the letters.'. /-u/, the inflection of the verb gaabu , is the formal reference to the antecedent ilwilaad 'the boys'. In the sentence :

da lgawaab illi gabuuh imbaariɦ.

'This is the letter which they brought yesterday.'

- the suffixed pronoun object of the verb gabuuh 'they brought it' refers to the antecedent.

In the sentence :

da lwalad illi ktaabu ḍaaʕ.

'This is the boy whose (his) book got lost.'

- the suffixed pronoun on kitaab is the reference.

In the sentence :

feen ilkitaab illi ʔultilak ʕaleeh ?

'Where is the book which I talked to you about (it) ?'

- the reference is through the suffixed pronoun object of the preposition ʕaleeh 'about it'.

Note that the above examples have definite antecedents. If the antecedent is indefinite, there is no relative pronoun in the construction.

ṛaagil sakan fimaṣr sanateen

'a man who lived in Egypt for two years'

*** *** ***

ARABIC

The most important Semitic (q.v.) language now spoken. It is the official language of Algeria, Bahrain, Chad, Egypt, Iraq, Jordan, Kuwait, Lebanon, Libya, Mali, Malta, Mauritania, Morocco, Qatar, Saudi Arabia, Somalia, the Sudan, Syria, Tunisia, Yemen, Democratic Yemen, Oman and the United Arab Emirates. Arabic is spoken by 100 million people. It is the religious language of 650 million Muslims.

Arabic is both a modern language and an ancient one, going back over 2,000 years. Classical Arabic is the language of the Holy

Koran and the vehicle of Arabic literature. It is universally acknowledged as the standard form of the language and is used in writing and speeches. Standard Arabic, also called Modern Standard Arabic is uniform all over the Arab World and is the language of education, the press, radio and TV as well as public lectures. In addition, an Arabic dialect is spoken in each of the Arab countries and varies to some extent from one Arab country to another. Arabists recognize two major dialect groups: "Western" and "Eastern"; the Western includes the Arab countries of North Africa through Libya and Malta, and the Eastern includes Egypt and all the Arab countries of the East.

*** *** ***

ARTICLE : VARIATION OF DEFINITE ARTICLE

(See : Definite Article : Form; and Definite Article : Meaning)

*** *** ***

ARTICULATION

a. "Point of Articulation" : The point of contact (or closest approach) of a speech organ to a part of the mouth or throat during the production of a sound. For example, in making the Egyptian consonant /t/, the apex of the tongue touches the back of the upper teeth; the point of articulation is referred to as dental. (Note that the English /t/ is slightly different : the apex of the tongue touches the alveolar ridge behind the upper teeth; the English /t/ is thus classed as alveolar).

Points of Articulation (A particular speech organ is generally associated with each point of articulation.)

1. Bilabial : lower lip and upper lip / p b m w /
2. Labiodental : lower lip and upper teeth / f v /
3. Dental : apex of tongue and upper teeth / t d s z n l /
4. Alveolar : apex of tongue and alveolar ridge / ṭ ḍ ṣ ẓ ḷ r ṛ /

5. Alveopalatal : blade of tongue and front part of palate / š ž /
6. Palatal : tongue blade and palate / y /
7. Velar : tongue dorsum and back of palate / k g /
8. Back-Velar (also "Post Velar") : tongue dorsum and velum / x ɣ /
9. Uvular : tongue dorsum and uvula / q /
10. Pharyngeal : root of tongue and pharynx forming a stricture / ɦ ʕ /
11. Glottal : produced in the <u>glottis</u> (opening at upper part of the larynx between the vocal cords) / ʔ h /

    The sound /ʔ/ <u>glottal stop</u> is produced by complete closure and release of the vocal cords.

b. <u>Manner of articulation</u> : The way in which the air passage is blocked or constricted during the production of a sound. For example, the lower and upper lips may form a complete closure, thus stopping the air flow, as in the case of a /b/ which is termed <u>stop</u>.

<u>Manners of articulation</u>

1. Stop : refers to consonants characterized by a complete closure of the air passage, thus blocking the air stream momentarily, e.g., closing of both lips in production of /b/: / p b t ṭ d ḍ k g q ʔ /
2. Fricative : refers to consonants produced by friction caused by the air moving through a narrowed passage in the vocal tract: / f v s ṣ z ẓ š ž x ɣ ɦ ʕ h /

   (Note : The term "Obstruent" includes Stops and Fricatives.)
3. Nasal : refers to consonants produced with the uvula lowered, allowing the air to excape through the nose, so that the nasal cavity acts as a resonator: / m n /
4. Lateral : refers to a consonant produced with the tongue touching only the middle of the palate, thus allowing the air flow to excape around one or both sides of the tongue: / l ḷ /
5. Flap : refers to a consonant produced by a single <u>tap</u> of the tongue in which the tip of the tongue makes a single rapid contact against the alveolar ridge: / r ṛ /

   (Note : A Trill is a double Flap: / rr ṛṛ /)

6. Semi-vowel : a vowel-like sound which functions as a consonant / w y / . Also often referred to as "Glides".

*** *** ***

ASPECTUAL-TEMPORAL FORMS

(See : Verb : Aspect ; and Verb : Tense)

*** *** ***

ASPIRATION

The puff of breath after a consonant, e.g., /t/ in English "top" is aspirated where that of English "stop" is <u>unaspirated</u>. Egyptian Arabic /t/ is also aspirated initially, e.g.,

/taani/ = [t^{h}ææni] 'again'

*** *** ***

ASSIMILATION

Assimilation is a phonetic process whereby a given sound acquires one or more characteristics of an adjacent sound or becomes identical to it, e.g., /xad/ + /t/ ----> /xatt/ 'I took'.

Another important instance of assimilation in EA is that of the /l/ of the definite article /il-/ when followed by one of the consonant phonemes / t ṭ d ḍ r ṛ s ṣ z ẓ š ž n l /. Assimilation of the definite article is optional when followed by either /k/ or /g/.

/ṛaagil/ 'man', /il/ + /ṛaagil/ -----> /iṛṛaagil/ 'the man'

In the following sequences : /td, sz, šž/, C_1 assimilates to C_2 only with respect to voice.

/ustaaz/ 'professor' -----> /asatza/ -----> /asadza/ 'professor'.

/xad/ 'to take' -----> /xadt/ -----> /xatt/ 'I took'

/ʔooḍa/ 'room' -----> /ʔoḍti/ -----> /ʔoṭṭi/ 'my room'

Note in the last example assimilation with respect to emphasis: /t/--> /ṭ/.

C_1C_2 Utterance Medially and Finally

Sequences of any two obstruents (i.e. stops or fricatives) are usually both voiced or both voiceless. Here C_1 assimilates to C_2 with respect to voice.

/xaṛagt/ ----->	/xaṛakt/	'I went out'
/lafaẓt/ ----->	/lafaṣṭ/	'I pronounced'
/fuzt/ ----->	/fust/	'I succeeded'

In sequences of a voiceless obstruent + /r/ or /l/, the latter assimilates to the obstruent with respect to voice; this is true utterance finally only (C̥ = devoiced consonant), e.g.,

ʔaṭṛ̥	train
ṛaṭḷ̥	pound
ʔifl̥	a lock
ʔaṣṛ̥	palace
našṛ̥	publication

The sequence C_1C_2 initially is very rare; e.g. /kwayyis ~ kuwayyis/ 'good', /bṛaavo/ 'bravo'.

*** *** ***

ASSIMILATION : /-l-/ OF DEFINITE ARTICLE

(a) Assimilation of /-l-/ of the definite article to the following consonants : / t ṭ d ḍ s ṣ z ẓ š ž n r ṛ / is obligatory, e.g., /iṭṭaalib/ 'the student', but /ilwalad/ 'the boy'.

(b) Assimilation of /-l-/ of the definite article to / k g / is optional in EA.

/ilkursi/ ~ /ikkursi/ 'the chair'

/ilgidiid/ ~ /iggidiid/ 'the new'

The form of the definite article is /l-/ rather than /il-/ when it follows a word ending in a vowel, e.g.,

/iṭṭaaliba lgidiida/ 'the new student'

This form of the definite article is also subject to the assimilation rules stated in (a) and (b) above, e.g.,

/iṭṭaaliba nnabiiha/ 'the intelligent student'
/ilkursi lgidiid/ ~ 'the new chair'
/ikkursi ggidiid/

*** *** ***

ASSIMILATION OF OBSTRUENTS

1. An obstruent is either a stop (e.g., /b/, /t/, /k/) or a fricative (e.g., /f/, /s/, /ɣ/). In a cluster of obstruents which is pronounced at normal conversational speed, the two constituent consonants are either both voiced or both voiceless. The formation of the word or the juxtaposition of words may bring together two obstruents, one of which is voiced and the other voiceless; when this takes place, the first obstruent changes to match the second in voicing unless such assimilation would obliterate the contrast between lexical items :

   yiḍħak (root: ḍħk) -----> /yiṭħak/ 'he laughs'
   agsaad (root: gsd) -----> /aksaad/ 'bodies'
   naas + zayyak -----> /naz zayyak/ 'people like you'

   Notice, however, that no such assimilation takes place in taħdiid 'specification; and aʕtirif 'I confess'; this is to keep the words in question distinct from taʕdiid 'mourning' and aħtirif 'I practice (a profession)' respectively.

2. When two different sibilants are brought together, the first is totally assimilated to the second :

   miš + zayyi -----> /miz zayyi/ 'not like me'
   ʕaaš + sana -----> /ʕas sana/ 'he lived for a year'

   In EA, the sibilants are /s/, /ṣ/, /z/, /ẓ/, /ž/ and /š/.

3. When the suffixed -ha and -hum are added to forms ending in

/x/, /ɣ/, /ɦ/, or /ʕ/, the resultant consonant cluster undergoes the following changes in the order given :

(a) The first consonant becomes voiceless (if not already voiceless) to match the second.

(b) The second consonant (i.e., the /h/) becomes identical to the first.

dawwax + -hum	----	/dawwaxxum/	'He made them dizzy.'
ṛooɦ + -ha	----	/ṛoɦɦa/	'her spirit'
dimaaɣ + -ha	----	/dimaxxa/	'her head' (after shortening long vowel)
yinfaʕ + -hum	----	/yinfaɦɦum/	'He benefits them.'

The assimilations discussed above are totally predictable; partly for that reason, and partly because it is desirable to indicate what the root consonants are, the transcription does not normally show these assimilations.

*** *** ***

AUXILIARY

(See : Verb : Auxiliaries)

- B -

BACK VOWEL

To produce a vowel sound, the tongue is arched High, Mid, or Low in the mouth. The arching of the tongue is either toward the Front of the palate or the Back. Thus, we describe the vowels in terms of these two parameters. We can, for example, say that EA /i/ is a high front vowel, EA /a/ is a low back vowel and EA /u/ is a high back vowel.

*** *** ***

BILABIAL

A place of articulation consisting of the lower and upper lips : / p b m w /.

*** *** ***

- C -

CLAUSE : RELATIVE CLAUSE

(See : Relative Clauses with illi)

*** *** ***

CLAUSE : STRUCTURE WITH DEMONSTRATIVES

da (ms) 'this, 'that'; di (fs) 'this,that'; and dool (p) 'these, those' may preceed or follow a noun or adjective with consequent significant differences in clausal structure :

They may stand alone as the subject of a sentence :

(a) da walad kibiir 'This is a big boy.'

(b) da kbiir 'This is big.'

Or they may follow a definite noun to form a phrase meaning "this ....:"

ilwalad da kbiir 'This boy is big.'

*** *** ***

COGNATE ACCUSATIVE CONSTRUCTION

There are two cognate accusative constructions in EA :

1. The first construction consists of a verb or an adjective followed by a verbal noun from the same root. The verbal noun is pronounced at a slower rate than the preceding words; moreover, the verbal noun is pronounced with a relatively high pitch and is followed by a sustained terminal juncture. In the following examples, the intonation is represented by a line :

ḍarabuu ḍarb.	'They beat him so viciously !'
akalt ʔakl.	'I ate so much !'
ilbint di ḥilwa ḥalaawa.	'This girl is so pretty !'

As can be seen from the examples, this construction signals strong emphasis.

2. The second construction consists of the following elements in the order given :

(a) A verb or an adjective,

(b) A verbal noun from the same root, and

(c) An expression modifying the verbal noun. The intonational peculiarities which characterize the first construction are not applicable here.

/nimt noom ɣawiiṭ/	'I slept soundly (literally : "I slept a deep sleep").'
/ɣaab ɣeeba ṭawiila/	'He was absent for a long time (literally : "He was absent a long absence").'
/ilbint di gamiila gamaal yigannin/	'This girl is beautiful to a dazzling degree.'

As the examples show, this construction specifies the type of whatever is designated by the verb or the adjective. The corresponding English expression is often an adverb of degree or manner.

*** *** ***

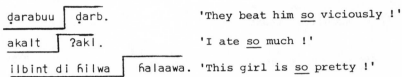

COLLECTIVE NOUNS

A collective is a noun that designates a class or mass of like things without counting the units that make up the mass. Things that can be measured or counted, like fruits and vegetables, have collective nouns as well as unit nouns and their plurals. Other things that can only be measured, like sugar and tea have only collective nouns. Things that can be counted or referred to as a group or "species", like trees, fish, sheep, also have collective nouns, unit nouns and their plurals.

A look at tuffaaḥ 'apples', tuffaaḥa 'an apple' and tuffaḥaat 'apples', shows that tuffaaḥa 'an apple' (here termed Unit Noun) is derived from tuffaaḥ 'apples' (here termed Collective Noun) by the suffixation of the feminine suffix /-a/, and that tuffaḥaat 'apples' (here termed Count Plural , i.e., the plural used after numerals 3-10) is derived from the unit noun by suffixation of /-aat/, like any other feminine plural. There are some collective nouns which form their unit noun by suffixing /-aaya/ and their count plural by suffixing /-ayaat/, e.g.,

manga 'mangos'; mangaaya 'a mango'; mangayaat 'mangos'
xaṣṣ 'lettuce'; xaṣṣaaya 'a head of lettuce'; xaṣṣayaat 'heads of lettuce'
ṭamaaṭim 'tomatoes'; ṭamaṭmaaya 'a tomato'; ṭamaṭmayaat 'tomatoes'

*** *** ***

CONDITIONAL SENTENCES

There are two types of conditional sentences : the simple, and the hypothetical.

A simple conditional sentence lays down a condition and states a result : the condition must be fulfilled before the result can take place, but the crucial fact is that both the condition and the result can occur.

A hypothetical sentence also lays down a condition and states a dependent result; the distinctive characteristic of this sentence is that the condition does not take place, and for that reason the result is not possible.

Of the following pair, the first is a simple conditional sentence while the second is a hypothetical conditional sentence :

iza ṛaaɦ ɦaṛuuɦ maʕaah.	'If he goes, I will go with him.'
law kaan ɦayṛuuɦ kunt aṛuuɦ maʕaah.	'If he were going to go, I would go with him.'

Conditional sentences (simple as well as hypothetical) encompass a large number of possible structures, and different speakers have different preferences. The rules given below define the most common usages. It is assumed that the condition and the result are derived from corresponding "source" sentences. Thus it is assumed that law raaɦ ɦaruuɦ maʕaah 'If he goes, I will go with him' has two source sentences : huwwa ɦayṛuuɦ 'He will go', and ana ɦaṛuuɦ maʕaah 'I will go with him'; it is also assumed that law kaan ɦayṛuuɦ kunt aṛuuɦ maʕaah 'If he were going to go, I would go with him' has the same source sentences.

Some widespread variations are described after the rules.

A. Simple Conditional Sentences

Condition	Result
Derived from the source sentence in the following manner :	
1. A conditional conjunction is added in sentence-initial position. The conjunction is usually iza 'if', but the synonymous conjunction in may also be used.	No change in the source sentence.
2. The constituent "Perfect" is obligatorily added before the verb. If the source sentence is equational, "Perfect" is added after the conjunction. The constituent "Perfect" is realized	

as a perfect form of *kaan* (e.g., *kaan*, *kunt*, *kaanit*, etc.) in an equational condition clause.

3. A future verb and a preceding perfect form of *kaan* are sometimes kept unchanged and sometimes replaced by a perfect verb : the replacement takes place if the *ɦa-* of the verb in question indicates simple futurity; no change takes place if the *ɦa-* indicates a future intention. Thus *iza + kaan + ɦayruuɦ* yields :
   (a) *iza raaɦ* 'if he goes', or
   (b) *iza kaan ɦayruuɦ* 'if he is going to go'

B. Hypothetical Sentences

Condition

Derived from the source sentence in the following manner :

1. The hypothetical conjunction *law* 'if' is added in sentence-initial position.

2. The constituent "Perfect" is optionally added before the verb. If the source sentence is equational, "Perfect" is added after the conjunction. "Perfect" is realized as a perfect form of *kaan* (e.g., *kunt*, *kaanit*, *kaan*, *kaanu*, etc.).

Result

Derived from the source sentence in the following manner :

1. The constituent "Perfect" is obligatorily added before the verb. If the source is equational, "Perfect" is added in initial position. "Perfect" is realized as a perfect form of *kaan* (e.g., *kunt*, *kaanit*, *kaan*, *kaanu*, etc.).

2. A perfect verb in the source sentence is left unaltered; an imperfect verb with an aspect prefix is replaced by the corresponding subjunctive form. If the source is equational, the subjunctive form to be used is *yikuun* (usually occuring after the subject). The pres-

ence of the subjunctive form signals the meaning 'not possible, not attainable'.

3. If the source sentence has kaan, the addition of "Perfect" would produce the sequence kaan kaan (e.g., law kaan kaan tilmiiz for 'if it were true that he used to be a student') This is avoided by :
   - (a) Exercising the option of not adding "Perfect", or
   - (b) Rephrasing; e.g., law kaan ṣaḥiiḥ innu kaan tilmiiz 'if it were true that he used to be a student'.

Note :

In simple as well as hypothetical conditional sentences, the carrier of "Perfect" may exchange positions with the subject of the clause; thus (b) in each of the following pairs is a structural paraphrase of (a) :

(a) law kaan ʕali ṛaaḥ, kaan miḥammad ʔablu.
'Had Ali gone, Mohammed would have met him.'
(b) law ʕali kaan ṛaaḥ, miḥammad kaan ʔablu.

(a) iza kaan ʕali hina, ismaḥli aʔablu.
'If Ali is here, allow me to see him.'
(b) iza ʕali kaan hina, ismaḥli aʔablu.

The following examples illustrate the application of the rules. In each case, the source sentences are given : the source sentence for the condition is labelled (a), and the source sentence for the result is labelled (b). Each source sentence is accompanied by very brief comments on the required transformations (no comments are included on the addition of conjunctions). The conditional sentence which results from combining the output of (a) and (b) is labelled (c). Optional constituents are enclosed in parentheses.

A. Simple Conditional Sentences

1.	(a)	ṛaaɦ ilbeet. Add kaan before raaɦ.	'He went home.'
	(b)	maṛuɦtiš mʕaah leeh ?	'Why didn't you go with him ?'
	(c)	iza/in kaan ṛaaɦ ilbeet, maṛuɦtiš maʕaah leeh ?	'If he went home, why didn't you go with him ?'
2.	(a)	bitidris ingiliizi figgamʕa di. Add kaanit before bitidris.	'She is studying English at this university.'
	(b)	ɦaʔabilha fyoom milʔayyaam.	'I will meet her someday.'
	(c)	iza/in kaanit bitidris ingiliizi figgamʕa di, ɦaʔabilha fyoom milʔayyaam.	'If she is studying English at this university, I will meet her someday.'
3.	(a)	bitiʔri ktaab kull yoom. Add kunti before bitiʔṛi.	'You (fs) are reading a book a day.'
	(b)	ɦatxaḷḷaṣi lkutub di fʔusbuuʕ.	'You (fs) will complete (reading) these books in a week.'
	(c)	iza/in kunti btiʔṛi ktaab kull yoom, ɦatxaḷḷaṣi lkutub di fʔusbuuʕ.	'If you are reading a book a day, you will complete (reading) these books in a week.'
4.	(a)	ɦatirgaʕu ʔabl iḍḍuhṛ. Add kuntu before ɦatirgaʕu. Keep kuntu ɦatirgaʕu unchanged to indicate future intention; replace it by rigiʕtu to indicate simple futurity.	'You (p) are going to return before noon.'
	(b)	ittiṣilu biyya.	'Get in touch with me.'
	(c)	iza/in kuntu ɦatirgaʕu ʔabl iḍḍuhṛ, ittiṣilu biyya.	'If you are going to return before noon, get in touch with me.'
		iza/in rigiʕtu ʔabl iḍḍuhṛ ittiṣilu biyya.	'If you return before noon, get in touch with me.'

5. (a) awlaadak taʕbaniin. — 'Your children are tired.'
Add kaanu before awlaadak.
(b) xalliikum hina. — 'Stay here.'
(c) iza/in kaanu awlaadak taʕbaniin, xalliikum hina. — 'If your children are tired, stay here.'

B. Hypothetical Sentences

1. (a) ṛaaɦ ilmadrasa. — 'He went to school.'
Add kaan optionally before ṛaaɦ.
(b) ṛuɦt maʕaah. — 'I went with him.'
Add kunt before ṛuɦt.
(c) law (kaan) ṛaaɦ ilmadrasa kunt ṛuɦt mʕaah. — 'If he had gone to school, I would have gone with him.'

2. (a) biyidris ingiliizi. — 'He is studying English.'
Add kaan optionally before biyidris.
(b) fihim illi ana ʔultu. — 'He understood what I said.'
Add kaan before fihim.
(c) law (kaan) biyidris ingiliizi kaan fihim illi ana ʔultu. — 'If he were indeed studying English, he would have understood what I said.'

3. (a) ɦayṛuuɦu maṣṛ. — 'They will go to Egypt.'
Add kaanu optionally before ɦayṛuuɦu.
(b) ʔalulna. — 'They told us.'
Add kaanu before ʔalulna.
(c) law (kaanu) ɦayṛuuɦu maṣṛ kaanu ʔalulna. — 'If they were going to go to Egypt they would have told us'

4. (a) kariim biyiktib maqaala kull usbuuʕ. — 'Karim writes an article every week.'
Add kaan optionally before biyiktib.

	(b)	baʔa mašhuuṛ. Add kaan before baʔa.	'He became famous.'
	(c)	law kariim (kaan) biyiktib maqaala kull usbuuʕ kaan baʔa mašhuuṛ.	'If Karim wrote an article every week, he would have become famous.'
5.	(a)	ṛaaħu min ɣeer izn. Add kaanu optionally before ṛaaħu.	'They went without permission.'
	(b)	ʕaqibtuhum bišidda. Add kunt before ʕaqibtuhum.	'I punished them severely.'
	(c)	law (kaanu) ṛaaħu min ɣeer izn kunt ʕaqibtuhum bišidda.	'If they had gone without permission, I would have punished them severely.'
6.	(a)	aṣħaabak fihmu lwaḍʕ. Add kaanu optionally before fihmu.	'Your friends understand the situation.'
	(b)	biyitkallimu kalaam ɣeer da Add kaanu before biyitkallimu, and replace biyitkallimu by its bare counterpart.	'They speak differently.'
	(c)	law aṣħaabak (kaanu) fihmu lwaḍʕ kaanu yitkallimu kalaam ɣeer da.	'If your friends had understood the situation, they would have spoken differently.'
7.	(a)	simʕu kalaamak. Add kaanu optionally before simʕu.	'They heeded your advice.'
	(b)	ħayathum gaħiim. Add kaanit in initial position, and add tikuun after ħayathum.	'Their life is hell.'
	(c)	law (kaanu) simʕu kalaamak kaanit ħayathum tikuun gaħiim.	'If they had heeded your advise, their life would now be hell.'

8. (a) ɦiseen ʕayyaan. 'Hussein is sick.'
Add kaan optionally before ɦiseen.

(b) abuuk ittaṣal bidduktooṛ. 'Your father contacted the doctor.'
Add kaan before ittaṣal.

(c) law (kaan) ɦiseen ʕayyaan kaan abuuk ittaṣal bidduktooṛ. 'If Hussein were sick, your father would have contacted the doctor.'

English employs a contrast which must be taken into consideration here. Compare the following sentences :

(a) If you visit Egypt, you'll change many of your opinions about the Egyptian people.

(b) If you visited Egypt, you'd change many of your opinions about the Egyptian people.

Both sentences are non-hypothetical, and thus both correspond to Arabic sentences of the type we have called "simple conditionals". There is a difference, however, between sentence (a) and sentence (b) : visiting Egypt and the change of opinion which would ensue are considered less probable in sentence (b) than they are in sentence (a). The point to be stressed is that the difference in question is not signalled by the grammatical structure of Arabic conditional sentences; instead, the difference is expressed lexically through the use of ɦaṣal inn, fuṛiḍ inn, or quddir inn (all translatable by "perchance"):

law zuṛt maṣṛ ɦatɣayyaṛ kitiir min aṛaaʔak ʕan iššaʕb ilmaṣṛi. 'If you visit Egypt, you'll change many of your opinions about the Egyptian people.'

law ɦaṣal/fuṛiḍ/quddir innak zuṛt maṣṛ ɦatɣayyaṛ kitiir min aṛaaʔak ʕan iššaʕb ilmaṣṛi. 'If you visited Egypt, you'd change many of your opinions about the Egyptian people' (literally: "If perchance you visit Egypt, you'll change many of your opinions about the Egyptian people.").

The following are some common variations :

1. Many Egyptians restrict the use of law to hypothetical sentences; the same speakers restrict the use of iza and in to simple conditional sentences. Some, however, use the three conjunctions interchangeably in both types of sentences :

law/iza/in ṛaaɦ ɦaṛuuɦ maʕaa.	'If he goes I will go with him.'
law/iza/in kaan ɦayṛuuɦ kunt aṛuuɦ maʕaa.	'If he were going to go I would go with him.'

2. In hypothetical sentences, some use law inn instead of law. The word inn here signals emphasis and frequently occurs with extra heavy stress:

law ʔinni makuntiš issabab fi mootu, kunt itʕazzeet.	'If only I were not the cause of his death, I would have found comfort .'

3. The invariable form yibʔa often introduces the result of a simple conditional sentence. The occurrence of yibʔa is by no means arbitrary, but neither are the rules governing such occurrence easily discernible; suffice it to say here that in many (though not all) instances, yibʔa occurs with the meaning 'then it is true, then it is a fact that, then it must be a fact that' :

iza kaan da ṛaʔyak yibʔa madarastiš ilmawḍuuʕ kuwayyis.	'If this is your opinion, then (it must be a fact that) you have not studied the matter sufficiently.'
iza kaan ilʔustaaz kamaan muxtalif maʕaaya fiṛṛaʔy, yibʔa ana ɣalṭaan.	'If the professor too differs with me in opinion, then (it must be a fact that) I am wrong.'

4. Although the condition usually precedes the result, it is possible to reverse the order; thus in each of the following pairs, (b) is a paraphrase of (a) :

(a)	iza rgiʕt badri ḥaḍṛablak tilifoon.	'If I return early, I will phone you.'
(b)	ḥaḍṛablak tilifoon iza rgiʕt badri.	'I will phone you if I return early.'
(a)	law kaan ʕandi fluus kunt ištareet ilbeet da.	'If I had (enough) money, I would have bought this house.'
(b)	kunt ištareet ilbeet da law kaan ʕandi fluus.	'I would have bought this house if I had (enough) money.'

*** *** ***

CONJOINING

Two sentences may be joined without subordinating one to the other -- i.e., without using one to fill a slot in the other. Such sentences are said to be "conjoined". Consider the following pair :

1.	ḥasan ṛaaḥ ilmaktab lamma ʕali rigiʕ milmadrasa.	'Hasan went to the office when Ali returned from school.'
2.	ḥasan ṛaaḥ ilmaktab wi ʕali rigiʕ milmadrasa.	'Hasan went to the office and Ali returned from school.'

In example 1, the main sentence may be represented as <u>ḥasan ṛaaḥ ilmaktab + T</u> where <u>T</u> stands for the adverbial slot <u>Time</u>. The sentence <u>ʕali rigiʕ milmadrasa</u> is used as a filler for the slot <u>T</u>. In example 2, the sentences <u>ḥasan ṛaaḥ ilmaktab</u> and <u>ʕali rigiʕ milmadrasa</u> are joined together (by the conjunction <u>wi</u>), but neither fills a slot in the other. In example 1, then, the sentence <u>ʕali rigiʕ milmadrasa</u> is "embedded" in another sentence, while in example 2, <u>ḥasan ṛaaḥ ilmaktab</u> and <u>ʕali rigiʕ milmadrasa</u> are "conjoined".

Sometimes the conjoined entities are sentence-like structures only on an abstract level. For example, the utterance ɦasan wi ʕali byidrisu lluɣa lʕarabiyya 'Hasan and Ali are studying the Arabic language' gives the impression that the conjoined entities are two nouns (ɦasan and ʕali), while this impression is correct on one level, it is incorrect on another level. The utterance in question may be considered the result of conjoining two sentences (ɦasan biyidris illuɣa lʕarabiyya and ʕali byidris illuɣa lʕarabiyya), then deleting the redundant constituents.

*** *** ***

CONJUNCTIONS

A conjunction is a word which connects words, phrases, clauses, or sentences, indicating the relationship of the connected elements. Some conjunctions are used for embedding one sentence in another, while some are used for conjoining sentences; the former are called coordinating conjunctions, and the latter are called subordinating conjunctions. Consider the following examples :

(a)	fariid hina wʕali miš hina.	'Farid is here and Ali is not here.'
(b)	fariid hina ʕašaan ʕali miš hina.	'Farid is here because Ali is not.'

In example (a), the two sentences fariid hina and ʕali miš hina are joined together without using one to fill a slot in the other; the conjunction which joins them (wi 'and') is therefore coordinating. In example (b), the sentence ʕali miš hina fills the adverbial slot in the sentence fariid hina + R (where R stands for the adverbial slot Reason); the conjunction which joins the two sentences (ʕašaan 'because') is therefore subordinating.

It is often the case that the entities joined by a conjunction are sentence-like structures on one level but not on another level. For example, in (c) below the joined entities (muniira and gamiila) are nouns; (c), however, is derived from (d) where the joined entities are clauses :

(c)	muniira wgamiila min iskindiriyya.	'Munira and Gamila are from Alexandria.'
(d)	muniira min iskindiriyya wgamiila min iskindiriyya.	'Munira is from Alexandria and Gamila is from Alexandria.'

In regard to the positions where they occur, EA conjunctions are divisible into three types :

1. Conjunctions of Type 1 are those which must occur between the joined entities. The majority of such conjunctions are coordinating. Example :

   axuuya duktoor̥ wana mdarris. 'My brother is a doctor, and I am a teacher.'

2. Conjunctions of Type 2 are those which may occur before or between the joined entities (the first position being more common). The majority of such conjunctions are subordinating. Example :

lamma l?ustaaz daxal, ittalamiiz sa??afu.	'When the professor entered, the students applauded.'
ittalamiiz sa??afu lamma l?ustaaz daxal.	'The students applauded when the professor entered.'

   Notice that when the position of the conjunction changes, the order of the joined entities changes accordingly.

3. Conjunctions of Type 3 are discontinuous forms. The first part of a discontinuous conjunction precedes the two joined entities, and the second part occurs between them. Example :

   ya tṣaaliħ xaliil ya tsiibu fħaalu. 'Either make up with Khalil or leave him alon̥e.'

Listed below are the most common conjunctions of EA. When two or more meanings are given for a conjunction, each meaning is identified by a letter.

A. Conjunctions of Type 1

1. wi 'and' : Elements joined by the conjunction wi must be of the same type; for example, two statements may be joined by wi but a statement and a question may not. When imperfect verbs are joined by wi, the aspect prefix is usually (though not necessarily) deleted from the second form if the first form has the same prefix. The following are examples :

ʔabilt ilʔustaaz wi ɦaddidt mʕaad maʕa lʕamiid.	'I met the professor and made an appointment with the dean.'
imtaɦant ɦseen wi fariida.	'I tested Hussein and Farida.'
ʔabiltu wšaṛaɦtilu lmawḍuuʕ.	'I met with him and explained the matter to him.'
ɦaʔablu w(ɦ)ašraɦlu lmawḍuuʕ.	'I will meet with him and (will) explain the matter to him.'
igtamaʕna mbaariɦ winnahaṛda.	'We met yesterday and today.'
ṛuuɦ wišṛaɦlu lmawḍuuʕ.	'Go and explain the matter to him.'

2. wi biṛṛaɣm min zaalik ~ wi maʕa zaalik 'yet, nevertheless, in spite of that' :

mukayyif ilhawa šaɣɣaal, wi maʕa zaalik ilɦaṛaaṛa ʕalya.	'The air conditioner is on and yet the temperature is high.'
madarastiš, wi biṛṛaɣm min zaalik nagaɦt fillimtiɦaan.	'I did not study; nevertheless, I passed the test.'
biyidris kitiir, wi biṛṛaɣm min zaalik miš ḅiyingaɦ.	'He studies a lot, and in spite of that he does not pass.'
xalliik muʔaddab fi kalaamak maʕaah, wi maʕa zaalik fahhimu nnak ɦatitṣaṛṛaf ɦasab ṛaʔyak ilxaaṣṣ.	'Be polite in talking with him; yet make it clear to him that you will act on your own opinion.'

3. aw 'or' : Sentences joined by aw are usually of the same type, but such sentences are rarely questions (walla, rather than aw, usually joins questions).

iftakaṛt innu baaʕ ilʕaṛabiyya aw ṛahan ilbeet.	'I thought he had sold the car or mortgaged the house.'
ħaštiri tiffaaħ aw ʕinab.	'I will buy apples or grapes.'
ħuṭṭ ilkutub filmaktab aw filfaṣl.	'Put the books in the office or in the classroom.'

4. wala 'nor, rather than; emphatic negative' : This conjunction has two common usages :

(a) It may replace the uninterrupted sequence wi miš; thus the first sentence of each pair below may be replaced by the second member :

(i)	miš ʕawziin niʔabilhum wi miš ʕawziin nišuuf wiššuhum.	'We do not want to meet them, and we do not want to see their faces.'
(ii)	miš ʕawziin niʔabilhum wala ʕawziin nišuuf wiššuhum.	'We do not want to meet them nor do we want to see their faces.'
(i)	ilmoot wi miš ilʕubudiyya.	'Death (is to be chosen) rather than slavery.'
(ii)	ilmoot wala lʕubudiyya. (preferable)	'Death (is to be chosen) rather than slavery.'

(b) It replaces wi ma-...-š when emphasis is to be signalled; in other words, wala may be interpreted as wi + ma-...-š + Emphasis. Of the following pair, the first sentence does not signal emphatic negation while the second one does :

(i)	rigiʕ wi masaʔalš fnaṣiħitna.	'He returned, paying no attention to our advice.'
(ii)	rigiʕ wala saʔal fi naṣiħitna.	'He returned, paying no attention whatsoever to our advice.'

As used in sentence (ii) above, wala denotes negation and emphasis, which distinguishes this use of wala from the use of ma- (in a sentence which contains ma-, emphasis is signalled by an oath particle, by inšaḷḷa, yareet, etc., but not by ma- itself. See "Negation : ma, ...").

5. walla 'or' : This conjunction is the counterpart of aw; as a general rule, walla occurs in questions and aw occurs elsewhere.

baaʕ ilʕaṛabiyya walla ṛahan ilbeet ?	'Did he sell the car or mortgage the house ?'
ɦatištiri tiffaaɦ walla ʕinab ?	'Will you buy apples or grapes ?'
bitidris walla btitfaṛṛag ʕa ttilifizyoon billeel ?	'Do you study or do you watch television at night ?'

6. laakin 'but (contrast)' :

gamʕit iskindiriyya kbiira, laakin gamʕit ilqaahiṛa akbaṛ minha.	'The University of Alexandria is large, but the University of Cairo is larger.'
katab ilmaqaala laakin manašaṛhaaš.	'He wrote the article but he did not publish it.'
ɦayṛuuɦ iskindiriyya laakin miš ɦayiɦḍaṛ ilmuʔtamaṛ.	'He will go to Alexandria, but he will not attend the conference.'
imši waṛaah laakin matkallimuuš.	'Follow him, but do not talk to him.'

7. bass 'but (contrast)' : This conjunction is usually interchangeable with laakin.

gamʕit iskindiriyya kbiira, bass gamʕit ilqaahiṛa akbaṛ minha.	'The University of Alexandria is large, but the University of Cairo is larger.'
katab ilmaqaala, bass manašaṛhaaš	'He wrote the article, but he did not publish it.'
ɦayṛuuɦ baɣdaad, bass miš ɦayiɦḍaṛ ilmuʔtamaṛ.	'He will go to Baghdad, but he will not attend the conference.'

imši waṛaah bass matkallimuuš.	'Follow him, but do not talk to him.'

8. <u>innama</u> 'but (contrast)' : This conjunction is usually interchangeable with <u>laakin</u>, but it occurs less frequently than <u>laakin</u> in a slot which immediately precedes a verb.

gamʕit iskindiriyya kbiira, innama gamʕit ilqaahiṛa akbaṛ minha.	'The University of Alexandria is large, but the University of Cairo is larger.'
katab ilmaqaala innama manašaṛhaaš.	'He wrote the article, but he did not publish it.'
ɦayṛuuɦ baɣdaad, innama miš ɦayiɦḍaṛ ilmuʔtamaṛ.	'He will go to Baghdad, but he will not attend the conference.'
imši waṛaah innama matkallimuuš.	'Follow him, but do not talk to him.'

9. <u>aɦsan</u> ~ <u>laɦsan</u> ~ <u>la</u> :

(a) 'lest' : The conjunction is translatable by 'lest' when followed by a clause which expresses an unreal or not yet realized state of affairs. The verb in the clause is in the subjunctive form.

idris laɦsan tisʔaṭ fi limtiɦaan.	'Study lest you should fail the test.'
matzaʕʕaluuš la yistaqiil.	'Do not offend him lest he should resign.'
ɦawarriihum ilmustanadaat aɦsan yiftikiru nni bakdib ʕaleehum.	'I will show them the documents lest they should think that I am lying to them.'

(b) 'because' : The conjunction is translatable by 'because' when it is followed by a clause which expresses a real state of affairs. If the clause contains a verb, it is in the indicative form.

matgiiš fi yulyu laɦsan iddunya bitkuun ɦaṛṛ ʔawi.	'Do not come in July because (during that month) the weather is very hot.'

iħtaris fi kalaamak maʕaah aħsan da ħassaas xaaliṣ.	'Mind what you say to him because he is very sensitive.'
yaḷḷa biina baʔa laħsan itʔaxxaṛna.	'Let's go because we're (already) late.'

10. illi 'for (indicating cause)' : This conjunction is usually (though not necessarily) followed by a verb.

ana ɣabi lli saddaʔtak.	'I am stupid for having believed you.'
ana mabsuuṭ illi ħaʔdaṛ azuṛhum ʔabl ma ysafru.	'I am glad I will be able to visit them before they leave.'

11. iyyaak : This conjunction expresses hope. It is preceded by a verb and followed by a verb or a verbal clause : the first verb is usually imperative or future; the second is a subjunctive form.

uṣbuṛ iyyaak titɣayyaṛ ilʔaħwaal.	'Be patient; hopefully the circumstances will change.'
ħaṣbuṛ iyyaak ilʔaħwaal titɣayyaṛ.	'I will be patient in the hope that circumstances will change.'
istanna iyyaak yiigi.	'Wait, maybe he'll come.'

B. Conjunctions of Type 2

As has already been stated, a sentence with a Type 2 conjunction has two structures : one in which the conjunction precedes the joined entities, and another in which the conjunction occurs between the joined entities. Although it occurs less commonly than the other, the second structure will be considered the source string; setting up the first structure as the source string would result in a relatively complicated transformation. The "first" of the joined entities is the one which occurs before the conjunction in the source string; similarly, the "second" of the joined entities is the one which occurs after the conjunction in the source string.

1. lamma ~ amma 'when' : each of the joined entities usually contains a verb. The verb of the second entity is usually

without an aspect prefix.

ḥaṛuuḥ amma ddunya tbaṭṭal maṭaṛ.	'I will go when the rain stops.'
amma ddunya tbaṭṭal maṭaṛ ḥaṛuuḥ.	'When the rain stops, I will go.'
baɣḍab lamma yiigi ilfaṣl min ɣeer ma yiʕmil wagbu.	'I get angry when he comes to class without having done his homework.'
lamma yiigi ilfaṣl min ɣeer ma yiʕmil wagbu baɣḍab.	'When he comes to class without having done his homework, I get angry.'
itʕaṛṛaft ʕaleeh lamma kunt ṭaalib fi gamʕit ilqaahiṛa.	'I got to know him when I was a student at the University of Cairo.'
lamma kunt ṭaalib fi gamʕit ilqaahiṛa tʕaṛṛaft ʕaleeh.	'When I was a student at the University of Cairo, I got to know him.'

2. iza, in, law 'if' : See "Conditional Sentences".

3. ʕašaan ~ ʕalašaan

(a) 'in order to (purpose)' : The conjunction is translatable by 'in order to' when followed by the subjunctive verb form.

ṛaaḥ issifaaṛa ʕašaan yiʔaabil ilmulḥaq issaqaafi.	'He went to the embassy in order to see the cultural attaché.'
ʕašaan yiʔaabil ilmulḥaq issaqaafi ṛaaḥ issifaaṛa.	'In order to see the cultural attaché, he went to the embassy.'

(b) 'because' : The conjunction is translatable by 'because' when not followed by a subjunctive verb form.

bitḥibbu ʕalašan biyitmallaqha.	'She loves him because he flatters her.'

ʕalašaan biyitmallaqha bitḥibbu.	'Because he flatters her she loves him.'
ana mṛawwaḥ ʕašaan ṛaasi wagʕaani.	'I am going home because I have a headache.'
ʕašaan ṛaasi wagʕaani ana mṛawwaḥ.	'Because I have a headache, I am going home.'

4. madaam 'since (cause)' :

ṛawwaḥ madaam iššuɣl xiliṣ.	'Go home since the work is done.'
madaam iššuɣl xiliṣ ṛawwaḥ.	'Since the work is done, go home.'
yišuflu šuɣla tanya madaam biyikṛah iššuɣla di.	'Let him find himself another job since he hates this one.'
madaam biyikṛah iššuɣla di, yišuflu šuɣla tanya.	'Since he hates this job, let him find himself another job.'
yaguuz aštiri ʕaṛabiyya madaam asʕaaṛ ilbanziin ḥatinxifiḍ.	'I may buy a car since the price of gas is going to go down.'
madaam asʕaaṛ ilbanziin ḥatinxifiḍ, yaguuz aštiri ʕaṛabiyya.	'Since the price of gas is going to go down, I may buy a car.'

This conjunction agrees in number, gender, and person with a preceding (but not a following) noun subject; it also agrees in number, gender, and person with a pronoun subject. The pronoun subject, when expressed, indicates emphasis and follows madaam, which agrees with the pronoun (unlike madaam + following noun subject). The forms of the conjunction are listed below, followed by a few illustrative contexts :

(huwwa)	madaam
(hiyya)	madaamit
(humma)	madaamu
(inta)	madumt
(inti)	madumti
(intu)	madumtu
(ana)	madumt
(iɦna)	madumna

madaam talamziti mabsuṭiin ana mabsuuṭ.	'As long as my students are happy, I am happy.'
madaam fariida mabsuuṭa ana mabsuuṭ.	'As long as Farida is happy, I am happy.'
talamziti madaamu mabsuṭiin ana mabsuuṭ.	'As long as my students are happy, I am happy.'
fariida madaamit mabsuuṭa ana mabsuuṭ.	'As long as Farida is happy, I am happy.'
ʕali mabsuuṭ madumti inti mabsuuṭa.	'Ali is happy as long as <u>you</u> (fs) are happy.'
madumti inti mabsuuṭa ʕali mabsuuṭ.	'As long as <u>you</u> (fs) are happy, Ali is happy.'
ʕali mabsuuṭ madumna ɦna mabsuṭiin.	'Ali is happy as long as <u>we</u> are happy.'
madumna ɦna mabsuṭiin ʕali mabsuuṭ.	'As long as <u>we</u> are happy, Ali is happy.'

Notice that before a noun subject only the <u>huwwa</u> form of the conjunction occurs.

5. mahma 'no matter what, regardless of what' : With mahma, an imperfect verb is subjunctive if it occurs in the second of the joined entities. Note that the verb in the clause following mahma can be imperfect or perfect with no change in time meaning.

matṣadda?uuš mahma y?ullak.	'Do not believe him no matter what he tells you.'
mahma y?ullak matṣadda?uuš.	'No matter what he tells you, do not believe him.'
ħaxaḷḷaṣ ilmašṛuuʕ da mahma kallifni l?amṛ.	'I will complete this project no matter what it costs me to do so.'
mahma kallifni l?amṛ ħaxaḷḷaṣ ilmašṛuuʕ da.	'No matter what it costs me to do so, I will complete this project.'

C. Conjunctions of Type 3

1. imma...(wi) imma ~ ya (imma) ... ya (imma) 'either...or' : Each of the joined entities usually contains a verb; neither the verb of the first entity nor that of the second can be an imperative form.

ilkitaab imma fmaktabi wi imma fmaktabak.	'The book is either in my office or in yours.'
ʕali imma byidris filmaktaba, wa imma biyʕuum finnaadi.	'Ali is either studying in the library or swimming at the club.'
ya imma maat ya imma miš ʕaawiz yiktib gawabaat.	'He is either dead or unwilling to write letters.'
ya tiigi maktabi ya aṛuuħ maktabak.	'Either you come to my office or I go to yours.'
ya taakul ya t?uum.	'Either eat or leave.'

2. la...wala 'neither...nor' : This conjunction occurs in a sentence whose source strings are negated and joined by wi

'and'. The form la is added to the first source string : it either (a) replaces the negative particle or (b) co-occurs with the negative particle and precedes an element to be contrasted. The form wala is added to the second source string : it replaces both wi and the negative particle. In each of the following examples, (b) and (c) are derived from (a); notice that, in each case, the derivation involves the deletion of a redundant verb form :

(a) miš biyidris filbeet wi miš biyidris filmaktaba.	'He does not study at home, and he does not study in the library.'
(b) la byidris filbeet wala filmaktaba.	'Neither does he study at home nor (does he study) at the library.'
(c) miš biyidris la filbeet wala filmaktaba.	'He does not study either at home or in the library.'

(a) mašuftuuš hina wmašuftuuš hinaak.	'I did not see him here and I did not see him there.'
(b) la šuftu hina wala hnaak.	'Neither did I see him here nor (did I see him) there.'
(c) mašuftuuš la hina wala hnaak.	'I did not see him either here or there.'

(a) matṛuḥš ilbeet wi matṛuḥš ilmadrasa.	'Do not go home, and do not go to school.'
(b) la tṛuuḥ ilbeet wala lmadrasa.	'Neither go home nor to school.'
(c) matṛuḥš la lbeet wala lmadrasa.	'Do not go either home or to school.'

Following is a list of the most common conjunctions in Egyptian Arabic with sentences illustrating only a certain number of them.

1.	in	if (possible)
		in gat badri ḥaṛuuḥ maʕaaha.
		'If she comes early, I'll go with her.'
2.	iza	if (possible)
		iza gat badri ḥaṛuuḥ maʕaaha.
		'If she comes early, I'll go with her.'
3.	law kaan	if (contrary to fact)
		law kaanit gat badri kunt ṛuḥt maʕaaha.
		'If she had come early, I would have gone with her.'
4.	illa in	except if; unless
5.	illa iza	except if; unless
		miš ḥaṛuuḥ illa iza gat badri.
		'I will not go unless she comes early.'
6.	illa law	except if; unless
7.	ḥatta in	even if
8.	ḥatta iza	even if
9.	ḥatta law	even if
		miš ḥaṛuuḥ ḥatta law gat badri.
		'I would not go even if she came early.'
10.	lamma	when, until
		ḥaṛuuḥ lamma tiigi.
		'I'll go when she comes.'
		ḥaʔʕud hina lamma tirgaʕ.
		'I'll stay here until you come back.'
11.	amma	when
12.	mahma	no matter what; regardless of what
		mahma ʔaalit miš ḥasmaʕ kalamha.
		'No matter what she says, I won't listen to her.'
13.	ʔabl ma	before
		iɣsil ideek ʔabl ma taakul.
		'Wash your hands before you eat.'
14.	baʕd ma	after
15.	liɣaayit ma	until
		uʔʕud hina liɣaayit ma tiigi.
		'Stay here until she comes.'

16. liħadd ma   until
17. waʔt ma   when
18. saaʕit ma   just as
                       šuftu saaʕit ma daxal.
                       'I saw him when he entered.'

19. awwil ma   as soon as
                       awwil ma daxal mišiit ana.
                       'As soon as he entered, I left.'

20. yadoob...wi...   no sooner...than; as soon as
                       yadoob daxal wana mšiit.
                       'No sooner had he entered, than I left.'

21. min ɣeer ma   without
                       kaltaha min ɣeer ma aʕṛaf eeh hiyya.
                       'I ate it (f) without knowing what it was.'

22. biduun ma   without
23. aħsan   lest, for fear that
24. laħsan   lest, for fear that
                       ʕaawiz aṛuuħ akallimu dilwaʔt laħsan yimši.
                       'I want to go talk to him now, lest he should leave.'

25. illi   because; that
                       ana farħaan illi šuftak.
                       'I am happy because (that) I saw you (ms).'

26. liʔann   because; for
                       magaaš innahaṛda liʔannu taʕbaan.
                       'He did not come today because he is tired.'
                       magatš liʔannaha nisyit.
                       'She did not come because she forgot.'
                       magatš liʔann axuuha nisi yiʔullaha.
                       'She did not come because her brother forgot to tell he

27. min ɣeer   without
                       nagaħt min ɣeer musaʕditu.
                       'I succeeded without his help.'

28 biduun   without

29. biṛṛaɣm min — in spite of

biṛṛaɣm min musaʕditu managahš.

'In spite of his help he did not succeed.'

30. lawla — but for

lawla musaʕditu makuntiš nagaht.

'But for his help I would not have succeeded.'

31. lawla in — but for

lawla innu saʕidni makuntiš nagaht.

'If it were not (but) for his help, I would not have succeeded.'

32. in — that; because

huwwa faṛhaan innu šaafak.

'He is happy because (that) he saw you.'

33. amma — as for; but

ana ṛuht, amma huwwa ʔaʕad hina.

'I went, but he stayed here.'

34. wi ~ w — and

ana darast whuwwa naam.

'I studied and he slept (wi = and = while)

ana darast wnimt.

'I studied and slept.'

35. aw — or

36. walla — or

inta maṣri walla suuri ?

'Are you Egyptian or Syrian?

inta hatiktib walla hatnaam ?

'Are you going to write or sleep?

37. ya ...ya ... — either...or

38. imma wi imma — either...or

39. imma aw — either...or

40. ya imma ya imma — either...or

ya imma huwwa ya imma hiyya hayṛuuhu maṣr fiṣṣeef .

'Either he or she will go to Egypt in the summer.'

ya imma tṛuuh maṣr ya imma tṛuuh lubnaan fiṣṣeef .

'She will either go to Egypt or Lebanon in the summer.'

41. ya imma...aw either...or

42. la...wala neither...nor

la lwalad wala lbint kaanu hina.

'Neither the boy nor the girl was here.'

la kal wala širib ḥaaga mbaariḥ.

'He neither ate nor drank anything yesterday.'

43. innama but as for; whereas

ilbint gat innama lwalad magaaš.

'The girl came but the boy didn't.'

kaltu innama maʕagabniiš.

'I ate it (ms) but I didn't like it.'

44. ʕašaan because; in order to; for

magaaš ʕašaan misaafir.

'He did not come because he is away (traveling).'

45. ʕalašaan because; in order to; for

gat ʕalašaan tidris maʕaaya.

'She came in order to study with me.'

46. laakin but

47. bass but; only

huwwa kuwayyis bass taʕbaan šuwayya.

'He is all right but he is a little bit (somewhat) tired.

gat bass madarasitš ḥaaga.

'She came but she didn't study anything.'

48. madaam since (= because)

49. ṭaalama as long as

*** *** ***

CONSONANT

A class of speech sounds characterized by constriction or closure of the air stream or friction at one or more point(s) in the breath channel; e.g., EA / b d t g /.

*** *** ***

CONSONANT : CLEAR /l/ VERSUS DARK /ḷ/

The Egyptian Arabic /l/ is like the "l" in English 'leave' and is called a clear "l". In some cases the dark /ḷ/ is used and it is the same as the "l" in the English word 'pull'. In EA the contrast between clear /l/ and dark or emphatic (q.v.) /ḷ/ is phonemic whereas in English they are allophonic variants of the phoneme /l/. The following minimal pair illustrates the phonemic nature of the distinction in EA :

walla 'or' : waḷḷa 'by God'

*** *** ***

CONSONANT : DISTRIBUTION

(a) In Egyptian Arabic (EA) any single consonant may occur at the beginning of a word, in the middle, or at the end; e.g., tiin 'figs', katab 'he wrote', faat 'he passed'.

(b) Doubled consonants may occur medially or finally; e.g., lissa 'not yet', bass 'enough'.

(c) A sequence of two different consonants may occur medially or finally; e.g., tiktib 'you (ms) write', malakt 'you (ms) owned'.

(d) A sequence of three or more consonants never occurs, either within a word or passing from the end of one word to the beginning of the next. This inadmissable sequence is avoided by the helping vowel /i/ (see Phonology 9). /i/ is the vowel of English bit. The helping vowel /i/ is always added between the second and third consonants; e.g. /iddars + sahl/ -----> /iddars i sahl/ 'the lesson is easy'.

*** *** ***

CONSONANT : DOUBLED

A doubled consonant has precisely twice the duration of a single consonant in any given utterance. All consonants may occur doubled in Egyptian Arabic.

*** *** ***

CONSONANT : EMPHATIC = VELARIZED = PHARYNGEALIZED = FLAT

Egyptian Arabic is characterized by having a set of emphatic consonants, which are sometimes referred to also as either "velarized", "pharyngealized", or "flat". An emphatic consonant is one which is produced by raising and backing the dorsum of the tongue concurrently with the primary dental or alveolar articulation so that the articulation is velarized and pharyngealized. The consonants / ṭ ḍ ṣ ẓ ḷ ṛ / are the emphatic counterparts of the PLAIN / t d s z l r /. The occurence of an emphatic consonant will cause a plain consonant in the same syllable (sometimes in the preceding and/or the following syllable) to become emphatic. The domain of the spread of emphasis is the syllable, which means that a syllable has all or none of its sounds emphatic. This also means that in Egyptian Arabic all of the consonants occur as both emphatic and plain consonants as explained above. Thus in

/ṭaab/ = [ṭạạḅ] 'to ripen'

the emphatic /ṭ/ caused plain /b/ to become emphatic [ḅ] and the vowel /a/ is colored with emphasis which means you'll hear an [a] similar to that of English father. As examples of the spread of the domain of emphasis to more than one syllable, we cite the following / - / denotes syllable boundary :

/rabaṭu/ = [ṛạ-ḅạ-ṭụ] 'he tied him'

/muɦaḍraat/ = [ṃụ-ɦ̣ạḍ-ṛạạṭ] 'lectures'

The influence of emphatic consonants on vowels is very noticeable to a non-native speaker. This is particularly clear with the back vowel /a/ which, when in the environment of an emphatic consonant is pronounced further back. In the environment of an emphatic consonant, /i/ is centralized and /u/ is lowered.

*** *** ***

CONSONANT : PLAIN

A non-velarized or non-pharyngealized consonant that is the counterpart of an emphatic consonant: / t d s z l r /

*** *** ***

CONSONANT : PRONUNCIATION

Egyptian Arabic has more consonants than does English. Most of the sounds are pronounced like their English counterparts, while a few are quite unlike anything in English and, therefore, require a great deal of practice on the part of the student.

<u>Egyptian Arabic consonants pronounced almost like their English counterparts</u> :

Egyptian Arabic	As in English
b	boy
p (occurs in borrowings)	pin
t	tea
d	dish
k	cat, king
g	go
f	fine
v (occurs in borrowings)	vine
s	see
z	zeal
š	<u>sh</u>e
ž (occurs in borrowings)	plea<u>s</u>ure, mea<u>s</u>ure
m	me

Egyptian Arabic	As in English
n	no
w	well
y	yet

The following sounds also exist in English, but please note:

/l/ : Egyptian /l/ is like the "l" in English 'leave' rather than the "l" of English 'feel'. Egyptian Arabic /l/ then is like the first "l" in the English word 'level' but never like the second unless velarized (i.e., /ḷ/).

To realize what this means, you might like to try to say 'pull', then start the word 'leave' where you finished 'pull'. Now you may realize that initial "l" in English is different from medial and final "l".

Thus Egyptian Arabic walla 'or' has an " " like that of English 'leave'; Egyptian Arabic waḷḷa 'by God' has an "l" like that of English 'pull'. The first "l" in 'level' is referred to as clear "l" and the last "l" is termed dark "l". Egyptian Arabic /l/ is clear and the emphatic /ḷ/ is dark. The distinction between EA plain /l/ and emphatic /ḷ/ is phonemic, whereas the distinction between clear "l" and dark "l" in English is allophonic (see : Consonant : Clear /l/ Versus Dark /ḷ/).

/h/ as in English 'he' : /h/ is not difficult when it begins a syllable or a word, e.g., Egyptian Arabic haaṭ 'give me' or mafhuum 'it is understood'. But the student may have difficulty pronouncing /h/ when it is at the end of a syllable or a word, e.g., ?ahwa 'coffee', ?eeh 'what?', or ?abuuh 'his father'.

/?/, the glottal stop, is a sound that should not give the English speaker any trouble. It is produced by complete closure and release of the vocal cords; it is sometimes found in English as in New York dialect pronounciation /bo?l/ 'bottle' or as the initial sound of English 'ouch', or between the two vowels of 'uh-oh'.

In Egyptian Arabic, words or utterances never begin with a vowel, whether short or long. In all cases where a non-native speaker hears what he thinks is an initial vowel, it is always /ʔ/ + vowel; thus :

/ana/ = /ʔana/ 'I'

/eeh/ = /ʔeeh/ 'what ?'

*** *** ***

CONSONANT : VOICED / VOICELESS

Refers to whether or not the vocal cords vibrate during the production of a sound. A voiced consonant is one which is accompanied by vibration of the vocal cords, for example, /v/ in the English word 'vine'. A voiceless consonant is one which is produced without any accompanying vibration of the vocal cords, for example, /f/ in the English word 'fine'.

The difference between voicing and voicelessness can be felt strongly if one covers one's ears with one's hands, then pronounces English 'fine' and 'vine', paying attention to the /f/ and /v/.

*** *** ***

CONSTRUCT PHRASE

1. Construct Phrases $N_1 + N_2 =$ the N_1 of N_2

   A construct phrase is either

   (a) definite, if N_2 is definite

/kitaab ilwalad/	'the boy's book'
/kitaab ilwalad ilkibiir/	'the book of the big boy'
/kitaab haani/	'Hani's book'
/kitaab uxti/	'my sister's book'

   or (b) indefinite, if N_2 is indefinite

/kitaab walad/	'a boy's book'

   In either case the construct phrase consists of two nouns $N_1 + N_2$ in a sequence meaning N_1 of N_2. Note that N_1 is definite in meaning, but cannot be definite in form; N_2 may be definite or indefinite in meaning and form.

Either N_1 or N_2 of a construct phrase can be modified by an adjective which is always placed after N_2 and agrees in gender, number and definiteness with the noun modified. Examples :

/kitaab ilbint ilkibiir/	'the girl's big book'
/kitaab ilbint ilkibiira/	'the big girl's book'
/kitaab bint kibiir/	'a girl's big book'

If both terms of a construct phrase are to be modified, a bitaaʕ construction is used, e.g.,

ilkitaab ilkibiir bitaaʕ ilbint ilḥilwa
'the pretty girl's big book'

2. Construct phrases where N_1 is a feminine noun ending in /-a/.
In this case, N_1 has a special form for the construct state (CS), e.g.,

/ʕaṛabiyya/ 'car' gives : /ʕaṛabiyyit nagwa/ 'Nagwa's car'
and /ṣuuṛa/ 'picture' gives : /ṣuurit ṣaḥbi/ 'my friend's picture'

(Notice /ṣaḥbi/ 'my friend' is made definite by possession.)

Compare the forms of /ṣuuṛa/ in the following :

/ṣuuṛa kbiira/	'a big picture'
/ṣuurit ṣaḥbi/	'my friend's picture'

where the first example is a noun-adjective phrase and the second is a construct phrase. (Note : /-a/ ---> /-it/ in a construct phrase.)

*** *** ***

CONSTRUCT STATE OF NOUNS

Note : for /ayyaam/ and /ušhuṛ/ the construct state after numerals 3 - 10 is /tiyyaam/ and /tušhuṛ/ :

/talat tiyyaam/	'three days'
/xamas tušhur/	'five months'

A few other words that belong to this limited class of nouns are :

alf - alaaf	thousand
sabaʕ talaaf	7,000
ṣaṭr - ṣuṭuur	line (in writing)
tisaʕ tuṣṭur	nine lines
xums - axmaas	fifth (fraction)
talat tixmaas	3/5

and other fractions, and optionally :

ʔalam - ʔilaam	pencil, pen
talat tiʔlaam ~ talat ʔilaam	three pencils

(See also : Construct Phrase)

*** *** ***

COUNT PLURAL NOUNS

(See : Collective Nouns)

*** *** ***

D

DEFINITE ARTICLE : FORM

In EA, the definite article is /il-/. The /l/ of the article is obligatorily assimilated to certain consonants, and optionally assimilated to certain other consonants :

1. The /l/ is obligatorily assimilated to a following dental consonant or a following /š/. The dental consonants are /t/, /ṭ/, /d/, /ḍ/, /s/, /ṣ/, /z/, /ẓ/, /r/, /ṛ/, and /n/. Examples,

ittaman	'the price'	izzibiib	'the raisins'
iṭṭaalib	'the student'	iẓẓaabiṭ	'the officer'
iddamm	'the blood'	irriħla	'the trip'
iḍḍuḍaʕa	'the frog'	iṛṛaagil	'the man'
issamaka	'the fish	innaas	'the people'
iṣṣabuuna	'the soap'	iššams	'the sun'

2. The /l/ is optionally assimilated to a following /k/ or /g/, e.g.:

ilkalb <u>or</u> ikkalb	'the dog'
ilgamal <u>or</u> iggamal	'the camel'

3. The form of the definite article is /l-/ when it follows a word ending in a vowel :

iṭṭaaliba lgidiida 'the new student (f)'

4. Usually the form of the definite article is /il-/ when it is prefixed to a word beginning with a vowel, e.g.:

(ʔ)arnab	'rabbit'	ilʔarnab	'the rabbit'
(ʔ)adab	'literature'	ilʔadab	'the literature'

However, with verbal nouns of Form VIII (see : Verbal Nouns) and colors of the form aFʕaL and such words as itneen 'two' the form of the definite article is /l-/ ~ /ill-/. Note the dropping of the /ʔ/ in these examples :

(ʔ)imtiħaan	'exam'	limtiħaan ~ illimtiħaan	'the exam'
(ʔ)aħmaṛ	'red'	laħmaṛ ~ illaħmaṛ	'the red'
(ʔ)itneen	'two'	litneen ~ illitneen	'the two'

*** *** ***

DEFINITE ARTICLE : MEANING

When it is prefixed to a given noun, the definite article indicates that the noun has an unambiguous referent. In regard to its referent, a noun is ambiguous if it is likely to elicit the question "Which one ?", and unambiguous if it would not normally elicit such a question. Compare, for example, the underlined nouns in the following sentences :

1. ištareet kitaab. 'I bought a book.'
2. ištareet ilkitaab. 'I bought the book.'

While kitaab in the first sentence is likely to elicit the question "Which book ?" or the question "What book ?", ilkitaab in the second sentence is not likely to do so; thus kitaab is ambiguous while ilkitaab is unambiguous.

In general, a noun is unambiguous if it has a specific referent (i.e., a particular referent set off in some way from similar referents), or a generic referent. The underlined nouns in the following sentences have generic referents :

1. ilʕaamil yistaħiʔʔ ugritu.	'A workman is worthy of his compensation.'
iṭṭayyaaṛa asṛaʕ min ilʔaṭr.	'A plane is faster than a train.'
ilkutub ahamm min iggaṛaayid.	'Books are more important than newspapers.'
ilʔaṭibbaaʔ miš ahamm min ilmudarrisiin.	'Doctors are not more important than teachers.'

2. ilmayya muhimma lilħayaat.	'Water is essential for life.'
izzeet ɣaali fmaṣṛ.	'Oil is expensive in Egypt.'
irraml anwaaʕ.	'There are different types of sand.'
3. ilħubb šarṭ asaasi liggawaaz.	'Love is a basic pre-requisite for marriage.'
ilfaʔr miš ʕeeb.	'Poverty is not shameful.'
ilʕamal aħsan min ilbiṭaala.	'Employment is better than unemployment.'

Some of the underlined nouns in group 1 imply a class while others denote a class : for example, ilʕaamil in the first sentence refers to any member of the class of people identified as workers, while ilʔaṭibbaaʔ in the fourth sentence denotes a class of people identified as doctors.

The underlined nouns of group 2, in contrast with those of group 1, denote mass (rather than countable) referents.

The underlined nouns of group 3, in contrast with those of the other two groups, denote abstract (rather than concrete) referents.

Since they are generic, the underlined nouns of all three groups occur with the definite article. Notice that the occurrence of the with English generic nouns is more restricted than the occurrence of il- with Arabic generic nouns : to be preceded by the, an English generic noun must be singular and countable (compare "Doctors are rich", "Work is a privilege", and "The car is a recent invention"). Notice too that, in English, singular generic nouns may be preceded by the indefinite article (e.g., "A plane travels faster than a car") while plural generic nouns are preceded by no article at all (e.g., "Books are important"); in Arabic, however, all generic nouns usually occur with the definite article.

*** *** ***

DEFINITE PHRASE

(See : Phrase Versus Sentence)

*** *** ***

DEFINITENESS

(See : Agreement in Construct Phrases; Definite Article : Form; Definite Article : Meaning)

*** *** ***

DEMONSTRATIVES

The demonstratives da (ms) 'this, that'; di (fs) 'this, that'; and dool (p) 'these, those' may preceed or follow a noun or adjective with consequent significant differences in clausal structure :

They may stand alone as the subject of a sentence :

(a) da walad kibiir. 'This is a big boy.'

(b) da kbiir. 'This is big.'

Or they may follow a definite noun to form a phrase meaning 'this ...' :

ilwalad da kbiir. 'This boy is big.'

da (m), di (f), dool (p) are for proximity, 'this, these'; dukha (m), dikha (f) and dukhum (p) are for remoteness, 'that, those'.

*** *** ***

DENTAL

A place of articulation at the upper teeth /t d s z n l /.

*** *** ***

DISCONTINUOUS MORPHEME

A broken sequence which together forms a morpheme of a certain function, e.g., /ma....š/ is the morpheme of negation in EA.

Example :

katab	'he wrote'
makatabš	'he did not write'

*** *** ***

DROPPING OF VOWELS

(See : Vowels : Contraction)

*** *** ***

DUAL NOUNS

The numeral "two" /itneen/ may be used before plural nouns, e.g.,

itneen wilaad	'two boys'
itneen banaat	'two girls'

and is used before plural adjectives :

itneen kubaaṛ	'two big (ones)'.

However, the use of the Dual Form of the Noun is preferable for most nouns. This is achieved by the suffixation of /-een/, the dual ending, to a ms noun or to the CS (Construct State) of fs nouns ending in -a #, e.g.,

waladeen	(< walad)	'two boys'
saħbiteen	(< saħba)	'two friends (f)'
fallaħteen	(< fallaaħa)	'two farmers (f)'
kitabeen	(< kitaab)	'two books'
binteen	(< bint)	'two girls'

The phrase N (dual) + itneen is a possible occurence, which has the effect of emphasizing the idea of duality.

waladeen itneen	'two boys (emphasizing duality)'

This is often accomplished in English by pronouncing 'two' with heavier-than-usual stress. With certain nouns it is preferable to have the word order itneen + N (p) for the dual expression. Examples :

itneen sawwa?iin	'two drivers'
itneen rassamiin	'two painters (artists)'
itneen fallaħiin	'two farmers'
itneen xaddamiin	'two servants'
itneen ħalla?iin	'two hairdressers'

(See also : Collective Nouns)

*** *** ***

DURATIVE FORM

(See : Frequentative Form)

*** *** ***

- E -

ELISION

(See : Vowels : Contraction)

*** *** ***

ELLIPSIS

An elliptic sentence or clause is one which is derived by deleting at least one redundant constituent from the source string. In each of the following examples, the source string contains a redundant expression (identified by an underscore) which is dropped by a deletion transformation :

ɣasalt wišši w <u>ɣasalt</u> riglayya	'I washed by face and I washed my feet'
---> ɣasalt wišši wriglayya	'I washed my face and my feet'
muṣṭafa akal wi baʕdeen <u>muṣṭafa</u> naam	'Mustapha ate and then Mustapha slept'
---> muṣṭafa akal wi baʕdeen naam	'Mustapha ate and then slept'

Elliptic sentences occur very commonly as short responses :

ʕali : darasti eeh baʕd iḍḍuhr ?	'Ali : What did you (fs) study in the afternoon ?'
suzaan : iddars ilxaamis.	'Susan : Lesson 5'

Notice that Susan's response is derived from darast iddars ilxaamis 'I studied Lesson 5' by deleting the contextually redundant expressions.

Although ellipsis is common in both English and EA, the deleted constituents are not always the same in the two languages. In the examples below, certain constituents are deleted from the English sentence (a) to produce the sentence (b); if the same constituents were deleted from the EA sentence (c), the result would be the ungrammatical sentence (d) :

(a) Sami read a book and Susan read an article.

(b) Sami read a book and Susan an article.

(c) saami ?ara ktaab wi suzaan ?arit maqaala.
'Sami read a book and Susan read an article.'

(d) *saami ?ara ktaab wi suzaan maqaala.

In EA, the major rules governing ellipsis are the following :

1. An expression cannot be deleted unless it is redundant. There are two types of redundancy :
   (a) Type 1 redundancy is defined as the occurrence in the answer of expressions which are totally predictable from the expressions in the question.
   (b) Type 2 redundancy is defined as repetition of expressions in the same sentence or across sentence boundaries which does not constitute Type 1 redundancy.
2. The constituents deleted on account of Type 1 redundancy are usually the same in English and EA.
   When an expression is repeated, it is usually the second occurrence which is considered redundant and which is therefore deleted.
3. An expression is usually not deleted on account of Type 2 redundancy if such deletion would produce a structural gap in the resultant sentence, (i.e., if a given slot in a clause were to be deleted).

As a result of Rule 3, deletion in set (a) below produces grammatical sentences while in set (b) it produces ungrammatical sentences :

a. (1)	ɦasan akal wi ɦasan naam	'Hasan ate and Hasan slept'
--->	ɦasan akal wi naam	'Hasan ate and slept'
(2)	kaan ʕaawiz yibiiʕ ilʕaṛabiyya wkaan ʕaawiz yiṛhan ilbeet	'He wanted to sell the car and he wanted to mortgage the house'
--->	kaan ʕaawiz yibiiʕ ilʕaṛabiyya wyiṛhan ilbeet	'He wanted to sell the car and mortgage the house'
(3)	fariid rigiʕ wi saami rigiʕ	'Farid returned and Sami returned'
--->	fariid wi saami rigʕu	'Farid and Sami returned'
b. (1)	ʕali štaṛa ktaab wi luṭfi štaṛa ʔalam	'Ali bought a book and Lutfi bought a pen'
--->	*ʕali štaṛa ktaab wi luṭfi ʔalam	
(2)	ana šaggaʕt ittilmiiz wi luṭfi daayiʔ ittilmiiz	'I encouraged the student and Lutfi bothered the student'
--->	*ana šaggaʕt ittilmiiz wi luṭfi daayiʔ	
(3)	huda bitɦibb ilʔadab ilʕaṛabi wi suheer bitɦibb ilʔadab ilʕaṛabi	'Huda likes Arabic literature and Soheir likes Arabic literature'
--->	*huda bitɦibb ilʔadab ilʕaṛabi wsuheer	

The output in b(1) is ungrammatical because it contains a sturctural gap : the output clearly consists of two clauses; to be a direct object, ʔalam 'pen' must co-occur in the same clause with a verb. In contrast, consider the output of the following transformation :

	ʕali štaṛa ktaab wi ʕali štaṛa ʔalam	'Ali bought a book and Ali bought a pen'
--->	ʕali štaṛa ktaab wi ʔalam	'Ali bought a book and a pen'

The output here is a single clause consisting of three slots : a subject slot filled by ʕali, a verbal slot filled by ištaṛa, and a direct object slot filled by the compound phrase kitaab wi ʔalam. This output therefore is grammatical : unlike the output of b(1), it does not contain a structural gap.

The output of b(2) comprises two clauses the second of which contains a transitive verb but no object; the lack of an object constitutes a structural gap.

In the output of b(3), suheer must function as subject if the desired meaning is to be denoted. The lack of a predicate after suheer not only constitutes a gap but also makes suheer the second term of a compound object :

huda bitħibb il?adab ilʕarabi wsuheer means 'Huda likes (both) Arabic Literature and Soheir'.

Here are two more examples where the output is ungrammatical on account of gaps :

katabt ilkitaab issana lli faatit wi katabt ilmaqaala ssanaadi
'I wrote the book last year, and I wrote the article this year'
---> *katabt ilkitaab issana lli faatit wilmaqaala ssanaadi

samiir biyidris filbeet wi fariid biyidris filmaktaba
'Samir studies at home, and Farid studies in the library'
---> *samiir biyidris filbeet wi fariid filmaktaba
(The output here would be grammatical if the meaning intended were 'Samir studies at home while Farid is in the library')

To avoid redundancy and structural gaps, EA substitutes a pronoun for a redundant noun. This fact accounts for the presence of the underlined pronouns in the sentences below (notice that the English translation does not contain equivalent pronouns) :

ilkanaba 'the sofa' + ʕali ?aʕad ʕa lkanaba 'Ali sat on the sofa'
---> ilkanaba lli ʕali ?aʕad ʕaleeha 'the sofa Ali sat on'

irriggaala 'the men' + nawaal šaafit irriggaala 'Nawal saw the men'
---> irriggaala lli nawaal šafithum 'the men Nawal saw'

Notes :

1. The pronominal subject of a verb is usually deleted; since the verb form indicates number, gender, and person, the pronominal subject is redundant.

ana darast iddars ---> darast iddars 'I studied the lesson'

2. If redundant, a definite modified noun may be deleted leaving only the modifier in the place of the attributive construction.

ʕandi tilmizteen. ittilmiiza lmaṣriyya smaha samiira, wittilmiiza lʔurduniyya smaha ʕayda.

'I have two students (f). The Egyptian student is called Samira, and the Jordanian student is called Aida.'

---> ʕandi tilmizteen. ilmaṣriyya smaha samiira, wilʔurduniyya smaha ʕayda.

'I have two students (f). The Egyptian (one) is called Samira, and the Jordanian (one) is called Aida.'

*** *** ***

EMBEDDING

Embedding is the process whereby a sentence is used to fill a slot in another sentence. For example, the sentence aṣ̌raf rigiʕ imbaariḥ 'Ashraf returned yesterday' contains an adverbial slot filled by imbaariḥ 'yesterday'; the same slot may be filled by a sentence :

aṣ̌raf rigiʕ lamma zeenab rigʕit. 'Ashraf returned when Zeinab returned.'

The sentence zeenab rigʕit is said to be embedded in another sentence.

Embedded sentences may be adverbial (as illustrated above), adjectival (as in irraagil illi zeenab itgawwizitu 'the man whom Zeinab married'), or nominal (as in simiʕt innak bitḥibbaha 'I heard that you are in love with her').

If adverbial, the embedded expression is usually introduced by a subordinating conjunction; if adjectival and modifying a definite noun, it is introduced by illi; if adjectival and modifying an indefinite noun, it is introduced by no particle; if nominal, it is introduced by a nominalizer in certain cases and by no particle in others (see "Nominalization") :

rigiʕ lamma zeenab rigʕit.	'He returned when Zeinab returned'
aʕṛaf ilʔustaaz illi biydarrisak.	'I know the professor who teaches you.'

aʕṛaf ustaaz biydarrisak.	'I know a professor who teaches you.'
simiʕt inn ʕali rigiʕ.	'I heard that Ali has returned.'
maʕṛafš byiʕmil ee.	'I do not know what he is doing.'

*** *** ***

EMPHASIS

(See : Consonant : Emphatic)

*** *** ***

EXCLAMATIONS AND OATHS / ittaʕaggub wilɦilfaan /

subɦaan aḷḷaah	How wonderful, praise be to God !
aḷḷaah	Well !
ya salaam	Fancy that !; My !; Wow !
aḷḷaah	How sweet !; Bravo !
amma ɣariiba	Strange !
šeeʔ ɣariib	Strange !
amma ʕagiiba	Strange !
šeeʔ ʕagiib	What a strange thing !
ya salaam ʕala kida	How strange ! How fancy ! How beautiful !
ya salaam ʕala dammak	How silly of you ! Shame on you !
ya ɦawl illaah	What a loss !
la ɦawla wala quwwata illa billaah	What a loss ! How helpless man is !
ʕaal	Excellent !
mudhiš	Excellent !
bṛaavo	Bravo !
ʕaẓiim	Excellent !
waḷḷaahi	By God ! Indeed ! Really !
wiɦyaat ṛabbina	By God ! (I swear ...)

winnabi	By God ! By the Prophet ! (I swear ...)
winnabi ?	Honestly ?
istaʕgib	to be amazed
istaɣṛab	to be amazed
ɦilif (i)	to swear
ixx ~ ixṣ	How disgusting !
ixṣ ʕaleek	Shame on you ! (ms)

*** *** ***

EXHORTATIVE PARTICLE

The exhortative particle /yaḷḷa/ 'let's' is used in constructions before imperfect forms to mean 'let's (do such and such)!'

yaḷḷa nimši	'Let's go !'
yaḷḷa biina	'Come on !, Let's ....'

*** *** ***

- F -

FEMININE NOUN IN CONSTRUCT

Construct phrases where N_1 is a feminine noun ending in /-a/. In this case, N_1 has a special form for the construct state (CS), e.g.,
/ʕaṛabiyya/ 'car' gives /ʕaṛabiyyit nagwa/ 'Nagwa's car' and
/ṣuuṛa/ 'picture' gives /ṣuurit ṣaḥbi/ 'my friend's picture'.
(Notice ṣaḥbi 'my friend' is made definite by possession).

*** *** ***

FLAP

Refers to a consonant produced by a single tap of the tongue in which the tip of the tongue makes a single rapid contact against the alveolar ridge; /r ṛ/ are flaps.

*** *** ***

FORM VS. FUNCTION

The terms "noun", "adjective", "verb", and "adverb" designate certain forms. On the other hand, the terms "nominal", "adjectival", "verbal", and "adverbial" designate functions (or slots). Nominal slots are typically filled by nouns, adjectival slots are typically filled by adjectives, verbal slots are typically filled by verbs, and adverbial slots are typically filled by adverbs. It must be stressed, however, that there is no one-to-one correlation between form and function : for example, a nominal slot may be filled by a sentence rather than a noun (see : "Nominalization"). In the first example below, the underlined sentence fills the subject slot; in the second example, the underlined sentence fills the object slot :

innu yingaɦ miš muɦtamal.	'That he will succeed is not probable.'
simiʕt inn ʕali rigiʕ.	'I heard that Ali has returned.'

*** *** ***

FREQUENTATIVE FORM

Consists of the imperfect (q.v.) form plus the frequentative prefix /bi-/. It expresses a habitual, repeated action, e.g.,

biyṛuuɦ ilmaktab kull yoom. 'He goes to the office every day.'

or an action which is simultaneous with regard to the time of speech or another definite moment (progressive aspect), e.g.,

biyzaakir dilwaʔti. 'He is studying now.'

With verbs of motion, e.g., /miši/ 'to go', the Frequentative never has a progressive meaning, e.g.,

biyimši min hina lilmaktab. 'He walks from here to the office.'

The Frequentative is also referred to as the Durative.

*** *** ***

FREQUENTATIVE PARTICLE

/bi-/, the frequentative particle, is prefixed to the imperfect (q.v.) to derive the frequentative form (q.v.). This particle has the variant forms /bi-/ after a consonant and /b-/ after a vowel, e.g.,

ilbint btiktib	'the girl writes'
samiir biyiktib	'Samir writes'
inta btiktib	'You (ms) write'

*** *** ***

FRICATIVE

Refers to consonants produced by friction caused by the air moving through a narrow passage in the vocal tract / f v s ṣ z ẓ š ž x ɣ ɦ ʕ h /.

*** *** ***

FRONT VOWEL

A vowel that is produced by arching the tongue to the front of the palate. We can, for example, say that /i/ is a high front vowel.

*** *** ***

- G -

GENDER

In Egyptian Arabic (EA), nouns (n) are either masculine (m) or feminine (f) in gender, e.g., walad (m) 'boy' bint (f) 'girl'. Henceforth, gender indicators will not be entered for those nouns where the sex of the referent clearly indicates the grammatical gender as in the examples above.

Adjectives (adj) show two genders, e.g., nabiih (m) 'intelligent', nabiiha (f) 'intelligent'.

Compare the following nouns and adjectives :

ṭaalib (m)	ṭaaliba (f)	'student'
nabiih (m)	nabiiha (f)	'intelligent'

Notice that the great majority of singular (s) feminine nouns and adjectives end in /-a/. Exceptions to this will be indicated by (f). Masculine singular nouns and adjectives will thus be identifiable by the absence of /-a/ or by the insertion of (m). This convention of indicating gender for singular forms will be followed regularly. Thus ṭaalib 'student' and ṭaaliba 'student' have no gender indicators, since it is clear that the first word is masculine and the second is feminine. Indicators, however, will be entered next to items such as arḍ (f) 'land' and mabna (m) 'building' since their endings do not follow the rule above.

(See also : Demonstratives; Plural; Nisba Adjectives; Agreement in Construct Phrases)

*** *** ***

GENDER : PRESENTATIONAL PARTICLES

ahó (ms), ahé (fs) 'here is' and ahóm (p) 'here are' are here referred to as Presentational Particles. The singular particles agree in gender with the singular noun referred to, e.g.,

aho ṭṭaalib innabiih.	'Here is the intelligent student (m).'
ahe ṭṭaaliba nnabiiha.	'Here is the intelligent student (f).'
ahom iṭṭuḷḷaab innubaha.	'Here are the intelligent students (m).
ahom iṭṭaalibaat innubaha.	'Here are the intelligent students (f).

*** *** ***

GLIDE

A Glide is a transitional sound produced when the vocal organs shift from the articulation of one sound (usually a vowel) to the articulation of another (vowel) sound. The glides in EA are /w/ and /y/. Glides are vocoids phonemicized as consonants.

GLOTTAL

A place of articulation in the glottis (opening at upper part of the windpipe between the vocal cords) : /ʔ, h/ are glottal consonants. The consonant /ʔ/ glottal stop is produced by complete closure and release of the vocal cords. The consonant /h/ is produced by the flow of air through the open vocal cords.

*** *** ***

GLOTTAL STOP

The consonant /ʔ/ glottal stop is produced by complete closure and release of the vocal cords (glottis). It is sometimes found in English as in New York City dialect pronunciation /boʔl/ 'bottle' or as in the initial sound of English 'ouch' before the ou, or between the two vowels of 'uh-oh'. From the phonetic point of view, EA has only one glottal stop. From the distributional point of view there are two word-initial glottal stops : the non-elidible and the elidible. Both are discussed below.

1. The non-elidible glottal stop is never deleted. EA words which contain this glottal stop usually correspond to Modern Standard Arabic words which begin with /q/ :

Egyptian Arabic		Standard Arabic
ʔalb	'heart'	qalb
ʔaam	'to rise'	qaam
ʔatal	'to kill'	qatal

Also nouns of the patterns ʔvCCaaC (e.g., /ʔasmaaʔ/ 'names') and ʔvCaaC (e.g., /ʔimaan/ 'faith') do not usually elide the initial glottal stop.

2. The elidible glottal stop is deleted from a word that is pronounced in close association with a preceding word or prefix, especially in fast speech :

/kitaab/ + /ʔibni/ --> [kitaab ibni] 'my son's book'

Such common forms as the personal pronouns (/ʔana/ 'I', /ʔinta/ 'you (ms)', etc.), the marker of first person singular imperfect verbs /ʔa-/ and the particles /ʔaywa/ 'yes', /ʔahó/ 'here it (m) is', /ʔahé/ 'here it (f) it' are particularly susceptible to such elision. Compare /ʔahwa/ (/ʔ = q/) 'coffee' and /ʔana/ 'I' in the following examples ([ ] denotes actual pronunciation) :

/širibt ɪ ʔahwa/ --> [širibt ɪ ʔahwa] 'I drank coffee'
/širibt ɪ ʔana/ --> [širibt ana] 'I drank'

Sometimes deletion of the elidible glottal stop results in the elision of a short vowel :

/maʕa/ + /ʔibni/ --> [maʕa] + [ibni] --> [maʕa bni] 'with my son'

In two instances, the glottal stop almost always elides : in the relative pronoun :

/ʔilli/ --> [illi] --> [lli] 'who, which, that'

and the definite article :

/ʔil-/ --> [il-] --> [l-] 'the'

For example :

/ʔilħaaga ʔilli maʕaak/ --> [ʔilħaaga lli mʕaak]
'the thing that you have'
/ḍarab ʔilwalad/ --> [ḍaṛab ilwalad] 'he hit the boy'
/rama ʔilkitaab/ --> [rama lkitaab] 'he threw the book'

Note that EA words or utterances never begin with a vowel, whether short or long. When an EA word is heard to begin with a vowel this means that the initial glottal stop has been elided.

Deletion of the elidible glottal stop does not take place in the following situations :

a. If the identity of a word or an expression would be obscured. Thus
/ʕawza/ + /ʔadxul/ = [ʕawza ʔadxul] 'I (f) want to enter.'
(no deletion takes place to keep the sentence distinct from [ʕawz adxul] 'I (m) want to enter.')

b. If the word containing the glottal stop in question is emphatic; compare [min awwil yoom] 'since the first day' and [min ʔáwwil yoom] (where ´ represents extra heavy stress) 'since the very first day'.

c. If deletion of the glottal stop would result in two adjacent long vowels :
/liih/ + /ʔaaxir/ = [liih ʔaaxir] 'It has an end.'

*** *** ***

GRAPHEME

A meaningful unit of the writing system of a language that distinguishes one lexeme (q.v.) or word from another, e.g., English /b/ and /t/ in 'boy' and 'toy'; Egyptian Arabic ب /b/ and ت /t/ in باب baab 'door' and تاب taab 'to repent'. Also referred to as "letter".

*** *** ***

- H -

HAAL ɦaal

A ɦaal is a modifier which indicates the state or condition of the noun modified at the time of the main clause. Consider for example the following sentences :

1. salwa naamit gaʕaana. 'Salwa slept hungry'
2. fariida šaafit ʕumaṛ miɦtaaṛ. 'Farida saw Omar perplexed.'

In sentence 1, the word gaʕaana 'hungry' indicates Salwa's state as she slept. In sentence 2, the word miɦtaaṛ indicates Omar's state when Farida saw him.

A ɦaal may also indicate the external circumstances surrounding the noun modified at the time of the main clause, as opposed to the state or condition of the subject or the object itself.

ṣiɦiit widdinya lissa ḍalma. 'I woke up while it was still dark.'

The ɦaal may be a single word, a phrase, or a clause consisting of an explicit subject and a predicate; in the last case, the ɦaal is always introduced by the particle wi which is often translatable by 'while, as, when' :

ʕali rigiʕ ɦaziin. 'Ali returned sad.'
ʕali rigiʕ yiḍɦak. 'Ali returned laughing.'
ʕali rigiʕ wi huwwa ɦaziin. 'Ali returned sad.'

ʕali rigiʕ wi mʕaah fluus kitiir. 'Ali returned with a lot of money.'

ʕali rigiʕ winta bṭistaɦamma. 'Ali returned while you were taking a bath.'

If the ɦaal is a verb, it is usually a present-tense form denoting progressive action.

*** *** ***

HARD PALATE

The hard palate is the portion of the roof of the mouth behind the alveolar ridge.

*** *** ***

HELPING VOWEL

(See : Vowel : Extra)

*** *** ***

HIGH VOWEL

A vowel that is produced with the tongue arched high in the mouth. The EA high vowels are /i/ and /u/.

*** *** ***

HOLLOW VERB

(See : Verb : Classification by Root Type)

*** *** ***

- *I* -

IMPERATIVE : FORMATION

Imperative forms are yielded by the corresponding second-person subjunctive forms. The traceability of the imperative form to the subjunctive is not surprising since the latter denotes possibility (as opposed to fact) and since a command or a request falls within the realm of possibility.

A second-person subjunctive form always begins with /t/ ; the imperative results from deleting that /t/ and the vowel which follows it; if this would result in a word-initial consonant cluster, only the /t/ is deleted.

<u>Subjunctive</u>	<u>Imperative</u>	
(inta) tiṛuuħ	ṛuuħ	'go !' (ms)
(inti) tiṛuuħi	ṛuuħi	'go !' (fs)
(intu) tiṛuuħu	ṛuuħu	'go !' (p)
(inta) tišaawir	šaawir	'consult !' (ms)
(inti) tišawri	šawri	'consult !' (fs)
(intu) tišawru	šawru	'consult !' (p)
(inta) tiʕallim	ʕallim	'teach !' (ms)
(inti) tiʕallimi	ʕallimi	'teach !' (fs)
(intu) tiʕallimu	ʕallimu	'teach !' (p)

(inta) tuxṛug	uxṛug	'go out !' (ms)
(inti) tuxṛugi	uxṛugi	'go out !' (fs)
(intu) tuxṛugu	uxṛugu	'go out !' (p)

(inta) titnaazil	itnaazil	'relinquish !' (ms)
(inti) titnazli	itnazli	'relinquish !' (fs)
(intu) titnazlu	itnazlu	'relinquish !' (p)

(inta) tiktib	iktib	'write !' (ms)
(inti) tiktibi	iktibi	'write !' (fs)
(intu) tiktibu	iktibu	'write !' (p)

Notes :

1. The subjunctive forms for 'you come' are tiigi (ms), tiigi (fs), and tiigu (p). Rather than the expected *gi and *gu, EA uses taʕaala, 'come !' (ms), taʕaali 'come !' (fs), and taʕaalu 'come !' (p).
2. The subjunctive forms for 'you bring' are tigiib (ms), tigiibi (fs), and tigiibu (p). The corresponding imperative forms are haat, haati, and haatu (although giib, giibi, and giibu are used occasionally) :

haat/giib ilkitaab maʕaak bukṛa ya ʕali	'Bring the book with you tomorrow, Ali.'
haat/giibi bintik maʕaaki	'Bring your daughter with you (fs).'
haatu/giibu aṣdiqaʔkum maʕaakum	'Bring your friends with you (p).'

In addition, the forms haat, haati, and haatu are used with the meaning 'give me'. In this context haat and haati are interchangeable with iddiini, while haatu is interchangeable with idduuni.

haat/ iddiini ʔalam ya ʕali.	'Give me a pencil, Ali.'
haati/iddiini lkitaab ya fariida.	'Give me the book, Farida.'
haatu/idduuni lkutub ya wlaad.	'Give me the books, children.'

3. The imperative forms <u>itfaḍḍal</u> (ms), <u>itfaḍḍali</u> (fs), and <u>itfaḍḍalu</u> (p) denote a polite invitation of any kind. Translatable by 'be so kind as (to do or accept something)', the three forms may be used with or without an object :

itfaḍḍal (said by someone who is eating)	'Please come and eat with me.'
itfaḍḍal (said upon opening the door)	'Please come in.'
itfaḍḍal (pointing to a chair)	'Please sit down.'
itfaḍḍal istirayyaɦ ya ʕali.	'Please sit down, Ali.'
itfaḍḍali uʔʕudi ya suzaan.	'Please sit down, Susan.'
itfaḍḍalu šaay ya asadza.	'Please have some tea, professors.'

*** *** ***

IMPERATIVE : IMPERATIVE FORMS IN THE VERB SEQUENCE

A verbal sequence which does not include <u>kaan</u> is made imperative in the following manner :

1. If it is a Class III auxiliary (see : Verb : Auxiliaries), the first verb assumes the imperative form; in addition, the second verb assumes the imperative form. If there is another verb in the sequence, that verb is a bare imperfect form :

itʕallim tiktib.	'Learn how to write.'
ibtidi titʕallim tiktib.	'Start learning how to write.'
iʔbal tibtidi titʕallim tiktib.	'Agree to start learning how to write.'
iʔbal tibtidi tṛuuħ titʕallim tiktib.	'Agree to start going to learn how to write.'
iʔbal yibtidi yṛuuħ.	'Agree (to the proposition) that he should go.'

All of the above verbal sequences may be preceded by a second-person perfect form of kaan (the form in question is usually translatable by 'you'd have done well to ...') :

kunt ṛuuħ itʕallim ṣanʕa.	'You'd (ms) have done well to go learn a trade.'
kunti ṛuuħi tʕallimi faṛansaawi.	'You'd (fs) have done well to go learn French.'
kuntu ṛuuħu tʕallimu ṣanʕa.	'You'd (p) have done well to go learn a trade.'
kunt itʕallim tiktib ʕaṛabi.	'You'd (ms) have done well to learn how to write Arabic.'
kunti tʕallimi tiktibi ʕaṛabi.	'You'd (fs) have done well to learn how to write Arabic.'
kuntu tʕallimu tiktibu ʕaṛabi.	'You'd (p) have done well to learn how to write Arabic.'

The imperative verb iwʕa (feminine : iwʕi, plural iwʕu) may introduce a verbal sequence to denote a warning or an admonition against something; the sequence in question may or may not contain a form of kaan :

1. If it occurs in the verbal sequence, kaan follows iwʕa and is a bare imperfect form. A verb which immediately follows kaan is an imperfect form with an aspect prefix; any other verb in the sequence is a bare imperfect form.

iwʕa tkuun ʕayyaan.	'I hope you (ms) are not sick.' Literally : "Be mindful of the possibility that you (ms) are sick."
iwʕi tkuuni bitħibbii.	'I hope you (fs) are not in love with him.' Literally : "Be mindful of the possibility that you (fs) are in love with him."
iwʕu tkuunu ħatibtidu tidrisu turki.	'I hope you (p) are not going to start studying Turkish.' Literally : "Be mindful of the possibility that you (p) will start to study Turkish."
iwʕa ykuun ʕayyaan.	'I hope he is not sick.' Literally : "You (ms) take heed lest he should be sick."
iwʕi ykuun biyħibbik.	'I hope he is not in love with you (fs).' Literally : "Take heed lest he should be in love with you (fs)."
iwʕu ykuunu ħayibtidu yidrisu turki.	'I hope they are not going to start studying Turkish.' Literally : "You (p) take heed lest they should be going to start studying Turkish."

2. If kaan does not occur in the verbal sequence, all the verbs which follow iwʕa are bare imperfect (= subjunctive) forms :

iwʕa tgiibu.	'Make sure you (ms) do not bring him.'
iwʕi tṛuuħi tʔablii.	'Make sure you (fs) do not go to meet him.'

iwʕu tibtidu tṛuuħu tidrisu turki.	'Make sure you (p) do not start to study Turkish.'
iwʕa yiigi.	'You (ms) make sure he does not come.'
iwʕi yṛuuħ yiʔabilha.	'You (fs) make sure he does not go to meet her.'
iwʕu yibtidu yṛuuħu yidrisu turki.	'You (p) make sure that they do not start to study Turkish.'

The imperative iwʕa may co-occur with a negative verb :

iwʕa matirgaʕš.	'Make sure you return.' Literally : "Guard against not returning."

*** *** ***

IMPERATIVE : NEGATIVE

A negative imperative form consists of the subjunctive second-person form plus the affixes ma-...-š :

tiktib	'you (ms) write'
ma-tiktib-š	'don't write (addressing a male)'
tiktibi	'you (fs) write'
ma-tiktibii-š	'don't write (addressing a female)'
tiktibu	'you (p) write'
ma-tiktibuu-š	'don't write (addressing more than one)'

The affirmative imperative forms of yiigi 'to come' are taʕaala (ms) taʕaali (fs), and taʕaalu (p); the corresponding negative imperatives are matgiiš (ms, fs) and matguuš (p).

Neither the negative nor the affirmative imperative form of kaan occurs in a verbal sequence; for this reason, the following comments are restricted to verbal sequences which include no form of kaan.

A verbal sequence may consist of only two members. If the first verb of such a sequence is negative imperative the second is an affirmative second-person bare form. If the second verb is negative, the first is an affirmative imperative form :

mati?balš truuħ.	'Don't agree to go.'
i?bal matruħš.	'Agree not to go.'

A verbal sequence may consist of more than two verbs. If the first verb of such a sequence is a negative imperative, the rest are affirmative second-person bare (subjunctive) forms. If a verb other than the first is negative, the first is an affirmative imperative, and the rest are affirmative second person bare (subjunctive) forms :

mati?balš truuħ titʕallim.	'Do not agree to go to learn.'
i?bal matruħš titʕallim.	'Agree not to go to learn.'

As the English translation shows, negating different constituents of the verbal sequence does not result in synonymous expressions. Most situations call for negating only the first verb :

mati?balš tibtidi truuħ.	'Don't agree to start going.'

A verbal sequence may contain one of the forms iwʕa (used in addressing a male), iwʕi (used in addressing a female), and iwʕu (used in addressing more than one person). The three forms in question imply undesirable consequences and are best translated by 'you'd better not (do something)'

iwʕa truuħ maʕaaha.	'Make sure you (ms) do not go with her.'
iwʕi truuħi maʕaaha.	'Make sure you (fs) do not go with her.'

iwʕu tṛuuħu maʕaaha.	'Make sure you (p) do not go with her.'

A negative imperative form may follow iwʕa, iwʕi, or iwʕu in the same verbal sequence :

iwʕa matṛuħš tʔablu.	'You'd better not fail to go to meet him.'
iwʕi tiʔbali matṛuħiiš.	'You'd better not agree not to go.'
iwʕu matħawluuš tihṛabu.	'You'd better not fail to attempt to escape.'

*** *** ***

IMPERATIVE : RESPONSES

The following five expressions are commonly used in responding to a request; they are interchangeable in most situations, and the idiomatic translation in each case is 'gladly' :

1.	ħaaḍir.	(literally : "(It's) Ready") (invariabl[e])
2.	bikull sṛuuṛ.	(literally : "With every pleasure")
3.	ʕala ʕeeni wṛaasi.	(literally : "On my eye and my head !" with the cultural implication that whatever is placed on the eye or the head is an obligation that can-not be taken lightly)
4.	ɣaali wiṭṭaḷab ṛixiiṣ.	(literally : "You are dear and the request is inexpensive")
5.	amṛak.	(literally : "Your order")

*** *** ***

IMPERATIVE : SOCIAL USAGE

The following sentences contain imperative verbs :

u?af gamb ilbaab.	'Stand (ms) next to the door.'
ṛuuħi maṣṛ.	'Go (fs) to Egypt.'
istaʕiddu lillimtiħaan.	'Get ready (p) for the test.'
i?ṛu lmaqaala kwayyis.	'Read (p) the article well.'

Although perfectly grammatical, the above sentences have restricted usage; they occur in one of the following situations :

1. When the speaker considers the addressee less than an equal.
2. When the speaker and the addressee are on familiar terms.

In formal situations, and when addressing equals or superiors, the speaker usually employs one of the following structures to express a request :

1. A question introduced by the auxiliary ti?daṛ (feminine : ti?daṛi, plural : ti?daṛu) 'could you' or the auxiliary tismaħ (feminine : tismaħi, plural : tismaħu) 'would you':

ti?daṛ tigibli kubbaayit mayya ?	'Could you (ms) bring me a glass of water ?'
ti?daṛi tšufiili huwwa feen ?	'Could you (fs) find him for me ?'
tismaħu tiigu baʕd iḍḍuhṛ ?	'Would you (p) come in the afternoon ?'

2. A question introduced by the modal mumkin 'could' :

mumkin tu?ʕud ʕa kkursi ttaani ?	'Could you (ms) sit on the other chair ?'
mumkin tiṭbaʕiili ggawaab da ?	'Could you (fs) type this letter for me ?'
mumkin tigiibu kutubkum maʕaakum bukṛa ?	'Could you (p) bring your books with you tomorrow ?'

3. An imperative construction combined with the polite expression min fadlak (feminine : min fadlik, plural : min fadlukum) 'please'. Less common than min fadlak, but equivalent to it in meaning, are the following expressions : wiħyaatak (feminine : wiħyaatik, plural : wiħyatkum), winnabi, iʕmil maʕruuf (feminine : iʕmili maʕruuf, plural : iʕmilu maʕruuf), yinuubak sawaab (feminine : yinuubik sawaab, plural: yinubkum sawaab, law samaħt (feminine : law samaħti, plural law samaħtum) :

iftaħ ilbaab min fadlak ya ʕali.	'Please open the door, Ali.'
iftaħi min fadlik ya fariida.	'Please open (the door), Farida.'
hatiili fingaal ?ahwa ynuubik sawaab ya fatħiyya.	'Please bring me a cup of coffee, Fathia.'
iddiini kkitaab da winnabi ya ħasan.	'Please give me this book, Hasan.'
uskutu ya wlaad iʕmilu maʕruuf.	'Please be quiet, children.'

4. One of the questions described in #1 and #2 above, combined with one of the polite expressions listed in #3 :

ti?dar tigibli fingaal ?ahwa min fadlak ?	'Could you (ms) please bring me a cup of coffee ?'
mumkin titbaʕiili ggawaab da winnabi ?	'Could you (fs) please type this letter for me ?'

*** *** ***

IMPERATIVE : SUPPLEMENTARY NOTES

1. The English expression "make so and so do such and such' is paralleled in EA by a construction which consists of the

following units in the order given :

(a) One of the imperative forms xalli (ms or fs) and xallu (p) 'make, have (someone do something)'.

(b) A noun or a third-person pronominal suffix functioning as subject of the following verb.

(c) A bare imperfect (subjunctive) verb.

The following are examples :

ya ʕali, xalli fariid yiṛuuḥ.	'Ali, make Farid go.'
ya samiira, xallii yṛuuḥ.	'Samira, make him go.'
ya asadza, xallu talamzitkum yinaḍḍafu lʔooḍa.	'Teachers, make your students clean up the room.'

The same construction can mean 'let (i.e., allow) so and so to do such and such'; here, however, constituent (b) may be a noun, a first-person pronominal suffix, or a third-person pronominal suffix :

ya fariid, xalli suzaan tiṛuuḥ.	'Farid, let Susan go (i.e., allow Susan to go).'
ya amaal, xalliini asaʕdik.	'Amal, let me help you (i.e., allow me to help you).'
ya wlaad, xalliihum yilʕabu mʕaakum.	'Children, let them play with you (i.e., allow them to play with you).'

2. The English construction with let's corresponds to an Arabic construction consisting of yaḷḷa and a following first-person plural verb :

yaḷḷa nirgaʕ.	'Let's return.'
yaḷḷa niʔli ssamak.	'Let's fry the fish.'

3. The sequence signal ma often occurs in contexts which denote commands or requests. All verbs which follow ma in such contexts are bare, imperfect, second-person forms :

ma tʔuum ya ʕali.	'Come on, Ali, get up !'
ma tʔuumi ya suzaan.	'Come on, Susan, get up !'
ma tʔuumu ya wlaad.	'Come on, children, get up !'
ma tʔuum taakul ya fariid.	'Come on, Farid, get up and eat !

The form ma is called a sequence signal because it may relate the sentence to a preceding portion of the discourse. Thus ma tʔuum taakul indicates annoyance at having to repeat the invitation.

*** *** ***

INDEFINITE PHRASE

(See : Phrase Versus Sentence)

*** *** ***

INDEFINITE SUBJECT

In EA, the subject of a sentence is usually definite :

ilkitaab ʕa ṭṭaṛabeeza.	'The book is on the table.'
ʕali filbeet.	'Ali is at home.'
inti min maṣṛ ?	'Are you from Egypt ?'

There are relatively few types of sentences with an indefinite subject; they consist of two groups :

1. Sentences whose predicate contains or consists of the word fii ~ fiih 'there is/are (denoting existence)'; an example is *ilaah fiih which, as will become clear from the discussion below, is the abstract source string for fiih ilaah 'There is a God.'
2. Sentences whose predicate neither contains nor consists of the word fii ~ fiih; an example is kalb ħayy aħsan min asad mayyit

'A living dog is more useful (literally : "better") than a dead lion.'

Sentences of the first group occur with the predicate preceding the subject; thus the source string *ilaah fiih undergoes an inversion transformation which produces fiih ilaah 'There is a God.' The inversion transformation in question is not applicable to sentences of the second group.

Sentences of the first group may be divided into the following sub-groups :

(a) Sentences where fii ~ fiih is followed by a modifier denoting place or possession. In the examples below, only the abstract source strings are given and the actual sentences will be derived later :

* kitaab fiih ʕa ṭṭaṛabeeza.	'There is a book on the table.'
* saaʕa fiih ʕandi.	'I have a watch.'
* ḍahṛ fiih liina.	'We have backing.'

(b) Sentences where fii ~ fiih is not followed by a modifier denoting place or possession. In the examples below, only the abstract source strings are given :

* ilaah fiih.	'There is a God.'
* kitaab ʕan maṣṛ fiih.	'There is a book about Egypt.'
* sitt btixbiz fiih.	'There is a woman who is baking.'

To produce concrete sentences (i.e., sentences which are actually pronounced by speakers), the abstract strings of sub-group (a) undergo one of the transformations described below :

1. The constituent fii ~ fiih is transposed to initial position :

* kitaab fiih ʕa ṭṭaṛabeeza ---> fiih kitaab ʕa ṭṭaṛabeeza
  'There is a book on the table.'
* saaʕa fiih ʕandi ---> fiih saaʕa ʕandi
  'I have a watch.'
* ḍahṛ fiih liina ---> fiih ḍahṛ liina
  'We have backing.'

2. The modifier is transposed to initial position and the minimum predicate fii ~ fiih is deleted :

 * kitaab fiih ʕa ṭṭaṛabeeza ---> ʕa ṭṭaṛabeeza ktaab
 'There is a book on the table.'
 * saaʕa fiih ʕandi ---> ʕandi saaʕa
 'I have a watch.'
 * ḍahṛ fiih liina ---> liina ḍahṛ
 'We have backing.'

To produce concrete sentences, the abstract strings of subgroup (b) undergo a transformation which transposes the predicate fii ~ fiih to initial position :

* ilaah fiih ---> fiih ilaah
 'There is a God'
* kitaab ʕan maṣṛ fiih ---> fiih kitaab ʕan maṣṛ
 'There is a book about Egypt'
* sitt btixbiz fiih ---> fiih sitt btixbiz
 'There is a woman who is baking.'

*** *** ***

INDEPENDENT PERSONAL PRONOUNS

(See : Pronoun : Personal)

*** *** ***

INDICATIVE MOOD

The indicative verb predicates an actual occurence or fact (as opposed to a wish, a conjecture, or a possibility). The actual occurence or fact may be either static, habitual, or progressive, as well as, according to the context, past, present, or future, e.g.,

/kaan biyiktib/	'he was writing'
/ḥaykuun biyiktib/	'he will be writing'
/biyiktib ʕaṛabi kwayyis/	'he writes Arabic well (script or language)'

*** *** ***

INTENSIFIER

Adverbs, interjections and other phrases that express a greater degree of something. Examples :

ʔawi	very
xaaḷiṣ	very
giddan	very
kitiir	a lot (after verbs or nouns)
abadan	never, not at all (independent or with negative verb)
mutašakkir xaaḷiṣ	Thank you very much.
mutašakkir ʔawi	Thank you very much.
mutašakkir giddan	Thank you very much.
innoom kitiir wiḥiš ʔawi	Sleeping a lot is very bad.
ʕumṛak širibt ilwiski ?	Have you ever drunk whiskey ?
abadan	Never
abadan xaaliṣ ?	Never ever at all ?
ʕumṛi	Never (in my whole life)
ʕumṛi ma šribt sagaayir.	I have never smoked cigarettes (Note : EA "drink" cigarettes)
ilḥamdu lillaah ʕumṛi mašribtiš sagaayir abadan.	Thank God, I never ever smoked at all.
ilbint di ḥilwa ʔawi, gamiila giddan.	This girl is very pretty, very beautiful.
inta akṛamtini ktiir ʔawi, wana mutašakkir giddan.	You were very hospitable to me, and I am very obliged to you.
imbaariḥ mišiit ʕašṛa miil.	Yesterday I walked for ten miles.
ʕašṛa miil miš kitiir ʔawi.	Ten miles is not very much.
la izzaay !	Oh, come on !
bṛaavo ! kuwayyis giddan.	Bravo, very good !

*** *** ***

INTERROGATIVE

(See : Questions : Alternative Questions,
Questions : Information Questions,
Questions : Tags,
Questions : Yes-or-No Questions)

*** *** ***

INTERROGATIVES

A word or a phrase used to ask questions. The most common interrogatives in Egyptian Arabic are :

eeh ?	'what ?'
feen ?	'where ?'
(ʕala) feen ?	'to where ?'
mineen ?	'from where ?'
leeh ?	'why ?'
emta ?	'when ?'
ʕalašaan eeh ?	'what for ?'
miin ?	'who ?'
eeh ?	'which ?'
bitaaʕ miin ?	'whose ?'
limiin ?	'whose ?'
kaam ?	'how many ? how much ?'
bikaam ?	'how much ? (price)'
ʔadd eeh ?	'how long (distance) ?'
izzaay ?	'how ?'
hal ?	'did, will ?' (question particle

*** *** ***

- L -

LABIODENTAL

A place of articulation consisting of the lower lip and upper teeth : /f v/.

*** *** ***

LATERAL

Refers to a consonant produced with the tongue touching only the middle of the palate, thus allowing the air flow to escape around one or both sides of the tongue : /l ḷ/.

*** *** ***

LEXEME

Also referred to as Lexical Item or Lexical Form or Word or Vocabulary Item or Dictionary Entry or Citation Form.

*** *** ***

LEXICON

A list of (all or certain) words in a language.

*** *** ***

LINKAGE

In many cases, word and syllable boundaries do not coincide in EA. Linkage is the formation of a syllable using the last phoneme(s) of one word and the initial phoneme of the following word. If we look at /ʔilgumla gdiida/ 'the sentence is new' in terms of syllable and word boundaries, we get /ʔil - gum - la͡g - dii - da/ (" - " here represents syllable boundary and ^ represents linkage between words). The most difficult part for a non-native speaker is the end of the first word and the beginning of the second word where linkage occurs : here, /la͡g/. This is particularly difficult in rapid speech.

*** *** ***

LONG VOWEL

(See : Vowels)

*** *** ***

LOW VOWEL

A vowel which is produced with the tongue arched low in the mouth. The EA low vowel is /a/.

*** *** ***

- M -

MANNER ADVERBS

(See : Adverbs of Manner)

*** *** ***

MAṢDAR

A term used by Arab grammarians to refer to the Verbal Noun (q.v.).

*** *** ***

MEASURES : DEFINITION

Compare the following words :

ɦammis	'to make (someone) enthusiastic'
kattib	'to make (someone) write'
sallim	'to greet'
sabbib	'to cause'

Although they have different roots, the words in question are structurally similar since each consists of the following elements in the order given : an initial radical, the vowel /a/, a doubled radical, the vowel /i/, and a final radical. Using F, ʕ, and L as cover symbols for any initial radical, any medial radical, and any final radical respectively, the shared structure may be represented as FaʕʕiL. Thus FaʕʕiL is a generalized shape which stands for all words of a given structure; such generalized shapes are called "measures".

Measures are usually associated with particular meanings in contrast with the lexical meanings of roots; for example, the verb measure FaʕʕiL frequently indicates causation (kattib 'to make someone write'); the noun measure FaaʕiL frequently indicates the doer (kaatib 'writer'); and the noun measure maFʕaL frequently indicates place (maktab 'office').

In addition to their particular meanings, measures also have a lexical designation; for example, the measure FaʕiiL frequently designates high-ranking positions while FaʕʕaaL frequently designates lowly occupations :

waziir	'(cabinet) minister'
amiir	'prince'
ʕaqiid	'colonel'
naqiib	'chairman of a guild'
safiir	'ambassador'
ṭabiib	'medical doctor'
ʕamiid	'dean'
ɦammaaṛ	'donkey driver'
gazzaaṛ	'butcher'
šayyaal	'porter'
naggaaṛ	'carpenter'
fallaaɦ	'farmer'
sabbaak	'smelter'
xabbaaz	'baker'
ɦallaaʔ	'barber'
sabbaak	'plumber'

Many measures have variants which are determined by general phonological rules; in other words, a measure is a class of patterns. For example, the following patterns belong to the same measure since they designate the same grammatical meanings (passivity, etc.) and since the structural differences which distinguish one from the other are predictable in terms of phonological changes in the root :

itFaʕaL	(from sound roots)
itFaʕʕ	(from doubled roots)
itFaaL	(from hollow roots)
itFaʕa	(from defective roots)

The "basic" shape (i.e., the shape which stands for the class as a whole) is the one which can yield the other shapes through the simplest and most general rules possible; in the case of triliteral verbs, the basic shapes are those which have sound roots (q.v.). It is for this reason that itFaʕaL stands for the class which includes itFaʕaL, itFaʕʕ, itFaaL, and itFaʕa; it follows that (unless further specification is necessary) itxaram, itʕadd, itbaaʕ and itrama are said to be of the measure itFaʕaL.

*** *** ***

MEASURES : INTUITIONAL REALITY OF

That the measure -- apart from the root -- is a psychological as well as a structural reality can be ascertained from two facts : the native's ability to coin new words by combining a familiar root with a familiar measure, and the native's ability to understand unfamiliar words which have familiar roots and familiar measures.

Knowledge of the root-and-measure system of Arabic makes it possible for students to guess with some degree of accuracy the meaning of unfamiliar words. Such knowledge may also prove useful in memorizing and remembering vocabulary items : the student may find it helpful to group together words with the same root or words with the same measure, and to study the entire list as sets at regular intervals. On the other hand, one should exercise caution in forecasting unfamiliar words by combining familiar roots with familiar measures : such an attempt may result in non-existent forms because no one root is capable of combining with every measure, and no measure can combine with every root.

*** *** ***

MID VOWEL

A vowel which is produced with the tongue arched at a mid-point in the mouth. EA [I] is a mid-vowel as in /ḍill/ --- [ḍIḷḷ] 'shade'.

*** *** ***

MINIMAL PAIR

(See : Phoneme)

*** *** ***

MODALS

A modal (or modal auxiliary) is a word that indicates the speaker's mood or psychological attitude toward the reality or truth value of the action or state denoted by the main verb with which it is used. Modals are usually followed by a bare (subjunctive) form, but certain modals (e.g., <u>laazim</u>, <u>gaayiz</u>) can be followed by a perfect verb. The perfect verb denotes a complete event while the subjunctive does not.

laazim aktib gawaab	'I must write a letter.'
laazim miši	'He must have left.'
labudd nimši	'We must leave.'
yimkin asaafir maṣṛ	'I may go to Egypt.'
gaayiz yiigi bukṛa	'He may come tommorow.'

Either the modal or the main verb in a sentence can be negated. Note the difference in meaning in the following sentences :

yimkin maktibš gawaab	'Maybe I won't write a letter.'
mayimkinš aktib gawaab	'I can't write a letter.'

Many modals are either active or passive participles, though some are nouns. The following is a list of the most common EA modals.

(a) Active participles :

ʕaawiz (-a, -iin)	'want to ...'
naawi (-a, -iin)	'intending to ...'
gaayiz	'it is possible that ...'
laazim	'it is necessary that ...'
ʔaaʕid (-a, -iin)	'continuing to ...'
ʕammaal (-a -iin)	'continuing to ...'

Note that <u>gaayiz</u> and <u>laazim</u> have the variant forms <u>yiguuz</u> and <u>yilzam</u> respectively.

(b) Passive participles :

mamnuuʕ	'it is forbidden to ...'
masmuuħ	'it is permitted to ...'
mustaʕidd (-a, -iin)	'is ready to ...'
mafṛuuḍ	'it is supposed that ...'
miṣammim (-a, -iin)	'is determined to ...'
mumkin	'may ...'

(c) Nouns:

nifs- + pro. suf.	'feel like ...'
ʔaṣd- + pro. suf.	'mean to ...'
zamaan- + pro. suf.	'must have ...'
tann- + pro. suf.	'continuing to ...'

(d) Others :

yareet- + pro. suf. (optional)	'wish ...'
yadoob- + pro. suf.	'must have ...'

labudd	'must ...'
rubbama	'may ...'
inšalla	'hope ...'
yalla	'let's ...'
iyyaa- + pro. suf.	'better not ...'

Notes :

1. Of the modals in categories (a) and (b), some are impersonal and therefore invariable in form, and others are personal and, as indicated, must agree in gender and number with the subject of the main verb.

   nawya tisaafir bukṛa 'She intends to leave tomorrow.'

2. Of the modals in categories (c) and (d), some, as indicated, take a following noun or pornoun suffix which agrees with the subject of the main verb. yareet can optionally take a pronoun suffix.

   nifsi aakul tiffaaɦ 'I feel like eating an apple.'

*** *** ***

MODIFIER

A word used to modify, describe, limit or qualify the meaning of a noun, verb or adjective. In Egyptian Arabic this class of modifiers consists of (a) adjectives (including participles used as adjectives and (b) adverbs. Examples :

(a)	walad kibiir	'a big boy'
	bint kbiira	'a big girl'
	awlaad kubaaṛ	'big boys'
	beet maftuuɦ	'an open house'

Notice number/gender agreement.

Note that participles used as adjectives (q.v.) are derived from verbs whereas the majority of adjectives are not. Many adjectives have the form FvʕiiL, e.g.,

kibiir	'big'
laṭiif	'nice'
laziiz	'delicious'

(b) Adverbs modify adjectives or verbs.

giri bsurʕa	'he ran fast'
ilbint nabiiha ʔawi	'the girl is very smart'

*** *** ***

ORPHEME

The minimal meaningful unit of speech in any language; it may be a word or part of a word, e.g., Egyptian Arabic katab 'to write' has one morpheme, katabt 'I wrote' has two and makatabtiš 'I did not write' has three. Notice that /ma- ...š/, the negative morpheme, is a Discontinuous Morpheme. Also note that / - / is referred to as a Morpheme Boundary.

*** *** ***

ORPHOPHONEME

A variant of a morpheme (q.v.). E.g., English /-s ~ -z ~ -iz/ as in "cats", "dogs" and "kisses", respectively, are all morphophonemic variants (or allomorphs, q.v.) of the noun plural morpheme. Their form is governed by the phonetic environment. In EA, /wi/ and /w-/ are morphophonemic variants of the conjunction "and". /wi/ is conditioned by a preceding consonant and /w-/ is conditioned by a preceding vowel.

*** *** ***

- N -

NASAL

Refers to consonants produced with the uvula lowered, allowing the air to escape through the nose, so that the nasal cavity acts as a resonator : /m, n/.

*** *** ***

NASAL CAVITY

One of the cavaties that serve as a resonator in speech.

*** *** ***

NEGATION : ma-, ma- ...-š, AND miš ~ muš

The forms ma-, ma-...-š and miš ~ muš are used to negate EA expressions; they are considered variants of the same unit since the choice between them is almost completely determined by the environment.

1. The form ma-

   The contexts where ma- occurs signal emphasis (emphatic negation, threat, or strong wish). The emphasis in question is not signalled by ma- alone : there is always some co-occurrent constituent which expresses emphasis. Specifically, ma- is used in the following environments :

(a) Prefixed to a verb (perfect or imperfect) which follows ʕumr 'ever' or an oath particle :

ʕumṛi ma-šuftu sakṛaan.	'I never saw him drunk.'
ʕumṛukum ma-ħatit?addimu.	'You (p) will never advance.'
bišaṛafi ma-ṛuħt.	'I swear (by my honor) that I did not go.'
waḷḷaahi ma-aħibbaha.	'I swear (by God) that I don't love her.'

(b) Prefixed to a verb (perfect or imperfect) after the form yareet 'I wish, would that, I hope' :

yareetu ma-ʕirif.	'I wish he had not known.'
yareet illi ħaṣal ma-ħaṣal.	'I wish what took place had not happened.'
yaritni ma-baħibbaha.	'I wish I were not in love with her.'
yareetu ma-yiigi.	'I hope he does not come.'

(c) Prefixed to a subjunctive verb after the expression ya ṛabb 'I hope' :

ya ṛabb ma-yiigi.	'I hope he will not come.'
ya ṛabb ma-tšuufu wiħiš abadan.	'I hope you will never encounter any evil.'

Notice that the imperfect after ya ṛabb, unlike the imperfect after yareet, may not take an aspect prefix.

(d) Prefixed to a perfect verb when the context is a conditional sentence expressing a threat :

makunš mdiir ilmaktab da law ma-ṭaṛadtak.	'I am not the director of this office if I don't fire you !'

(e) Prefixed to a perfect verb after one of the forms ʕann- and inšalla ~ šalla which denote annoyance and indifference :

ʕannak ma-kalt.	'I don't give a damn if you don't eat !'
inšalla/šalla ma-ḥawwišna.	'To hell with saving money !'

2. The form ma- ...-š

The form ma- ...-š is used in three environments excluding the contexts for ma-.

(a) Affixed to all verb forms except those which have the prefix ḥa- :

ma-katab-š	'he did not write'
ma-byakul-š	'he does not eat'
ma-yiʕraf-š yruuḥ	'He does not know how to go.'
ma-titkallim-š	'Don't talk !'

(b) Affixed to an inverted predicate consisting of (i) fii 'there is/are' or (ii) a preposition and a pronominal suffix :

ma-fii-š ḥadd hina.	'There is no one here.'
ma-ʕandukum-š fluus ?	'Don't you (p) have any money ?'
ma-ʕalik-š zanb .	'You (ms) are not to blame.'
ma-lik-š ḍahr.	'You (ms) have no one to back you up.'

(c) Affixed to a pronoun when the whole sentence -- not the pronoun alone -- is negated. The pronoun in question is usually one which functions as subject :

ma-ntaa-š fahimni.	'You (ms) don't understand me.'

Notice, however, that ma- ...-š is not used to negate the pronoun alone (i.e., apart from the rest of the sentence) :

ʕali : miin illi kasar ilkubbaaya ?	'Ali : Who broke the glass ?'

suzaan : miš ana lli kasaṛtaha.	'Susan : I am not the one who broke it.'

Notes

1. The suffix -š (which constitutes the second part of ma- ...-š) occurs after all other suffixes :

ma-katab-haa-š	'he did not write it (f)'
ma-katab-ha-l-ak-š	'he did not write it (f) for you'
ma-baʕattu-hum-lu-hum-š	'I did not send them to them'

2. Provided it is preceded by a consonant, the suffix -š (which constitutes the second part of ma- ...-š) may be replaced by -ši in sentence final position :

ʕali margiʕš or ʕali margiʕši.	'Ali did not return.'

The optional occurrence of -ši in sentence-final position after a consonant may be the result of a tendency to generalize : in sentence medial position, -Cš is replaced by -Cš^{i} when the next word begins with a consonant :

/makatabš/	'he did not write'
/makatabš^{i} ktaab/	'he did not write a book'

Less frequently, sentence final -š is replaced by -ši after a long vowel :

mašuftahaaš. or mašuftahaaši.	'I did not see her.'
maṛaɦuuš. or maṛaɦuuši.	'They did not go.'

The optional occurrence of -ši in sentence-final position after a long vowel may be the result of a tendency to generalize. In sentence-medial position, a long vowel rarely occurs in a closed syllable. For that reason most speakers replace -VVš by -Vš before a word which begins with a consonant, and some replace -VVš by -VVši in the same position; it is usually the latter group of speakers who use -VVši in sentence-final position.

The validity of the above explanation is supported by the fact that a sentence-final -š is not replaced by -ši after a short vowel; thus the form makatabtiši does not occur as an alternative to sentence-final makatabtiš.

3. The form miš ~ muš

The form miš ~ muš is used (a) before bi- as an alternative to the use of ma- ...-š, and (b) in all environments other than those for ma- and ma- ...-š, including rhetorical questions and exhortations.

miš bašuufu yoom ilħadd or ma-bašufuu-š yoom ilħadd.	'I do not see him on Sunday.'
illuɣa lʕaṛabiyya miš ṣaʕba.	'The Arabic language is not difficult.'
fahmi miš ustaaz.	'Fahmi is not a professor.'
issabab miš maʕṛuf.	'The reason is not known.'
tanfiiz awamru miš mumkin.	'Carrying out his orders is not possible.'
miš ħaṛuuħ maṣṛ issanaadi.	'I will not go to Egypt this year.'
iššaxṣ illi kunt aʔṣudu miš inta.	'The person to whom I was referring is not you.'
iggaṛaayid miš filmaktab.	'The newspapers are not in the office.'
ilħaʔʔ miš ʕaleek.	'The fault is not yours.'
ilfuluus miš ʕandi.	'The money is not with me.'
miš ħazzaṛtak ?	'Haven't I warned you ?' (rhetorical)
miš tiʔuum takullak luʔma ?	'Won't you get up and eat a bite ?' (exhortation)

*** *** ***

NEGATION : NEGATING A VERBAL NOUN

Two forms occur as negators of verbal nouns : ʕadam and balaaš; of these, the more frequent is ʕadam. The forms in question are not interchangeable since they signal different meanings.

1. ʕadam negates the existence of what the verbal noun designates. Translatable by non-, un-, in-, dis-, lack of, etc., the word ʕadam is placed before the verbal noun to be negated.

ana mutaʔakkid min ʕadam wuguud ilħayaat filmarriix.	'I am certain of the non-existence of life on Mars.'
muškilitna hiyya ʕadam littifaaʔ ʕa lmabaadiʔ ilʔasasiyya.	'Our problem is disagreement on the basic principles.'
miš ʕagibni ʕadam ihtimaamak bidruusak.	'I do not like your lack of interest in your studies.'

2. The form balaaš expresses a request to refrain or desist from the action denoted by the following verbal noun; thus balaaš akl means 'Stop eating'. Notice that in this context the verbal noun is usually, though not always, indefinite. (See : Negation : The Form balaaš)

*** *** ***

NEGATION : NEGATING A VERBAL SEQUENCE

In EA, a verbal sequence may consist of as many as six verbs (beginning with a form of kaan and ending with the main verb) :

kaan yiħibb yibtidi yṛuuħ yitʕallim yitmallaq innaas.	'He would have liked to start going to learn how to flatter people.'

Any verb in the sequence may be negated : thus one may say makanš yħibb ... 'He would not have liked ...', kaan mayħibbiš ... 'He would have not liked ...', kaan yiħibb mayibtidiiš ... 'He would have liked not to start ...', etc.

As the English translation indicates, negating different verbs in the sequence does not result in synonymous expressions. Most situations call for negation of only the first verb in the sequence.

*** *** ***

NEGATION : NEGATING CONDITIONAL SENTENCES

The constituents of a conditional sentence are negated in accordance with the general rules of negation. The following are examples :

iza ʕali ṛaaħ ħazʕal.	'If Ali goes, I will be upset.'
iza ʕali maṛaħš ħazʕal.	'If Ali does not go, I will be upset.'
iza ʕali ṛaaħ miš ħazʕal.	'If Ali goes, I will not be upset.'
iza ʕali maṛaħš miš ħazʕal.	'If Ali does not go, I will not be upset.'

Some conditional sentences are derived by adding a form of the perfect verb kaan to one or more constituents; negation of that form may be substituted for negation in the source constituent; thus the following pairs are equivalent :

iza kaan ʕali maṛaħš... iza makanš ʕali ṛaaħ ...	'if Ali has not gone'
law kaan ʕali miš tilmiiz... law makanš ʕali tilmiiz...	'if Ali were not a student'
law rigʕu, kaan maṛaħš... law rigʕu, makanš ṛaaħ...	'If they had returned he would not have gone.'

*** *** ***

NEGATION : NEGATING THE SEQUENCE MODAL + VERB

In a sequence consisting of a modal and a following verb, it is usually possible to negate either the modal or the verb. Thus labudd yṛuuɦ 'he must go' may yield miš labudd yṛuuɦ 'it is not necessary for him to go' or labudd mayṛuɦš 'it is necessary for him not to go; he must not go' (notice that the two negative expressions are not identical in meaning). There are, however, some modals which cannot be negated; the main ones are inšaḷḷa 'I hope', iyyaak 'had better not (threat)', and rubbama 'might'.

*** *** ***

NEGATION : THE FORM balaaš

1. If followed by a verbal noun or a subjunctive form, balaaš is an instruction to refrain or desist from an action :

balaaš ziʕiiʔ.	'Stop shouting !'
balaaš tiṛuuɦ innahaṛda.	'Don't go today !'

Notice that in this context the verbal noun is usually, though not necessarily, indefinite.

2. When used as an exclamatory sentence, balaaš indicates compliance with a refusal :

ʕali: laazim tigiib ilkutub.	'Ali: You must bring the books.'
fariid: miš gayibha.	'Farid: I won't bring them.'
ʕali: balaaš.	'Ali: Fine, don't !'

3. Elsewhere, balaaš is an instruction to exclude what follows :

iʔṛa garidt ilʔahṛaam laakin balaaš garidt ilʔaxbaaṛ.	'Read the newspaper Al-Ahram, but forget about the newspaper Al-Akhbar.'
mistaktaṛ innu dabaɦɦa wširib min dammaha ? balaaš širib	'Do you find it too much to believe that he cut her throat and drank

min dammaha. tistaktaṛ innu dabaḥḥa ?	her blood ? Well, forget about drinking her blood. Do you find it too much to beleive that he cut her throat ?'

*** *** ***

NEGATION : THE FORM wala

(See : Conjunctions)

*** *** ***

NEGATIVE IMPERATIVE

(See : Imperative : Negative)

*** *** ***

NEGATIVE PARTICLES

(See : Negation : ma-, ma- ...-š, miš ~ muš)

*** *** ***

NISBA ADJECTIVES

In English, adjectives are often formed by the addition of certain affixes to nouns (a process which sometimes requires a change in the noun) :

Noun	Adjective
America	American
Rome	Roman
Spain	Spanish
face	facial

In EA, an adjective may be formed by adding the suffix -i to a noun :

Noun	Adjective
maṣṛ 'Egypt'	maṣṛi 'Egyptian'
mawḍiʕ 'place'	mawḍiʕi 'local'

Adjectives derived in this manner are called "nisba adjectives" or "relative adjectives" because they show relationships. The termination -V or -(Vy)V is deleted before suffixing /-i/. Examples :

madrasa ++ -i --> madrasi 'scholastic'
baljiika + -i --> baljiiki 'Belgian'
turkiya + -i --> turki 'Turkish'

A noun which invariably occurs with the definite article loses that article when the nisba suffix is added :

ilyabaan + -i --> yabaani 'Japanese'
ilʔurdun + -i --> urduni 'Jordanian'

The definite article may, of course, be added to yabaani or urduni if the modified noun is definite; the fact being stressed is that yabaani and urduni are possible while yabaan and urdun are not.

Upon receiving the nisba suffix, a handful of nouns (mostly defective) undergo changes which cannot be predicted by the above rules; for example, sana 'year' becomes sanawi 'annual', nabi 'prophet' becomes nabawi 'prophetic', and asya 'Asia' becomes asyawi 'Asian'. The nisba adjectives corresponding to such nouns should be learned as items.

The feminine singular form of the nisba adjective is obtained by adding -yya to the masculine singular form; the plural form, by adding -yyiin. :

Masculine Singular	Feminine Singular	Plural
maṣṛi 'Egyptian'	maṣṛiyya	maṣṛiyyiin

Notice, however, that some nisba adjectives have broken plurals, e.g., atṛaak 'Turkish (p)', ingiliiz 'British (p)'.

In a sequence of adjectives, a nisba adjective must come first :

karafatta ingiliizi ħamṛa 'a red English tie'

For contexts where nisba adjectives designate color, type of product, or social status, see "Adjective : Attributive Construction".

A nisba adjective can be used as a noun, as can other adjectives, e.g.:

ilmaṣri	'the Egyptian (man)'
suuriyya	'a Syrian (woman)'

*** *** ***

NOMINALIZATION : DEFINITION

Nominalization is the use of a sentence to fill a slot which is typically filled by a noun. For example, the object slot in simiʕt ilxabar 'I heard the news' is typically filled by a noun; however, the sentence ʕali rigiʕ 'Ali has returned' may be used to fill the same slot :

simiʕt inn ʕali rigiʕ.	'I heard that Ali has returned.'

More examples are given below. In each case, the filler of the nominal slot is underlined :

ʔaal inn fathi kaslaan.	'He said that Fathi is lazy.'
ʕirift inn fariida raahit maṣr.	'I learned that Farida went to Egypt.'
iftakaṛu inn iggamʕa ṣγayyaṛa.	'They thought that the university was small.'
fikrit innak tiṛuuh faṛansa miš kuwayyisa.	'The idea of your going to France is not a good one.'

In the last example, the nominalized sentence is the second term of a noun construct, which explains the final -it of fikrit.

Certain nominalized expressions must be introduced by a nominalizer (in the above examples, the nominalizer is inn), others may or may not be introduced by a nominalizer, and still others are never introduced by a nominalizer (see : "Nominalizers" and "Nominalization Without Nominalizers").

A nominalized expression may occur in various nominal slots; it may, for example, function as subject of the sentence, object of a verb, object of a preposition, or second term of a noun construct :

miš ṣaḥiiḥ inn almanya ḥtallit maṣṛ.	'It is not true that Germany occupied Egypt.'
simiʕt innak itraʔʔeet.	'I heard that you have been promoted.'
itʕaggibt min innak maṛuḥtiš.	'I was surprised that you did not go.'
iṣṣinaaʕa lyabaniyya tʔaddimit lidaṛagit inn ilyabaan bitṣaddaṛ ilʕaṛabiyyaat.	'Japanese industry has progressed to the extent that Japan exports cars.'

Notice that a nominalized subject is often transposed to the position which follows the predicate. This transposition is the norm when the predicate is short and verbless, it is frequent when the predicate is a verb or a short expression containing a verb, and it is infrequent otherwise.

	inn almanya ḥtallit maṣṛ miš ṣaḥiiḥ.	'That Germany occupied Egypt is not true.'
----->	miš ṣaḥiiḥ inn almanya ḥtallit maṣṛ.	'It is not true that Germany occupied Egypt.'
	inn basma maxaḷḷaṣitš iššuɣl narfizni.	'That Basma did not finish the work upset me.'
----->	narfizni inn basma maxaḷḷaṣitš iššuɣl.	'It upset me that Basma did not finish the work.'
	inn ilḥurriyya tḥaddidit asnaaʔ ilḥaṛb ilʕalamiyya lʔuula sabbib lilmaṣṛiyyiin mašaakil kitiira giddan.	'That freedom was restricted during World War I created a large number of problems for the Egyptians.'

For the purpose of agreement, a nominalized subject is considered third-person masculine singular :

zaʕʕalni innak šatamtaha	'It upset me that you insulted her.'
ṣaḥiiḥ inn maṣr it?addimit.	'It is true that Egypt has progressed.'

*** *** ***

NOMINALIZATION WITHOUT NOMINALIZERS : IMPERATIVES

Imperative sentences are embedded in nominal slots without the use of a nominalizer after verbs of saying. An imperative verb form in the sentence to be embedded may remain unchanged or it may be replaced by the subjunctive form. The following utterances result from embedding the sentence ruuḥ iddukkaan 'Go to the shop' in the nominal slots following ?ultilu 'I said to him; I told him', ?ultilha 'I said to her; I told her', etc.

1.	?ultilu ruuḥ iddukkaan.	'I said to him, Go to the shop.'
	?ultilha ruuḥi ddukkaan.	'I said to her, Go to the shop.'
	?ultilhum ruuḥu ddukkaan.	'I said to them, Go to the shop.'
	?ultilak ruuḥ iddukkaan.	'I said to you (ms), Go to the shop.'
	?ultilik ruuḥi ddukkaan.	'I said to you (fs), Go to the shop.'
	?ultilkum ruuḥu ddukkaan.	'I said to you (p), Go to the shop.'
	?alli ruuḥ iddukkaan.	'He said to me (m), Go to the shop.'
	?alli ruuḥi ddukkaan.	'He said to me (f), Go to the shop.'
	?allina ruuḥu ddukkaan.	'He said to us, Go to the shop.'
2.	?ultilu yruuḥ iddukkaan.	'I told him to go to the shop.'
	?ultilha truuḥ iddukkaan.	'I told her to go to the shop.'
	?ultilhum yuruuḥu ddukkaan.	'I told them to go to the shop.'
	?ultilak turuuḥ iddukkaan.	'I told you (ms) to go to the shop.'
	?ultilik turuuḥi ddukkaan.	'I told you (fs) to go to the shop.'
	?ultilkum turuuḥu ddukkaan.	'I told you (p) to go to the shop.'
	?alli aruuḥ iddukkaan.	'He told me to go to the shop.'
	?allina nruuḥ iddukkaan.	'He told us to go to the shop.'

Notice that in group 2 the subjunctive form agrees with its subject in number, gender and person, whereas in group 1 the embedded sentences are direct discourse and do not affect the syntax of the sentence.

Negative imperative sentences contain (or consist of) negated verb forms such as matruħš 'do not go (ms)', matruħiiš 'do not go (fs)', and matruħuuš 'do not go (p)'. Such forms may (1) be embedded in a nominal slot without being changed; they may also (2) be changed to agree with a subject of the third or the first person :

1. ʔultilu matruħš iddukkaan. 'I said to him, Do not go to the shop.'
   ʔultilha matruħiiš iddukkaan. 'I said to her, Do not go to the shop.'
   ʔultilhum matruħuuš iddukkaan. 'I said to them, Do not go to the shop.'
   ʔultilak matruħš iddukkaan. 'I said to you (ms), Do not go to the shop
   ʔultilik matruħiiš iddukkaan. 'I said to you (fs), Do not go to the shop
   ʔultilkum matruħuuš iddukkaan. 'I said to you (p), Do not go to the shop.
   ʔalli matruħš iddukkaan. 'He said to me (m), Do not go to the shop.
   ʔalli matruħiiš iddukkaan. 'He said to me (f), Do not go to the shop.
   ʔallina matruħuuš iddukkaan. 'He said to us, Do not go to the shop.'

2. ʔultilu mayruħš iddukkaan. 'I told him not to go to the shop.'
   ʔultilha matruħš iddukkaan. 'I told her not to go to the shop.'
   ʔultilhum mayruħuuš iddukkaan. 'I told them not to go to the shop.'
   ʔultilak matruħš iddukkaan. 'I told you (ms) not to go to the shop.'
   ʔultilik matruħiiš iddukkaan. 'I told you (fs) not to go to the shop.'
   ʔultilkum matruħuuš iddukkaan. 'I told you (p) not to go to the shop.'
   ʔalli maruħš iddukkaan. 'He told me not to go to the shop.'
   ʔallina manruħš iddukkaan. 'He told us not to go to the shop.'

In both cases, the difference between sentences of Group 1 and those of Group 2 is the difference between direct and indirect quotes.

*** *** ***

NOMINALIZATION WITHOUT NOMINALIZERS : QUESTIONS

Questions are usually embedded in nominal slots without the use of a nominalizer. The first sentence below results from embedding the question rigiʕ leeh ? 'Why did he return ?' in the subject slot; the second sentence results from embedding the same question in the object slot :

rigiʕ leeh miš muhimm.	'Why he returned is not important.'
maʕṛafš rigiʕ leeh.	'I do not know why he returned.'

A question which is embedded in a nominal slot usually implies a noun; e.g., in the above sentences rigiʕ leeh implies issabab 'the reason'. There may be a relationship between this fact and the fact that questions are usually embedded in nominal slots without a nominalizer (nouns are used as fillers of nominal slots with no need for nominalizers). The following sentences provide additional examples :

miš ʕaarif ṛaaħ feen.	'I do not know where he went.'
xammin miin bitħibbu.	'Guess who loves him.'
mas?alit rigiʕ imta di mathimminiiš.	'This question of when he returned is of no interest to me.'
?ulli štareet eeh ?	'Tell me what (it is that) you bought.'

Embedding a yes-or-no question in a nominal slot usually involves the addition of the expression walla la? 'or not' at the end of the slot :

ʕaawiz aʕṛaf inta ṛuħt walla la?.	'I want to know whether you went or not.'

Besides, one of the expressions in kaan and iza kaan (both translatable by 'whether') may be added at the beginning of the slot; in this context, kaan agrees with its subject in number, gender, and person :

ʕaawiz aʕṛaf (iza kaan) ʕali ṛaaħ walla la?	'I want to know whether Ali went or not.'
ʕaawiz aʕṛaf (in kaanit) fariida ṛaaħit walla la?.	'I want to know whether Farida went or not.'
ʕaawiz aʕṛaf (iza kuntu) intu ṛuħtu walla la?.	'I want to know whether you (p) went or not.'

When an alternative question is embedded in a nominal slot, one of the expressions in kaan and iza kaan may be added at the beginning of the slot; in this context, kaan agrees with its subject in number, gender, and person :

maʕṛafš (iza kaan) ʕaawiz yidris hina walla ffaṛansa.	'I do not know whether he wants to study here or in France.'
maʕṛafš (in kaanit) ʕawza tidris hina walla ffaṛansa.	'I do not know whether she wants to study here or in France.'

*** *** ***

NOMINALIZED SENTENCES : POSSIBILITY OF REPLACING CERTAIN CONSTITUENTS BY A NOUN

A nominalizer plus the predicate of the nominalized expression may usually be replaced by a noun which then enters into construct with the subject. This transformation is restricted to instances where the predicate in question is one of the following :

1. A verb or a form which is derived from a verb. Replacement here is by a verbal noun :

ʔaṛeet xabaṛ ʕan inn ilwaziir itgawwiz.	'I read an item in the news about the fact that the (cabinet) minister got married.'
ʔaṛeet xabaṛ ʕan gawaaz ilwaziir.	'I read an item in the news about the marriage of the (cabinet) minister.'
koonak mašhuuṛ ɦayḍuṛṛak.	'Your being famous will harm you.'
šuhṛitak ɦatḍuṛṛak	'Your fame will harm you.'

ʔabiltu baʕd <u>ma rigiʕ</u>.	'I met him after he returned.'
ʔabiltu baʕd <u>rguuʕu</u>.	'I met him after his return.'

2. A noun or an adjective which is not derived from a verb but which yields a noun of quality. Replacement here is by the noun of quality :

mafiiš šakk f-<u>inn ʕali waṭani</u>.	'There is no question that Ali is patriotic.'
mafiiš šakk f-<u>waṭaniyyit ʕali</u>.	'There is no question in regard to Ali's patriotism.'
suzaan muʕgaba b-<u>koonu raagil</u>.	'Susan admires the fact that he is manly.'
suzaan muʕgaba bi-<u>ruguuliyyitu</u>.	'Susan admires his manliness.'

*** *** ***

NOMINALIZER : <u>inn</u>

The nominalizer <u>inn</u> introduces an embedded clause in contexts other than those where the nominalizer <u>ma</u> occurs (see "Nominalizer : <u>ma</u>") :

simiʕt <u>inn</u> nḍaal itxaṭabit.	'I heard that Nidal got engaged.'
muħtamal <u>inn</u> ašṛaf rigiʕ.	'It is possible that Ashraf has returned.'
matnazilš ldaṛagit <u>inn</u>-i aʕmil ʕamal zayy da.	'I would not stoop to the point of doing such a thing.'
itʕaggibt min <u>inn</u>-ak zaʕʕaltaha.	'I was surprised at the fact that you upset her.'

EA contains a set of close-knit expressions each consisting of a verb and a closely associated preposition (or a "phrasal verb"); e.g., <u>daʕa li-</u> 'to wish well to (someone)', <u>nizil fi</u> 'to attack (someone) vigorously', <u>daħħa bi-</u> 'to sacrifice (something)', and <u>katab ʕala</u>

'for God to decree (something) on (someone)'. These expressions are followed by inn. Note the following alternatives :

1. The preposition may be deleted .
2. The sequence Preposition + inn + subject of a subjunctive form may be deleted. In most cases, this transformation does not apply unless -- in the source string -- the verb after inn expresses a possibility further delineated by the verb form which precedes inn. The result of the transformation is a verbal phrase, and is therefore restricted by the rules which govern auxiliaries (see "Verb : Auxiliaries").

The following are examples :

ʕali ṣammim ʕala innu yiigi. ʕali ṣammim innu yiigi. ʕali ṣammim yiigi.	'Ali was determined to come.'
ʕali ṣammim ʕala innina nzuuṛu. ʕali ṣammim innina nzuuṛu. ʕali ṣammim nzuuṛu.	'Ali was determined to have us visit him.'
ʕali mayṣuub ʕala innu yṛuuɦ. ʕali mayṣuub innu yṛuuɦ. ʕali mayṣuub yiṛuuɦ.	'Ali is forced to go.'

Listed below are some common close-knit expressions which are formed after the pattern Verb + Preposition and which designate subjunctive meanings :

itẓaahiṛ bi-	'to feign (something)'
naṣaɦ bi-	'to advise (someone) to'
ṛiḍi bi-	'to be satisfied with'
waʕad bi-	'to promise (something to someone)'
samaɦ bi-	'to allow (something)'
aṣaṛṛ bi-	'to insist on'

fakkaṛ fi	'to reflect on'
itʔakkid min	'to be certain of'
manaʕ min	'to prevent (someone) from'
xaaf min	'to be afraid of'
aṛɣam ʕala	'to compel (someone) to do (something)'
ittafaʔ ʕala	'to agree on'
waafiʔ ʕala	'to agree to'
waṣṣa ʕala	'to bequeath (something) to (someone)'
ɣaṣab ʕala	'to force (someone) to do (something)'

For the deletion of inn after other verbs, see Verb : Auxiliaries .

*** *** ***

NOMINALIZER : koon

The nominalizer koon is used interchangeably with inn in many but not in all contexts :

1. koon is frequently substituted for inn when the nominalized expression is verbless :

ahamm ħaaga fṣalħu nnu ẓaabiṭ or ahamm ħaaga fṣalħu koonu ẓaabit.	'The most important thing in his favor is the fact that he is an officer.'

2. koon is occasionally substituted for inn when the nominalized expression contains a verb denoting a fact (rather than a possibility) :

innu biɣɣiib kitiir miš fi ṣalħu or koonu biɣɣiib kitiir miš fi ṣalħu.	'The fact that he is often absent is not in his favor.'

3. koon is not substituted for inn when the nominalized expression indicates a possibility rather than a fact :

yaguuz inn hyaam tirgaʕ bukṛa.	'Hiyam may return tomorrow.'

but not *yaguuz koon hiyaam tirgaʕ bukṛa.

*** *** ***

NOMINALIZER : ma

Like inn, ma introduces an embedded clause. ma occurs after certain prepositions and nouns, and inn occurs elsewhere.

The following differences must be noted :

1. inn is usually followed by a noun or a pronoun functioning as subject. The same is true of the nominalizer ma; the difference is that ma may be followed immediately by a verb form.

simiʕt inn ʕeeša tgawwizit.	'I heard that Aisha got married.'
simiʕt innaha tgawwizit.	'I heard that she got married.'
rigiʕt baʕd ma ʕadnaan rigiʕ.	'I returned after Adnan did.'
rigiʕt baʕd ma huwwa rigiʕ.	'I returned after he did.'
rigiʕt baʕd ma rigiʕ.	'I returned after he did.'

2. A pronoun which follows inn is a suffix; one which follows ma is independent :

yaguuz innaha rigʕit.	'Perhaps she has returned.'
rigiʕt baʕd ma hiyya rigʕit.	'I returned after she did.'

3. In most (though not all) cases, an imperfect verb form which follows ma is bare (= subjunctive) :

simiʕt innu ɦayiigi bukṛa.	'I heard that he will come tomorrow.'
simiʕt innu byiigi kull yoom.	'I heard that he comes every day.'
ɦawṣal ʔabl ma yiwṣal.	'I will arrive before he does.'
bawṣal ʔabl ma yiwṣal.	'I usually arrive before he does.'

Generally speaking, the forms which precede the nominalizer ma are prepositions or nouns. Listed below are the most common combinations of a preposition or noun and ma. Notice that, in the majority of instances, each expression corresponds to an English conjunction.

1. baʕd ma 'after' : A verb which follows this expression may be perfect or imperfect.

rigiʕt baʕd ma rigiʕ.	'I returned after he did.'
rigiʕt baʕd ma rigiʕ ʕali.	'I returned after Ali did.'
rigiʕt baʕd ʕali ma rigiʕ.	'I returned after Ali did.'
ɦargaʕ baʕd ma yirgaʕ.	'I will return after he does.'
ɦargaʕ baʕd ma yirgaʕ ʕali.	'I will return after Ali does.'
ɦargaʕ baʕd ʕali ma yirgaʕ.	'I will return after Ali does.'

2. ʔabl ma 'before' : A verb which follows ʔabl ma is usually an imperfect form; the temporal designation of that verb is the same as that of the verb which precedes ma.

kallimtu ʔabl ma rgaʕ.	'I talked to him before I returned.'
bastaɦamma ʔabl ma naam.	'I take a bath before I go to bed.'
ɦayiktib ilmaqaala ʔabl ma yṛuuɦ faṛansa.	'He will write the article before he goes to France.'

3. liɦadd ma 'until' :

sakan fi bitna lɦadd ma naʔal liʔaswaan.	'He lived in our house until he moved to Aswan.'
ɦayuskun maʕaana lɦadd ma yunʔul liʔaswaan.	'He will live with us until he moves to Aswan.

4. liɣaayit ma 'until' : This expression is interchangeable with liħadd ma.

5. min ɣeer ma 'without' :

xaṛag min ɣeer ma yistaħamma.	'He went out without taking a bath.'

6. ʕand ma 'when' :

igru ʕand ma tismaʕu ṣṣuffaaṛa.	'Run when you hear the whistle.'

7. waʔt ma 'when, the moment that' :

ħašṛaħlu lmawḍuuʕ waʔt ma yirgaʕ.	'I will explain the matter to him when he returns.'

8. saaʕit ma 'when, the hour that' :

ittiṣil biyya saaʕit ma tiwṣal.	'Get in touch with me when you arrive.'

9. nahaaṛ ma 'the day that' :

kunt fiskindiriyya nahaaṛ ma tgawwizit.	'I was in Alexandria the day she got married.'

10. yoom ma 'the day that' : This expression is usually interchangeable with nahaaṛ ma.

11. sanit ma 'the year that' :

kunt fsurya sanit ma tammit ilwiħda been maṣṛ w libya.	'I was in Syria the year that Egypt and Libya united.'

12. maṭṛaħ ma 'the place that, where, anywhere that, wherever' :

la?a lmahfaẓa maṭraḥ ma sabha.	'He found the wallet where he had left it.'
maṭraḥ ma ṭruuḥ aṛuuḥ.	'Wherever you go, I will go.'

13. makaan ma and maḥall ma : Both expressions are interchangeable with maṭraḥ ma.

14. mi?daaṛ ma : 'the degree to which, the extent to which' :

indahašt min mi?daaṛ ma hiyya gamiila.	'I was astounded by how beautiful she is (literally : "by the degree to which she is beautiful").'

Three more expressions which contain ma, and which are translatable by English conjunctions, are : fiima 'while', baynama 'while', and kull ma 'whenever'. Of these, the first two are usually followed by a clause which contains a form of the perfect verb kaan and (a) an imperfect indicative (with the /bi-/ prefix or (b) an equational clause. The third (kull ma) is usually followed by a bare imperfect (subjunctive) verb.

fiima kunna bnitgaadil, innuuṛ iṭṭafa.	'While we were arguing, the lights went off.'
issawṛa ?aamit baynama kaan ṛa?iis iggumhuriyya baṛṛa lbalad.	'The rebellion took place while the president of the republic was out of the country.'
kull ma yiigi, a?fil ilbaab fi wiššu.	'Whenever he comes, I slam the door in his face.'

*** *** ***

NOUN

In Egyptian Arabic (EA), nouns (n) are either masculine (m) or feminine (f) in gender. Most feminine nouns end in /-a/, and most masculine nouns do not. For other nouns, the sex of the referent clearly indicates the grammatical gender, e.g., /bint/ (f) 'girl'. Henceforth, gender need not be indicated when it is clear from the form of the noun or the sex of the referent. Indication of gender is only needed for such nouns as /mabna/ (m) 'building' or /naaṛ/ (f) 'fire' since gender is not clear from their forms. Most nouns inflect for the dual and all nouns (except collectives, q.v.) inflect for plural.

(See also : Collective Nouns; Verbal Nouns; Plural; Dual Nouns; Gender)

*** *** ***

NOUN : BASIC

A noun that has no relation to any verb or verb stem (q.v.) from which it could be derived; e.g., /katab/ 'to write' has /kitaab/ 'book' as a derived noun. /mayya/ 'water', on the other hand, is a basic noun since there is no verb from which it is derived in EA.

*** *** ***

NOUNS : HUMAN AND NON-HUMAN

A human noun is one that in its singular form refers to human beings. With <u>human plural</u> nouns, adjectives agree in number : /awlaad kubaaṛ/ 'big boys'; /banaat kubaaṛ/ 'big girls'. However, with <u>non-human plural</u> nouns, either plural adjectives or feminine singular adjectives may be used :

/kutub kubaaṛ/ 'big books'
/kutub kibiira/ 'big books'

The latter form is sometimes applied even to modify <u>human</u> plural nouns by <u>some</u> speakers of EA, e.g.,

/awlaad kutaaṛ/ 'many boys'
/awlaad kitiira/ 'many boys'

and /banaat kutaaṛ/ 'many girls'
/banaat kitiira/ 'many girls'

Human Plurals

S# 1 : ilbanaat dool ṭuwaal walla ?uṣayyaṛiin ?
'Are these girls tall or short ?'
S# 2 : ilbanaat dool ṭuwaal miš ?uṣayyaṛiin.
'These girls are tall; not short.'

Non-Human Plurals

(a) S# 1 : ilkutub di gdiida walla ?adiima ?
:'Are these books new or old ?'
S# 2 : ilkutub di gdiida
:'These books are new.'
(b) S# 1 : ilkutub dool gudaad walla ?udaam
'Are these books new or old ?'
S# 2 : ilkutub dool gudaad
'These books are new.'

Remember that demonstratives and adjectives must agree in number with the Human Plural nouns they modify.

Here, "Non-Human Plurals", e.g., book, table, etc., preferably are treated as feminine singular syntactically only. That is to say, they are plurals, but in terms of gender and number they take (fs) demonstratives and adjectives. However, it is possible to treat them as plurals syntactically; that is to say, to use plural demonstratives and adjectives as in the variant examples above (b).

Demonstratives and adjectives must agree in gender as well as number with the singular nouns they modify, whether the noun has a human or non-human referent.

*** *** ***

NOUN OF CHARACTER

A word (derived in most cases from a verb (q.v.)) that refers to a characteristic of a person. They are formed on the measure (q.v.) FaʕʕaaL, e.g.,

kizib	'to tell lies'	kazzaab	'liar'
nisi	'to forget'	nassaay	'forgetful'

*** *** ***

NOUN OF INSTRUMENT

/muftaaɦ/ 'key' and /munšaaṛ/ 'saw' are nouns of instrument derived from the verbs /fataɦ/ 'to open' and /našaṛ/ 'to saw' respectively, on the measure muFʕaaL. Other nouns of instrument are /maḍrab/ 'racket' and /mabšaṛa/ 'peeler' derived from /ḍarab/ 'to hit' and /bašaṛ/ 'to peel' respectively, on the measure maFʕal(-a).

*** *** ***

NOUN OF PROFESSION OR OCCUPATION

A noun derived, usually from a verb, but in some cases from a noun, and which denotes a profession or occupation. Most of these are of the measure FaʕʕaaL, e.g. :

xabaz	'to bake'	xabbaaz	'baker'
bana	'to build'	banna	'mason'
xaṭṭ	'handwriting'	xaṭṭaaṭ	'calligrapher'
ɦadiid	'iron'	ɦaddaad	'blacksmith'
baab	'door'	bawwaab	'doorman, concierge'

The following nouns of profession are of the measure muFaʕʕiL(-a) (an active participle measure) :

darris 'to teach'	mudarris(-a) 'teacher'
marraḍ 'to nurse'	mumarriḍ(-a) 'nurse'
fattiš 'to inspect'	mufattiš(-a) 'inspector'

There are other measures for nouns of profession or occupation, but those shown above are among the most common.

*** *** ***

NOUN OF PLACE

/maṭbax/ 'kitchen' is a noun of place derived from the verb /ṭabax/ 'to cook' on the measure maFʕaL (m); /maktab/ 'office' is another noun of place derived from the verb /katab/ 'to write'. /maktaba/ 'library, bookstore' is a noun of place derived from the same verb on the measure maFʕaLa (f).

*** *** ***

NOUN REPLACER ma : DIFFERENCE FROM NOMINALIZERS

While the replacer ma implies a noun, nominalizers are semantically empty. This fact becomes clear when the following sentences are compared.

1. da aḥsan min inn ʕali yirgaʕ. — 'This is preferable to having Ali return.'
2. fariida agmal mimma (= min ma) ʕali yẓunn. — 'Farida is prettier than Ali imagines.'

In sentence 1 the object of the preposition is ʕali yirgaʕ, and for that reason inn ʕali yirgaʕ may be replaced by ruguuʕ ʕali 'Ali's return'. In sentence 2 the object of the preposition is ma, and for that reason ma ʕali yẓunn cannot be replaced by ẓann ʕali 'Ali's imagination' (in other words, Farida is not prettier than Ali's imagination; rather, she is prettier than what Ali imagines).

The replacer ma should not be confused with the nominalizer ma : the former implies a noun while the latter is semantically empty. Compare the following sentences :

3. rigiʕt baʕd ma ʕali rigiʕ — 'I returned after Ali did.'
4. fariida agmal mimma (= min ma) ʕali yẓunn. — 'Farida is prettier than Ali imagines.'

In sentence 3 the object of the preposition is ʕali rigiʕ, and for that reason ma ʕali rigiʕ may be replaced by ruguuʕ ʕali 'Ali's return.' In sentence 4 the object of the preposition is ma, and for that reason ma ʕali yẓunn cannot be replaced by ẓann ʕali 'Ali's imagination'.

The replacer ma differs from inn and koon in two major respects :

1. The replacer ma may occur directly before a verb (in addition to the fact that it may occur before a noun or a pronoun functioning as subject); inn and koon must occur before a noun or a pronoun functioning as a subject.'

ʕamalu zayy ma ʔaalit.	'They did as she said.'
ʕamalu zayy ma zeenab ʔaalit.	'They did as Zeinab said.'
ʕamalu zayy ma hiyya ʔaalit.	'They did as she said.'
iftakaṛt inn ʕali min lubnaan.	'I thought that Ali was from Lebanon.'
iftakaṛt innak min lubnaan.	'I thought you were from Lebanon.'

2. The pronoun which follows the replacer ma is independent; the pronoun which follows inn and koon is a suffix.

iʕmil zayy ma nta ʕaawiz.	'Do as you (ms) wish.'
ẓanneet innaha ʕayyaana.	'I thought she was sick.'

***   ***   ***

NOUN REPLACER ma : FUNCTION

The replacer ma is substituted for a definite non-human noun which is modified by a relative clause; this fact becomes clear when one compares sentences such as the following :

1.	ḥaʕmil aktaṛ min ilḥaaga illi yiṭlubha.	'I will do more than the thing he requests.
2.	ḥaʕmil aktaṛ mimma (= min ma) yiṭlub or ... mimma yiṭlubu.	'I will do more than he requires.'

The transformation which derives sentences like 2 from sentences like 1 involves :

(a) Substitution of ma for the definite modified noun.

(b) Deletion of illi.

(c) Optional deletion, from the modifier, of the pronoun which functions as direct object of a verb and which refers to the replaced noun. If retained, the pronoun in question must be masculine singular since the form ma is considered masculine singular.

More examples are given below; in each case, sentence (a) is the source string of sentence (b).

(a)	da aʕgab šeeʔ šuftu.	'This is the strangest thing I have seen.'
(b)	da aʕgab ma šuft(u).	'This is the strangest thing I have seen.'
(a)	iʕmil zayy iššeeʔ illi tḥibbu.	'Do in accordance with the thing that you like.'
(b)	iʕmil zayy ma tḥibb.	'Do as you like.'
(a)	da fooʔ ilmiʔdaaṛ illi atṣawwaṛu.	'This is more than the amount I envisioned.'
(b)	da fooʔ ma kunt atṣawwaṛ(u).	'This is more than I envisioned.'
(a)	da aktaṛ min ilkimmiyya lli ṭaḷabtaha.	'This is more than the amount I requested.'
(b)	da aktaṛ mimma (= min ma) ṭalabt(u).	'This is more than I requested.'

In the foregoing examples, ma replaces a singular non-human noun which is modified by a relative clause; as the following sentences show, ma may also replace a plural non-human noun which is modified by a relative clause :

da aħsan ilħagaat illi ʕandi.	'This is the best of the things I have.'
da aħsan ma ʕandi.	'This is the best thing I have (literally : "the best of what I have").'

The replacer ma occurs most commonly as the object of a preposition, the object of a verb, or the second term of a construct phrase; its occurrence as the subject of a sentence is restricted to a handful of idiomatic expressions such as binhum ma ṣanaʕ ilħaddaad 'There is a great deal of animosity between them.'

*** *** ***

NOUN REPLACER ma : MEANING

The replacer ma is translatable by 'what, the thing(s) that' :

kul ma tħibb	'Eat the thing(s) you like.'
da aħsan ma ʕandi	'This is the best I have (literally : "the best of the thing(s) I have").'

Although it replaces a noun which is definite in form, ma is indefinite in meaning : the nouns which it replaces (iššee?'the thing', il?ašyaa? 'the things', ilħaaga 'the thing', ilħagaat 'the things') are semantically indefinite in the sense that each designates a class of unspecified referents. Compare, for example, the nouns of the first column below with the nouns of the second column.

iššee?	'the thing'	ilkitaab	'the book'
ilħaaga	'the thing'	il?alam	'the pencil'
il?ašyaa?	'the things'	ilkutub	'the books'
ilħagaat	'the things'	illa?laam	'the pencils'

All of the nouns in the list have non-human referents. The difference is that while each of the nouns on the right denotes a distinct object which is clearly differentiated from other non-human referents, the corresponding noun on the left denotes any non-human referent; in this sense, the nouns on the left are semantically indefinite.

*** *** ***

NOUN : SINGULAR COUNT

(See : Numerals : Singular Count Nouns)

*** *** ***

NUMERALS : CARDINAL HUNDREDS -- INDEFINITE CONSTRUCTION

The forms for the hundreds are listed below. Notice that, with the exception of 200, each numeral has two forms : one which ends in -a and another which ends in -t; the latter is used before a counted noun, and the former is used elsewhere.

miyya	miit	'100'
miteen	miteen	'200'
tultumiyya	tultumiit	'300'
ṛubʕumiyya	ṛubʕumiit	'400'
xumsumiyya	xumsumiit	'500'
suttumiyya	suttumiit	'600'
subʕumiyya	subʕumiit	'700'
tumnumiyya	tumnumiit	'800'
tusʕumiyya	tusʕumiit	'900'

The counted noun is singular and follows the numeral :

miit ṛaagil	'100 men'
miit sitt	'100 women'
miit gineeh	'100 pounds (money)'
miteen kitaab	'200 books'

xumsumiit beet	'500 houses'
subʕumiit faddaan	'700 (Egyptian) acres'

*** *** ***

NUMERALS : CARDINAL MILLIONS & BILLIONS -- INDEFINITE CONSTRUCTION

The form for 'one million' is milyoon and the form for 'one billion' is bilyoon, both being singular counted nouns (q.v.). The words milyoon and bilyoon are counted as follows :

1. 'Two million' and 'two billion' are expressed by itneen milyoon, and itneen bilyoon, respectively.
2. Millions and billions are expressed by phrases in which the long forms of 3 - 10 precede one of the singular forms milyoon and bilyoon.

ar̥baʕ talaaf	'four thousand'
ar̥baʕa milyoon	'four million'
ar̥baʕa bilyoon	'four billion'

*** *** ***

NUMERALS : CARDINAL 'ONE' -- INDEFINITE CONSTRUCTION

The cardinal numeral 'one' has two forms : waaɦid (m) and waɦda (f). Singularity is usually indicated by the singular form of the noun without use of the numeral (e.g., kitaab 'a book, one book'); consequently, waaɦid and waɦda have restricted occurrence. The following are the most common contexts where waaɦid and waɦda are used :

1. waaɦid may be used to modify a preceding masculine singular noun, and waɦda may be used to modify a preceding feminine singular noun. Since the noun itself indicates singularity, the effect of the numeral is to emphasize -- rather than merely to denote number.

ʕandi ktaab waaħid.	'I have a single book.'
ʕandi šanṭa waħda.	'I have only one suitcase.'

2. The forms waaħid and waħda are sometimes used as nouns with the meaning 'someone, somebody, a certain person'. In this usage, the numeral may also occur in apposition with a following singular noun :

fiih waaħid mistanniik.	'There is someone waiting for you.'
ʔabilt waħda fallaaħa.	'I met a certain peasant woman (literally : "a woman who is a peasant").'

3. The masculine form waaħid also occurs in the following contexts :

(a) Before singular counted nouns (q.v.) which are used in ordering food, drinks, etc.

waaħid šaay	'one (cup of) tea'
waaħid laħma	'one (serving of) meat'

(b) In compound numerals before the forms milyoon 'million' and bilyoon 'billion' :

waaħid milyoon wi tultumiit alf	'1,3000,000'
waaħid bilyoon xumsumiit milyoon wi suttumiit alf	'1,500,600,000'

(c) At the end of a compound numeral :

miyya wwaaħid	'101'
miyya wwaaħid kitaab	'101 books'

(d) In counting and mathematical calculation :

waaħid, itneen, talaata,...	'one, two, three, ...'
miyya wwaaħid, miyya witneen,...	'101, 102, ...'
itneen naaʔiṣ waaħid yisaawi waaħid.	'2 - 1 = 1'

*** *** ***

NUMERALS : CARDINAL NUMERAL 'TWO' -- INDEFINITE CONSTRUCTION

The cardinal numeral 'two' is itneen.

Duality is usually indicated by the dual form of the noun without use of a numeral; consequently, itneen has restricted occurrence. The following are the most common contexts where itneen is used :

1. The form itneen may be used to modify a preceding dual (masculine or feminine) noun. Since the noun itself indicates duality, the effect of the numeral is to emphasize -- rather than merely to show -- duality :

ʕandi ktabeen itneen.	'I have just two books.'
ʕandi šanṭiteen itneen.	'I have just two suitcases.'

2. The form itneen is sometimes used as a noun; in this usage, the numeral may be in apposition with a following plural noun :

(a) ištareet itneen.	'I bought two.'
(b) ʔabilt itneen fallaħiin.	'I met two peasants (literally : "two who are peasants").'

The usage illustrated by sentence (b) is the norm with nouns of occupation whose singular is FaʕʕaaL. With other nouns, however, this usage is possible, but rare; thus it is possible but uncommon to say itneen talamza 'two students'.

3. The form itneen occurs before a singular counted noun (q.v.) to make that noun dual.

hatlina tneen šaay.	'Bring us two teas.'
maʕaaya tneen gineeh.	'I have two pounds (money).'
misaħtu tneen mitr mrabbaʕ.	'Its area is two square meters.'
fi gišna tneen milyoon ʕaskari.	'There are two million soldiers in our army.'

4. The form itneen occurs at the end of a compound numeral :

miyya witneen	'102'
miyya witneen kitaab	'102 books'
an acceptable variant is :	
miit kitaab witneen	'102 books'

5. The form itneen occurs in counting and in mathematical calculation :

waaħid, itneen, talaata, ...	'one, two, three, ...'
miyya witneen, miyya wtalaata, ...	'102, 103, ...'
xamsa naaʔiṣ talaata ysaawi itneen.	'5 - 3 = 2'

*** *** ***

NUMERALS : CARDINALS 3 - 10 -- INDEFINITE CONSTRUCTION

Each of the cardinal numerals 3 - 10 has two forms : a long form which ends in -a, and a short form which ends in a consonant. These forms are listed below (the long forms are on the left, and the short counterparts are on the right) :

talaata	talat	'3'
aṛbaʕa	aṛbaʕ	'4'
xamsa	xamas	'5'
sitta	sitt	'6'
sabʕa	sabaʕ	'7'
tamanya	taman	'8'
tisʕa	tisaʕ	'9'
ʕašaṛa	ʕašaṛ	'10'

The short forms occur before counted nouns other than singular count nouns (SCN, q.v.) ; the long forms occur elsewhere :

talat kutub	'three books'
talat banaat	'three girls'
talaata gneeh	'three Egyptian pounds (money)'
ʕandi talaata	'I have three' (Here the numeral is used as a noun.)

The following facts should be noted :

1. The counted noun follows the numeral.

2. Unless it is an SCN, the counted noun is plural.
3. When used as counted nouns, the forms aFʕaaL and aFʕuL are changed to tiFʕaaL and tuFʕuL respectively :

awlaad maṣṛiyyiin	'Egyptian boys'
talat tiwlaad	'three boys'
aẓṛuf kibiira	'large envelopes'
xamas tuẓṛuf	'five envelopes'

Educated Egyptians sometimes (though not commonly) use aFʕaaL and aFʕuL as counted nouns without making such changes :

talat awlaad	'three boys'
talat azṛuf	'three envelopes'

*** *** ***

NUMERALS : CARDINALS 11 - 19 -- INDEFINITE CONSTRUCTION

The cardinals 11 - 19 are :

ḥiḍaašaṛ	'11'
itnaašaṛ	'12'
talattṭaašaṛ	'13'
aṛbaʕṭaašaṛ	'14'
xamasṭaašaṛ	'15'
sitṭaašaṛ	'16'
sabaʕṭaašaṛ	'17'
tamanṭaašaṛ	'18'
tisaʕṭaašaṛ	'19'

The counted noun is singular and follows the numeral :

tisaʕṭaašaṛ walad	'nineteen boys'
tisaʕṭaašaṛ bint	'nineteen girls'
sabaʕṭaašaṛ gineeh	'seventeen pounds (money)'

*** *** ***

NUMERALS : CARDINALS 20, 30, 40, ... 90 -- INDEFINITE CONSTRUCTION

The tens above 19 are :

ʕišriin	'20'
talatiin	'30'
arbiʕiin	'40'
xamsiin	'50'
sittiin	'60'
sabʕiin	'70'
tamaniin	'80'
tisʕiin	'90'

The counted noun is singular and follows the numeral :

ʕišriin kitaab	'twenty books'
ʕišriin ṭaṛabeeza	'twenty tables'
ʕišriin gineeh	'twenty pounds (money)'

*** *** ***

NUMERALS : CARDINAL THOUSANDS -- INDEFINITE CONSTRUCTION

The form for 1,000 is alf, and the form for 2,000 is alfeen (consisting of alf and the dual suffix -een). The thousands above 2,000 are formed by counting the word alf. In this context, alf has the plural talaaf which follows the short forms of 3 - 10. The singular form alf follows all numerals above 10.

aṛbaʕ talaaf	'4,000'
ħiḍaašaṛ alf	'11,000'
waaħid wi xamsiin alf	'51,000'
miit alf	'100,000'
xumsumiit alf	'500,000'
suttumiyya wwaaħid alf	'601,000'
subʕumiyya witneen alf	'803,000'
tumnumiyya wtalaata alf	'815,000'

subʕumiyya wsittiin alf	'760,000'
tusʕumiyya tisʕa wtisʕiin alf	'999,000'

The counted noun is singular and follows the numeral. Thus raagil 'man' or sitt 'woman' can be added after each of the foregoing numerals without changing the numerical expression in any way.

*** *** ***

NUMERALS : COMBINATIONS OF 1 - 99 WITH THE CARDINAL HUNDREDS -- INDEFINITE CONSTRUCTION

The sequence is as follows : the hundreds occur first, followed by (a) one of the numerals 1 - 19, (b) one of the tens above 19, or (c) one of the combinations 21 - 99. The forms used in this context are the following : the form miyya, or miteen, or the forms of 300 - 900 ending in -a and the long forms of 3 - 10. The conjunction wi 'and' occurs only once in each sequence -- before the last word.

miyya wwaaɦid	'101'
miteen witneen	'202'
tultumiyya wxamsa	'305'
ṛubʕumiyya wsabʕa	'407'
xumsumiyya witnaašaṛ	'512'
suttumiyya wsabʕiin	'670'
subʕumiyya sabʕa wtalatiin	'737'
tusʕumiyya tisʕa wtisʕiin	'999'

The counted noun is singular and follows the numeral (Also note Variants) :

tultumiyya wwaaɦid kitaab ~ tultumiit kitaab wiwaaɦid	'301 books'

tultumiyya wwaaħid šanṭa	'301 suitcases'
ṛubʕumiyya witneen kitaab	'402 books'
ṛubʕumiyya witneen šanṭa ~ ṛubʕumiit šanṭa witneen	'402 suitcases'
xumsumiyya wtalaata ṛaagil	'503 men'
suttumiyya xamsa wsabʕiin ṣafħa	'675 pages'
tusʕumiyya sabʕa wtamaniin ṣaṭr	'987 lines'

*** *** ***

NUMERALS : COMBINATIONS OF (1) THE CARDINAL MILLIONS WITH NUMERALS BELOW ONE MILLION AND OF (2) THE CARDINAL BILLIONS WITH NUMERALS BELOW ONE BILLION -- INDEFINITE CONSTRUCTION

(1) The millions precede the other numerals. The expression waaħid milyoon (rather than milyoon) stands for 'one million'.

(2) Similarly, the billions precede the other numerals, and the expression for 'one billion' is waaħid bilyoon rather than bilyoon.

In (1) and in (2), the conjunction wi precedes the last word of the numeral as well as the last word of a combination which counts alf, milyoon, or bilyoon.

(waaħid) milyoon wi waaħid	'1,000,001'
(waaħid) milyoon witneen	'1,000,002'
(waaħid) milyoon miyya xamsa wʕišriin alf suttumiyya talaata wtisʕiin	'1,125,693'

subʕumiyya talaata wsittiin milyoon tusʕumiyya tneen wi sabʕiin alf miyya talaata wtalatiin	'763,972,133'
(waaɦid) bilyoon wi waaɦid	'1,000,000,001'
(waaɦid) bilyoon witneen	'1,000,000,002'
tultumiyya talaata wsittiin bilyoon tusʕumiyya witneen milyoon xumsumiyya ṛbaʕa warbiʕiin alf miteen xamsa wʕišriin	'363,902,544,225'

The counted noun is singular and follows the numeral. Thus <u>saṭr</u> 'line' or <u>kilma</u> 'word' may be added to any of the above combinations without changing the numerical expression in any way.

*** *** ***

NUMERALS : COMBINATIONS OF THE CARDINAL THOUSANDS WITH NUMERALS BELOW ONE THOUSAND -- INDEFINITE CONSTRUCTION

The thousands precede the other numerals in such combinations. The conjunction <u>wi</u> 'and' precedes the last word in the numeral, as well as the last word in a combination which counts <u>alf</u>.

alf wwaaɦid	'1,001'
talat talaaf witneen	'3,002'
sabaʕ talaaf wi sabʕa	'7,007'
taman talaaf witnaašaṛ	'8,012'
ɦiḍaašaṛ alf wtisaʕṭaašaṛ	'11,019'
waaɦid wi xamsiin alf tisʕa wxamsiin	'51,059'
miyya xamsa wtalatiin alf tusʕumiyya sabʕa wsittiin	'135,967'

The counted noun is singular and follows the numeral. Thus kitaab 'book' or ṣafḥa 'page' can be added to any of the above combinations without changing the numerical sequence in any way.

*** *** ***

NUMERALS : COMBINATIONS OF UNITS WITH THE CARDINAL TENS ABOVE 19 -- INDEFINITE CONSTRUCTION

The forms waaḥid, itneen, and the long forms of 3 - 9 combine with the tens above 19. The unit precedes the ten, and the form wi is used as a conjunction. The combination is thus like the archaic English "four and twenty", "seven and sixty", etc. The following are examples :

waaḥid wi ʕišriin	'21'
itneen wi talatiin	'32'
talaata warbiʕiin	'43'
arbaʕa wxamsiin	'54'
xamsa wsittiin	'65'
sitta wsabʕiin	'76'
sabʕa wtamaniin	'87'
tamanya wtisʕiin	'98'

The counted noun is singular and follows the numeral :

waaḥid wi ʕišriin ṛaagil	'21 men'
waaḥid wi ʕišriin bint	'21 girls'
sabʕa wtamaniin kitaab	'87 books'
sabʕa wtamaniin gineeh	'87 pounds (money)'

*** *** ***

NUMERALS : CONJUNCTION wi 'and' IN NUMERICAL EXPRESSIONS

The conjunction wi 'and' precedes (1) the last word of a compound number provided that word is not itself a counted noun, as well as (2) the last word of a combination which counts alf, milyoon, or bilyoon.

waaɦid wi ʕišriin	'21'
miyya wwaaɦid	'101'
tultumiyya xamsa wsittiin	'365'
alfeen xumsumiyya tneen wi ʕišreen	'2,522'
suttumiyya wʕišriin milyoon tultumiyya xamsa wʕišriin alf miteen wi ʕašaṛa	'620,325,210'
subʕumiyya wwaaɦid bilyoon miyya waaɦid wi sittiin milyoon tusʕumiyya wsabʕiin alf miyya tisʕa wtisʕiin	'701,161,970,199'

*** *** ***

NUMERALS : COUNT NOUNS WITH CARDINAL NUMERALS -- INDEFINITE CONSTRUCTION

1. The masculine form waaɦid may precede a singular count noun (SCN, q.v.) of Class (a); it may also precede an SCN of Class (d).

waaɦid biira	'one serving of beer'
waaɦid milyoon wi tultumiyya	'1,000,300'

Both of the forms waaɦid and waɦda may be used as intensifiers modifying a preceding noun other than an SCN; the noun in question is singular and the numerical modifier agrees with it in gender :

kitaab waaɦid	'a single book'
ṭayyaaṛa waɦda	'a single plane'

2. The form itneen precedes an SCN to make that noun dual :

itneen šaay	'two teas'
itneen malliim	'two milliemes'
itneen buuṣa mṛabbaʕa	'two square inches'
itneen milyoon	'2,000,000'

The form itneen can also be used as an intensifier modifying a preceding dual noun; since itneen is invariable, there is no gender agreement between the noun and the numeral :

waladeen itneen	'only two boys'
binteen itneen	'only two girls'

3. With the numerals 3 - 10, the counted nouns are plural unless they are SCN's. In regard to position, the counted noun follows the numeral. There is no gender agreement between the numeral and the counted noun.

talat riggaala	'three men'
talat sittaat	'three ladies'
talaata gneeh	'three pounds (money)'

If the noun to be counted is a plural of the measure aFʕaaL, it is usually changed to tiFʕaaL; if the noun to be counted is a plural of the measure aFʕuL, it is usually changed to tuFʕuL. Educated speakers sometimes use aFʕaaL and aFʕuL as counted nouns without these changes.

xamas tiʔlaam or xamas aʔlaam	'five pencils'
xamas tuzṛuf or xamas azṛuf	'five envelopes'

4. With numerals above 10, the counted noun is singular. In this case the numeral precedes, and shows no gender agreement with, the counted noun.

xamasṭaašar walad	'fifteen boys'
xamasṭaašar bint	'fifteen girls'
miyya xamsa wʕišriin walad	'125 boys'
miyya xamsa wʕišriin bint	'125 girls'

*** *** ***

NUMERALS : DEFINITE CARDINAL CONSTRUCTIONS

A construction consisting of a numeral and a counted noun may be made definite in accordance with the rules given below.

1. The construction consisting of waaħid (feminine waħda) and a preceding noun may be made definite by prefixing the definite article to the numeral as well as the noun. The more common practice, however, is to replace ilwaaħid (feminine : ilwaħda) by the adjective ilwaħiid (feminine : ilwaħiida) 'the only'.

ilkitaab ilwaaħid illi ʕandi	'the one book that I have'
iššanṭa lwaħda lli ʕandi	'the one suitcase I have'
ilkitaab ilwaħiid illi ʕandi	'the only book I have'
iššanṭa lwaħiida lli ʕandi	'the only suitcase I have'

2. The construction consisting of itneen and a preceding noun is made definite by prefixing the definite article to the numeral as well as the noun :

ilkitabeen illitneen	'the two books'
iššanṭiteen illitneen	'the two suitcases'

3. Constructions consisting of any other numeral and a following count noun are made definite in one of the following ways :

(a) The definite article may be prefixed to the numeral; in a numerical sequence, it is the first word which takes the definite article. Except for the addition of the definite article, the construction remains unchanged.

sabaʕ kutub	'seven books'
issabaʕ kutub	'the seven books'
miyya wʕišriin bint	'120 girls'
ilmiyya wiʕišriin bint	'the 120 girls'

alf suttumiyya wtalatiin beet	'1630 houses'
il?alf suttumiyya wtalatiin beet	'the 1630 houses'
waaɦid laɦma	'one (serving of) meat'
ilwaaɦid laɦma	'the one (serving of) meat'
itneen gineeh	'two pounds (money)'
illitneen gineeh	'the two pounds'
talaata biira	'three beers'
ittalaata biira	'the three beers'

(b) The definite article may be prefixed to the numeral in the manner specified in 3(a) above, <u>and</u> to the counted noun as well. Here, however, the counted noun must be plural, and it must precede the numeral. The construction described in 3(a) is the usual one, whereas the construction described here emphasizes a totality which is translatable by 'all'.

sabaʕ kutub	'seven books'
issabaʕ kutub	'the seven books'
ilkutub issabʕa	'the seven books, all of the seven books'
miyya wʕišriin bint	'120 girls'
ilmiyya wʕišriin bint	'the 120 girls'
ilbanaat ilmiyya wʕišriin	'the 120 girls, all of the 120 girls'
alf suttumiyya wtalatiin beet	'1630 houses'
il?alf suttumiyya wtalatiin beet	'the 1630 houses'
ilbuyuut il?alf suttumiyya wtalatiin	'the 1630 houses, all of the 1630 houses'

talaata gineeh	'three pounds (money)'
ittalaata gineeh	'the three pounds'
ilginehaat ittalaata	'the three pounds'

*** *** ***

NUMERALS : FRACTIONS

1 as numerator and 2 - 10 as denominators

The forms involved here are listed in the following table. To the right of each singular fraction, the plural form is given.

nuṣṣ	'one-half'	anṣaaṣ
tilt	'one-third'	atlaat
ṛubʕ	'one-fourth'	arbaaʕ
xums	'one-fifth'	axmaas
suds	'one-sixth'	asdaas
subʕ	'one-seventh'	asbaaʕ
tumn	'one-eighth'	atmaan
tusʕ	'one-ninth'	atsaaʕ
ʕušṛ.	'one-tenth'	aʕšaaṛ

2 as numerator and 3,5,7,9, as denominators

The forms involved here are the duals of tilt, xums, subʕ, and tusʕ :

tilteen	'two-thirds'
xumseen	'two-fifths'
subʕeen	'two-sevenths'
tusʕeen	'two-ninths'

3 - 9 as numerators and 4 - 10 as denominators

Each of the simple fractions involved is expressed by a phrase consisting of (a) one of the short forms for 3 - 9, and (b) a denominator functioning as a counted noun. Since the noun in question is a plural of the measure aFʕaaL, the denominator is of the shape tiFʕaaL (see :

"Numerals : The Cardinals 3 - 10"). Notice, however, that tirbaʕ occurs in the place of the expected tirbaaʕ.

Listed below are the denominators :

tirbaʕ	'fourths'
tixmaas	'fifths'
tisdaas	'sixths'
tisbaaʕ	'sevenths'
titmaan	'eighths'
titsaaʕ	'ninths'
tiʕšaaṛ	'tenths'

The following are examples of the fractions involved :

talat tirbaʕ	'three-fourths'
talat tixmaas	'three-fifths'
aṛbaʕ tixmaas	'four-fifths'
aṛbaʕ tisbaaʕ	'four-sevenths'
xamas tisdaas	'five-sixths'
xamas tisbaaʕ	'five-sevenths'
tisaʕ tiʕšaaṛ	'nine-tenths'

Denominators above 10

Each of the simple fractions in this category is expressed by a phrase consisting of (a) a numerator, (b) the preposition ʕala 'over', and (c) a denominator. The numerators and the denominators are identical to the cardinals.

waaħid ʕala sabaʕṭaašaṛ	'1/17'
tisʕa ʕala tneen wi ʕišriin	'9/22'
miyya w sabʕa ʕala tultu-miyya xamsa wsittiin	'107/365'

Fractions in construct with nouns or pronouns

As nouns, fractions of the measure FVʕL may occur in construct with a following noun or pronoun :

nuṣṣ saaʕa	'half an hour'
nuṣṣukum	'half of you (p)'

Fractions combined with Cardinals

Each of the combinations in question consists of (a) a cardinal whole number, (b) the conjunction wi 'and', and (c) a fraction.

sitt wṛubʕ	' 6 1/4 '
itneen wi talatiin wi tilt	' 32 1/3 '
suttumiyya waaħid wi sittiin wi talatṭaašaṛ ʕala sabʕa wʕišriin	'661 13/27'

The use of illa 'less' to express fractions

A phrase consisting of (a) a whole number, (b) illa 'less' and (c) a fraction is a common alternative for expressing a fraction or a whole number plus a fraction. For example, instead of talat tirbaʕ 'three quarters' we may say waaħid illa ṛubʕ 'one less a quarter'; again, instead of waaħid wi talat tirbaʕ 'one and three-quarters' we may say itneen illa ṛubʕ 'two less a quarter'. Theoretically, any fraction may follow illa; in practice, however, only rubʕ 'a quarter' and tilt occur frequently in this position. This construction is most frequently used in telling time.

*** *** ***

NUMERALS : ORDINALS 1 - 10

The ordinals 1 - 10 have both masculine and feminine forms. In the following table, the masculine forms are listed on the left, and the feminine forms are listed on the right.

Masculine		Feminine
awwil or awwilaani	'first'	uula or awwalani
taani	'second'	tanya
taalit	'third'	talta
ṛaabiʕ	'fourth'	ṛabʕa
xaamis	'fifth'	xamsa
saatit ~ saadis	'sixth'	satta ~ sadsa
saabiʕ	'seventh'	sabʕa
taamin	'eighth'	tamna
taasiʕ	'ninth'	tasʕa
ʕaašir	'tenth'	ʕašra

Notice that :

1. There are two forms for 'first'. As will be explained below, awwal and uula may be used as nouns or adjectives, while awwalaani and awwalaniyya may be used only as adjectives.
2. The ordinals 2 - 10 are derived from the corresponding cardinals, the measure being FaaʕiL for the masculine form and FaʕLa for the feminine form.

In general, the ordinals 1 - 10 may be used as nouns or as adjectives; both usages are discussed and illustrated below.

The ordinals 1 - 10 as nouns

1. Except for awwalaani, the masculine forms of the ordinals 1 - 10 enter into construct with a following singular indefinite noun. The second term of the construct phrase may be either masculine or feminine; the ordinal number on the other hand, shows no contrast for gender.

daxalt awwil beet.	'I entered the first house.'
daxalt awwil ooḍa.	'I entered the first room.'
kunt xaamis ṛaagil wiṣil.	'I was the fifth man to arrive.'
kaanit xaamis sitt wiṣlit.	'She was the fifth woman to arrive.'

2. Except for awwalaani and awwalaniyya, the ordinals 1 - 10 enter into construct with a following definite plural noun. The second term of the construct may be masculine or feminine (depending on the referent); the first term too may be masculine or feminine (depending on the referent).

ʕali xaamis ilawlaad illi nagaḥu.	'Ali ranks fifth among the boys who passed (the test).'
faarida xamsit ilbanaat illi nagaḥu.	'Farida ranks fifth among the girls who passed (the test).'

3. Except for awwalaani and awwalaniyya, the ordinals 1 - 10 enter into construct with a following plural pronoun. The ordinal in this usage may be masculine or feminine (depending on the referent).

huwwa ṛabiʕhum.	'He is the fourth among them.'
hiyya ṛabʕithum.	'She is the fourth among them.'

The ordinals 1 - 10 as adjectives

The ordinals 1 - 10 (including the forms awwalaani and awwalaniyya) may follow singular nouns, the construction being that of a noun and its modifier. The ordinal agrees with the modified noun in gender and definiteness.

ilkitaab il?awwal or ilkitaab il?awwalaani	'the first book'
iṣṣafḥa l?uula or iṣṣafḥa l?awwalaniyya	'the first page'
ilyoom ilxaamis	'the fifth day'
issana lxamsa	'the fifth year'

Phrases consisting of an indefinite noun and a following adjectival ordinal are usually idiomatic expressions; e.g., sana uula means 'first grade (of school)' rather than 'a first year'.

*** *** ***

NUMERALS : ORDINALS ABOVE 10

The ordinals above 10 are identical to the corresponding cardinals. Like the ordinals 1 - 10, they may be used adjectivally; unlike 1 - 10, however, they are never used as nouns.

Although the modified noun may be masculine or feminine, the ordinals above 1- 10 show no contrast for gender.

ilyoom ilxamsa wtalatiin	'the thirty-fifth day'
issana lxamsa wtalatiin	'the thirty-fifth year'

Note

Six forms are used to express the meaning 'last'; those forms and their usages are described below.

1. The form aaxir is used as a noun in construct with a following form. The second member of the construct may be a singular indefinite noun (masculine or feminine), a definite plural noun (masculine or feminine), or a plural pronoun. In all of these contexts, the form aaxir shows no contrast for gender.

aaxir tilmiiz	'the last student (m)'
aaxir tilmiiza	'the last student (f)'
aaxir il?awlaad	'the last of the boys'
aaxir ilbanaat	'the last of the girls'
axirhum	'the last (one) of them'
axirna	'the last (one) of us'

2. The forms axiir (feminine : axiiṛa) and axraani (feminine : axraniyya, plural : axraniyyiin) are used adjectivally. The modified noun may be definite or indefinite.

?aṛeet iṣṣaṭr il?axiir ?	'Have you read the last line ?'
eeh ikkilma l?axiiṛa ?	'What is the last word ?'
haat lwalad il?axraani.	'Bring the last boy.'
haat ilbint il?axraniyya.	'Bring the last girl.'

haat ilbanaat il?axraniyyiin. 'Bring the last girls.'

haat il?awlaad il?axraniyyiin. 'Bring the last boys.'

Phrases like su?aal axiir (where the modified noun is indefinite) are usually idiomatic; e.g., su?aal axiir is translatable by 'a final question' rather than 'a last question'.

*** *** ***

NUMERALS : SINGULAR COUNT NOUNS (SCN)

Singular count nouns are a small set of forms which are invariably singular after a numeral; they may be divided into four classes :

(a) Nouns which share no structural identity but which are used in ordering food, drinks, etc.; e.g., ?ahwa 'coffee', šaay 'tea', laħma 'meat', wiski 'whiskey'.

hatlina xamsa wiski. 'Bring us five whiskies.'

(b) Certain nouns (largely loan words) which designate weight, measurement, or monetary value; e.g., giraam 'gram', kilugraam 'kilogram', miil 'mile', kilumitr 'kilometer', santimitr 'centimeter', gineeh 'Egyptian pound (money)', malliim 'millieme (an Egyptian coin)', taʕriifa 'five milliemes', saay 'piastre (ten milliemes)', šilin 'five piastres', riyaal 'twenty piastres'.

maysawiiš talaata malliim 'It is not worth three milliemes.'

(c) All nouns designating measurement when followed by murabbaʕ 'square' (feminine : murabbaʕa) or mukaʕʕab 'cubic' (feminine : mukaʕʕaba).

tisʕa mitr mṛabbaʕ 'nine square meters'

sitta buuṣa mkaʕʕaba 'six cubic inches'

(d) The forms milyoon 'million' and bilyoon 'billion'

itneen milyoon 'two million'

aṛbaʕa bilyoon 'four billion'

*** *** ***

- O -

ATH

(See : Exclamations and Oaths)

*** *** ***

BSTRUENTS

A speech sound which is produced by the obstruction of the breath passage completely or to the point of producing friction : a stop or a fricative (q.v.).

*** *** ***

IISSION OF VOWELS

(See : Vowels : Contraction)

*** *** ***

TATIVE STRUCTURES

Egyptian Arabic has a number of optative structures expressing a wish or a desire, e.g. "May God bless you". These structures all refer to the present and future whether they have a perfect or imperfect verb form, e.g.,

aḷḷaah yixalliik	'May God keep you'
ṣalla ḷḷaahu ʕalayhi wi sallam	'May God pray for and give peace to him (The Prophet)'

*** *** ***

ORAL CAVITY

The mouth, which is one of the resonance cavities, is called the oral cavity.

*** *** ***

ORGANS OF SPEECH

The stream of air expelled by breathing passes out of the lungs and is used for speech. The larynx is a cartilaginous box at the upper end of the trachea or windpipe. The importance of the larynx in speech is that it contains the vocal cords, or vocal folds, which are essentially two horizontal folds of elastic tissue. The triangular space enclosed by two vocal cords is referred to as the glottis. The tongue has four sections : the apex or tip, the blade or front, the dorsum or back, and the root, which forms the front wall of the pharynx. The tongue is one of the most important movable articulators. The upper front teeth are important in speech formation. Both the lips are of importance in speech. The roof of the mouth may be divided into four parts : the alveolar ridge, the convex portion of the mouth just behind the front teeth; the hard palate, the portion behind the alveolar ridge; the velum or soft palate, the area behind the hard palate; and finally, the uvula, the small appendage that hangs down from the very edge of the velum.

There are three major resonance cavities : the mouth, which is known as the oral cavity; the nose, or nasal cavity, and the throat, or pharynx; their main function in speech is to serve as resonators.

*** *** ***

- P -

PALATAL

A place of articulation consisting of the tongue blade and the palate : /y/.

*** *** ***

PARTICLE

A word, usually uninflected and invariable, used to indicate syntactical relationships. In Egyptian Arabic, particles are adverbs (q.v.), conjunctions (q.v.), prepositions (q.v.), presentational particles (q.v.), pronouns (q.v.), and the vocative particle (q.v.). One thing to remember is that no Egyptian particle is exactly the equivalent of any given gloss in English.

*** *** ***

PASSIVE : MEANING

The passive construction always denotes one of the following :

1. That the agent is unknown.
2. That the agent is concealed for some reason.
3. That the agent is obvious and therefore need not be mentioned e.g.,

itħakam ʕalee bilʔiʕdaam 'He was sentenced to death.'

The above constraints show why the EA passive construction does not contain a phrase such as the underlined one in the following English sentence :

The fugitive was shot by a policeman.

In some contexts, the passive construction denotes potentiality :

baʕḍ innabataat tittaakil wi baʕḍ innabataat matittakilš.	'Some plants are edible and some are not edible.'
ʕali yitḍiħik ʕalee bishuula.	'Ali can be easily decieved.'
samya miš gamiila, laakin titħabb.	'Samia is not pretty, but she is likeable.'

Notice that the passive verbs in the above sentences are subjunctive in form.

The instrument used to perform the act can usually be expressed in the Arabic passive construction by the preposition /bi-/; thus the sentence 'This letter must be written by hand.' can be rendered in Egyptian Arabic as follows :

iggawab da laazim yitkitib bilyadd.

*** *** ***

PASSIVE : PASSIVIZABLE VERBS

The active verbs which may be made passive are those which have a recipient of their action, i.e., those which are transitive or ditransitive (having two recipients), and those whose action is passed on to a noun be means of a preposition (a verb of the second group and the following preposition will be called a "phrasal verb").

1. That transitive and ditransitive verbs may be passivized is illustrated by the following examples :

ʕali <u>fihim</u> iddars.	'Ali understood the lesson.'
iddars <u>itfaham</u>.	'The lesson was understood.'
fariid <u>fahhim</u> ʕali ddars.	'Farid explained the lesson to Ali.'
iddars <u>itfahhim</u> liʕali.	'The lesson was explained to Ali.'

2. That phrasal verbs may be passivized is illustrated by the following examples :

fariid ʔaʕad ʕa kkursi.	'Farid sat on the chair.'
ilkursi tʔaʕad ʕaleeh.	'The chair was sat on.'
ʕali katab ʕa ssabbuuṛa.	'Ali wrote on the board.'
issabbuuṛa tkatab ʕaleeha.	'The board was written on.'

As used here, the term "phrasal verb" does not embrace <u>every</u> sequence which consists of a verb and a following preposition; unless the preposition transmits the action to a following noun, the sequence is not a phrasal verb. Thus the underlined sequence in the example below is not a phrasal verb :

ʕali <u>rigiʕ baʕd</u> illigtimaaʕ. 'Ali returned after the meeting.'

It must be pointed out, however, that the recipient of a phrasal verb is rather loosely defined. In each of the following sentences, the underlined word is a recipient for the reason stated after the sentence :

1. ʕali ʔaʕad ʕa <u>kkursi</u> 'Ali sat on the chair' : The chair received the action denoted by the verb.
2. ʕali katab bi-<u>lʔalam</u> 'Ali wrote with the pencil' : The pencil was used.
3. makanš mumkin ilmuɣanniyyaat yiɣannu li-<u>lxaliifa</u> law kaan ilʔislaam yiḥaṛṛam ilɣuna 'Singing girls could not have sung for the Caliph if singing had not been permissible in Islam' : The Caliph received the benefit of singing.
4. ʕawziin yiwṣalu li-lʔamaṛ fi xamas saʕaat. il-ʔinsaan mayiwṣalš li-<u>lʔamaṛ</u> bissurʕa di 'They want to reach the moon in five hours.

Man cannot reach the moon in such a short time.' : The moon is the object to be reached, and therefore the object which would receive the action denoted by the verb.

5. innaas mumkin yiskunu f-ʔaṣwaan fiššita laakin miš fiṣṣeef
'People can live in Aswan in the winter but not in the summer.' : Aswan is the place to be inhabited, and therefore the place which would receive the action denoted by the verb.

It is thus seen that the recipient is often the object of a preposition in a phrase which indicates instrument, beneficiary, destination, or place. The passive counterparts of the foregoing five sentences are as follows :

1. ilkursi tʔaʕad ʕaleeh.	'The chair was sat on.'
2. ilʔalam itkatab biih.	'The pencil was written with.'
3. makanš mumkin yitɣanna lilxaliifa law kaan ilʔislaam yiɦaṛṛam ilɣuna. ~ makanš mumkin ilxaliifa yitɣanna liih law kaan ilʔislaam yiɦaṛṛam ilɣuna.	'The Caliph could not have been sung for if singing were not permissible in Islam.'
4. ʕawziin yiwṣalu lilʔamaṛ fi xamas saʕaat. ilʔamaṛ mayitwiṣilluuš bissurʕa di.	'They want to reach the moon in five hours. The moon cannot be reached in such a short time.'
5. aṣwaan mumkin titsikin fiššita laakin miš fiṣṣeef. ~ aṣwaan mumkin yitsikin fiiha fiššita laakin miš fiṣṣeef.	'Aswan is habitable in the winter, but not in the summer.'

A verb, then, is passivizable when it has a direct object; in addition, it is often passivizable when it has an item occurring as object of a preposition and which is an instrument, beneficiary, destination, or place.

*** *** ***

PASSIVE : SYNTAX

1. Given an active construction where the direct object of the verb is the only recipient : The direct object becomes the subject of the passive construction. The passive verb agrees with its subject in number, gender, and person.

suʕaad katabit ilmaqaala	'Su'ad wrote the article'
---> ilmaqaala tkatabit	'The article was written'
bahdiluuni mbaariɦ	'They treated me contemptously yesterday'
---> itbahdilt imbaariɦ	'I was treated contemptously yesterday'

2. Given an active construction where the verb has both a direct object and an indirect object : Either the direct object or the indirect object becomes the subject of the passive construction. If the first option is selected, the preposition <u>li-</u> must be prefixed to the indirect object. Whether the first or the second option is chosen, the passive verb agrees with its subject in number, gender, and person.

fahhimt fariid iddars	'I explained the lesson to Farid'
---> iddars itfahhim lifariid	'The lesson was explained to Farid'
<u>or</u> fariid itfahhim iddars	'Farid was helped to understand the lesson.'

3. Given an active construction with a phrasal verb : The object of the preposition becomes the subject of the passive construction. The passive verb form shows no agreement with the subject of the passive construction; the preposition takes a pronominal suffix whose antecedent is the subject of the passive construction.

ilmaɦkama ɦakamit ʕala aṣdiqaaʔak	'The court sentenced your friends'
---> aṣdiqaaʔak itɦakam ʕaleehum	'Your friends were sentenced'

ilmaħkama ħakamit ʕalayya	'The court sentenced me'
---> itħakam ʕalayya	'I was sentenced'

In English, the subject of the active construction may occur in the passive construction as object of the preposition by (e.g., The hunter shot the tiger ---> The tiger was shot by the hunter); in EA, the subject of the active construction does not occur in the passive construction.

*** *** ***

PASSIVE : VERB FORMATION

A verb becomes passive when the active form is replaced by the corresponding passive form. The passive verb form takes the prefix it- (~ in-).

katab	'to write'	itkatab	'to be written'
ʕirif	'to know'	itʕaṛaf	'to become known'
ṣaḷḷaħ	'to fix'	itṣaḷḷaħ	'to be fixed'
baarik	'to bless'	itbaarik	'to be blessed'
bahdil	'to treat contemptuously'	itbahdil	'to be treated contemptuously'

It must be emphasized, however, that not all verbs with the prefix it- are passive (see "Measures : Meaning"); consider, for example, the following sentences :

1.	faṛuuʔ naṭṭaṭ ʕali.	'Farouk made Ali jump up and down.'
2.	ʕali tnaṭṭaṭ milfaṛaħ.	'Ali jumped up and down out of joy.'
3.	fataħ ilbaab.	'He opened the door.'
4.	zaʔʔ ilbaab fa-tfataħ	'He pushed the door and so it opened'

Comparing sentences 1 and 2 shows that itnaṭṭaṭ designates reflexivity rather than passivity; comparing sentences 3 and 4 shows that itfataħ designates yielding rather than passivity.

There are instances where an active form has a recipient but does not correspond to a form with the prefix it-. To compensate for the expected but non-existent colloquial passive, a Standard Arabic passive is used :

Active		Passive
iħtaṛam	'to respect'	uħturim
ixtaaṛ	'to choose'	uxtiir
istaʕmil	'to use'	ustuʕmil

In Standard Arabic, the passive form of perfect verbs always has /i/ as the stem vowel; a preceding vowel is /u/ if short and /uu/ if long. The imperfect passive of Standard Arabic always has /u/ as the vowel of the prefix; every other vowel in the stem is /a/ if short and /aa/ if long. In the speech of many Egyptians, it- and in- are interchangeable (see : "Verb Measures").

*** *** ***

PASSIVE PARTICIPLES : DEFINITENESS

If it denotes a semantic extension (see : "Passive Participles : Meaning"), a passive participle is made definite by prefixing il- to it :

miš baħibb ilmaħši. 'I do not like stuffed cabbage.'

If it denotes the basic designation (see : "Passive Participles : Meaning"), a passive participle is made definite by placing il- or illi before it (il- being the more common of the two) :

Indefinite

ṭaṛabeeza mitṣanfara 'a sandpapered table'

Definite

iṭṭaṛabeeza lmitṣanfaṛa or 'the sandpapered table'
iṭṭaṛabeeza lli mitṣanfaṛa

*** *** ***

PASSIVE PARTICIPLES : DERIVATION

The passive participles of Measure I triliteral verbs have the following forms :

1. maf؟uul from sound roots; e.g., katab 'to write' : maktuub, ؟irif 'to know' : ma؟ruuf.
2. maf؟uu؟ from doubled roots, e.g., ḥaṭṭ 'to put' : maḥṭuuṭ, kabb 'to spill' : makbuub, ḥabb 'to love' : maḥbuub.
3. maf؟i from defective roots; e.g., da؟a 'to invite' : mad؟i, bana 'to build' : mabni, nisi 'to forget' : mansi.

The passive participle of verbs other than Measure I triliterals frequently has the same form as the active participle : it is usually derived by substituting mi- for the yi- of the imperfect huwwa form, e.g.,

Imperfect Verb Form		Active Participle	Passive Participle
yidalla؟	'he spoils (a child)'	midalla؟	midalla؟
yiḥtall	'to occupy (a territory)'	miḥtall	miḥtall
yidaḥṛag	'he rolls (something)'	midaḥṛag	midaḥṛag
yiḥalli	'to sweeten'	miḥalli	miḥalli

A given verb does not yield the passive participle unless that verb co-occurs with a form which designates a recipient. Thus the passive participle is derived from :

1. Transitive verbs :

؟ali garaḥ ḥasan.	'Ali wounded Hasan.'
ḥasan magruuḥ.	'Hasan is wounded.'

2. Verbs whose action is transmitted to a recipient by means of a preposition :

ilmaḥkama ḥakamit ؟ala ؟ali bil?i؟daam.	'The court sentenced Ali to death'
؟ali maḥkuum ؟aleeh bil?i؟daam.	'Ali is sentenced to death.'

3. Passive verbs. (Note that Passive Verbs have only one participle which is passive in meaning.)

ilʕeeš itbaarik.	'The bread was blessed.'
ilʕeeš mitbaarik.	'The bread is (in a state of having been) blessed.'

As has already been mentioned, the passive participle often has the same form as the corresponding active participle. This means that it is sometimes difficult to determine whether a form in isolation is the active or the passive participle. For example, midallaʕ may mean '(of a child) spoiled' or 'spoiling (a child)', depending on whether the participle in question is the passive or the active. When the source verb is a passive one, such ambiguity is hardly possible : passive verbs usually yield passive participles, but on rare occasions they may yield active participles.

Two interesting observations should be noted :

1. No passive participles are derived from verbs of the hollow form FaaL; instead, the participles of the corresponding passive verbs are used. Thus there is no passive participle from baaʕ 'to sell', but the meaning which such a participle would denote is expressed by mitbaaʕ (from itbaaʕ 'to be sold').
2. Passive participles are rarely derived from sound, doubled, and defective verbs of the passive measure itFaʕaL; instead, the passive participles of the corresponding Measure I verbs are used. For example, itkatab 'to be written' seldom yields a passive participle, but the meaning which such a participle would denote is expressed by maktuub (from katab 'to write').

The following statement emerges from these two observations and from the fact that passive verbs rarely yield the active participle : only a few verbs of the passive measure itFaʕaL yield a participle; those are the hollow forms, and it is the passive participle which they usually yield.

Influence of Standard Arabic

Under the influence of Standard Arabic, educated Egyptians in the majority of cases substitute mu- (rather than mi-) for the initial yi- of the imperfect; this "classicism" is often accompanied by two other imitations of Standard Arabic :

1. Deriving the passive participle takes into consideration the vowel which precedes the last radical of the imperfect verb form : if not already /a/ or /aa/, the vowel in question is replaced by /a/ if short and by /aa/ if long. This produces a contrast which exists in Standard Arabic : /a/ or /aa/ (in the specified position) for the majority of passive participles, and /i/ or /ii/ for the corresponding active participles. Examples :

Imperfect Verb Form		Active Participle	Passive Participle
yiʔaddib	'he disciplines'	muʔaddib ~ miʔaddib	muʔaddab
yistaʕmil	'he uses'	mustaʕmil ~ mistaʕmil	mustaʕmal
yisammi	'he names'	musammi ~ misammi	musamma
yistagiib	'he responds'	mustagiib	mustagaab

Due to certain phonological rules, Standard Arabic includes some active participles which -- like their passive counterparts -- have /aa/ before the last radical; the participles worthy of mention in this context are the participles derived from hollow triliterals of Measure VII and Measure VIII. The lack of distinction exists in EA as well.

2. /a/ is inserted before the F of Measure V and Measure VI triliterals in the process of deriving a participle.

Imperfect Verb Form		Active Participle	Passive Participle
yiṭṭaḷḷab	'he requires'	mutaṭallib	mutaṭaḷḷab
yitnaafis	'he competes (with)'	mutanaafis	mutanaafas

As may be expected, such "classicism" usually occurs when the EA participle is identified with a Standard Arabic participle (i.e., when the two participles in question are derived from the same root and the same verbal measure). Since verbs of Measure IV are usually borrowings from Standard Arabic, it is not surprising to find that the passive participles of those verbs are usually of the measure muFʕaL (rather than miF̣ʕiL); e.g., aṛhaq 'to overburden' : muṛhaq.

Differentiating the Passive Participles of Derived Verbs from the Active Counterparts

Sometimes a passive participle cannot be differentiated from the corresponding active participle by the classicism explained above under Influence of Standard Arabic. For example, yidallaʕ 'he spoils (a child)' has /a/ as the stem vowel, and for that reason the replacement described in item 1 under Influence of Standard Arabic cannot be used as a means of differentiating the participles; again, yixtaaṛ 'he chooses' like other hollow triliterals of Measure VIII, yields an active participle and a passive participle both of which have /aa/ before the last radical (this is true in Standard Arabic as well as in EA).

In this situation, educated speakers often resort to one of the following devices :

1. Deriving the active participle from the active verb form, and the passive participle from the passive verb form, e.g., midallaʕ 'having spoiled (a child)' but mitdallaʕ 'spoiled'.

2. Using mi- for the active participle and mu- for the passive participle; e.g., mixtaaṛ 'having chosen' but muxtaaṛ 'chosen'. This device is usually employed when the verb is an active form with no corresponding passive form.

***   ***   ***

PASSIVE PARTICIPLES : GENDER OF SINGULAR

A singular passive participle shows contrast for gender. The feminine singular form results from adding -a to the corresponding masculine form :

Masculine		Feminine
maktuub	'written'	maktuuba
mustaʕmal	'used'	mustaʕmala
masguun	'imprisoned'	masguuna

If the masculine form ends in /i/, /-yya/ is added to produce the feminine form :

Masculine		Feminine
mansi	'forgotten'	mansiyya
mabni	'built'	mabniyya

Under the influence of Standard Arabic, some masculine singular forms (derived from verbs other than the Measure I triliterals) end in /a/ rather than /i/. The feminine singular of such participles is formed by substituting -aah for the final -a :

Masculine		Feminine
musamma	'named'	musammaah
mustasna	'excepted'	mustasnaah

*** *** ***

PASSIVE PARTICIPLES : MEANING

1. "Basic" Meaning

EA verbs are divisble into two types (see "Verbs : Aspect") :

1. Those with which bi- does not indicate continuity (continuity being viewed as the feature of an action or an event in progress). Included here are verbs which denote a state e.g., biyifham 'he understands', biyiʕraf 'he (usually) knows'. Included also are verbs which denote fixation of location; e.g., biyuskun 'he (usually) resides'.
2. Those with which bi- indicates continuity (as well as repetitiveness, habituality); e.g., biyidris 'he is studying', biyiktib 'he is writing'.

For verbs of the first type, the passive participle designates a current state (usually translatable by an English expression which consists of 'is / am / are' and a following past participle); e.g., ʕirif 'to know' : maʕruuf 'is known', fihim 'to understand' : mafhuum 'is understood'.

(a) ilbeet da maskuun. 'This house is inhabited.'

(b) inta maʕruuf. 'You are well known.

For verbs of the second type, the passive participle means 'in a state of having been ___' where the blank stands for the meaning of an English past participle; e.g., katab 'to write' : maktuub 'is in a state of having been written', ʔaṭaʕ 'to cut' : maʔṭuuʕ 'is in a state of having been cut', rabaṭ 'to tie up' : marbuuṭ 'is in a state of having been tied up'.

(c) laʔeetu marbuuṭ. 'I found him tied up (literally : "in a state of having been tied up").'

The difference between the two meanings of passive participles becomes clear when sentence (a) is compared with sentence (c) : in sentence (a), the act of inhabiting is current; in sentence (c), it is not the act of cutting but the result of that act which is current.

Thus, the passive participle shares certain semantic elements with the active participle : from Type 1 verbs, both express a current state; from Type 2 verbs, both express a current state brought about by a past act (see : "Active Participles : Meaning").

To obtain the correct English translation, one must make sure that the Arabic participle and the English equivalent occur in comparable slots; one must also choose as the English equivalent an expression which is appropriate for the slot :

irrisaala maktuuba.	'The message is (now) written.'
irrisaala lmaktuuba	'the written message'
ilbeet mabni.	'The house has (now) been built.'
ilbeet ilmabni	'the house which has been built'

2. Semantic Extension

Some passive participles may be used either with the basic designation or with a meaning (called the "extension") which is similar to but not identical with the basic designation. For example, masguun can mean 'imprisoned ("in a state of having been imprisoned"), but it can also mean 'a prisoner'; likewise, maħši can mean 'stuffed (in a state of having been stuffed)', but it can also mean 'stuffed cabbage'.

simiʕt innu masguun.	'I heard that he is imprisoned.'
ilmasguun hirib.	'The prisoner escaped.'

Difference in regard to aspect (i.e., verbal force) is part of what distinguishes the basic designation from the extension : while the basic designation includes aspect, the extension does not. Compare, for example, the participles in the following sentences :

ilmawḍuuʕ da mafhuum min zamaan.	'This subject has been clear ("understood") for a long time.'
mafhuum ilkilma di ɣeer mafhuum ilkilma dukha.	'The designation of this word differs from that of the other word.'

3. Absence of Person Designation

Unlike verbs, passive participles do not designate person. Thus in isolation the form maʕruuf does not indicate whether reference is to first, second, or third person; the same is true of maʕruufa and maʕrufiin.

4. In some contexts the EA passive participle denotes a potentiality which is often expressed in English by the suffix -able. The following are examples :

laazim titkallim biṣoot masmuuʕ.	'You must speak in an audible voice.'
ilwaḍʕ wiħiš laakin muħtamal.	'The situation is bad but tolerable.'
mawqifak mafhuum.	'Your attitude is understandable.'

*** *** ***

PASSIVE PARTICIPLES : NUMBER

A. Passive Participles Which Denote a Semantic Extension (Typically Nominal)

If a passive participle denotes a semantic extension (see : "Passive Participles : Meaning"), it may be singular, dual, or plural. The dual is formed by adding -een to the singular form :

Singular		Dual
masguun	'a prisoner (m)'	masguneen
masguuna	'a prisoner (f)'	masgunteen
muwaẓẓaf	'an employee (m)'	muwaẓẓafeen
muwaẓẓafa	'an employee (f)'	muwaẓẓafteen
mašṛuub	'a drink'	mašṛubeen
musaddas	'a pistol'	musaddaseen

Provided it is derived from a verb other than a Measure I triliteral, and provided it denotes a human being, each of the passive participles being discussed typically has two plural forms : the sound masculine, and the sound feminine; the former results from adding -iin to the masculine singular, while the latter results from adding -aat to the feminine singular.

Singular		Plural
muwaẓẓaf	'an employee (m)'	muwaẓẓafiin
muwaẓẓafa	'an employee (f)'	muwaẓẓafaat

Provided it is derived from a verb other than a Measure I triliteral, and provided that it designates a non-human referent, each of the passive participles in question typically has a sound feminine plural form :

Singular		Plural
mudaṛṛag	'lecture room (in a university)	mudaṛṛagaat
murakkab	'a (chemical) compound'	murakkabaat

musallas	'a triangle'	musallasaat
musaddas	'a pistol'	musaddasaat

If derived from Measure I triliteral verbs, the passive participles in question typically have broken plurals; in this context, one of the most common plural measures is maFaʕiiL.

Singular		Plural
maʕguun	'a paste'	maʕagiin
masguun	'a prisoner'	masagiin
maḥṣuul	'a crop'	maḥaṣiil
maʔmuuṛ	'a commissioner'	maʔamiir
magmuuʕa	'a collection (e.g., of stamps)'	magamiiʕ

B. Passive Participles Which Denote the Basic Designation (Typically Adjectival)

If it denotes the basic designation, a passive participle may be singular or plural (the dual is rarely used). The plural is typically a sound form which results from adding -iin to the masculine singular, and which may modify a masculine or a feminine noun.

Certain masculine singular forms undergo specifiable changes upon the addition of -iin; those changes are as follows :

1. If the masculine singular form ends in /i/, /-yyiin/ is added to make it plural :

Masculine Singular		Feminine Singular	Plural
madʕi	'invited'	madʕiyya	madʕiyyiin
mitṛabbi	'brought up well'	mitṛabbiyya	mitṛabbiyyiin

iṛṛaagil illi madʕi	'the man who is invited'
iṛṛagleen illi madʕiyyiin	'the two men who are invited'
irriggaala lli madʕiyyiin	'the men who are invited'

issitt illi madʕiyya	'the woman who is invited'
issitteen illi madʕiyyiin	'the two women who are invited'
issittaat illi madʕiyyiin	'the women who are invited'

2. If the masculine singular form ends in /a/, /-yiin/ is added to make it plural :

Masculine Singular		Feminine Singular	Plural
muṣaffa	'filtered'	muṣaffaah	muṣaffayiin

saaʔil muṣaffa	'a filtered liquid'
saaʔileen muṣaffayiin	'two filtered liquids'
sawaaʔil muṣaffaah	'filtered liquids'

Combining number and gender contrasts, we get the following forms :

1. For participles with a semantic extension (typically nominal)

   (a) Masculine singular; e.g., masguun 'a prisoner', muwaẓẓaf 'an employee'.

   (b) Feminine singular; e.g., masguuna, muwaẓẓafa.

   (c) Masculine dual; e.g., masguneen, muwaẓẓafeen.

   (d) Feminine dual; e.g., masgunteen, muwaẓẓafteen.

   (e) Plural

      (i) Sound masculine; e.g., muwaẓẓafiin.

      (ii) Sound feminine; e.g., muwaẓẓafaat.

      (iii) Broken; e.g., masagiin.

2. For participles with the basic designation (typically adjectival)

   (a) Masculine singular; e.g., muʔaddab 'polite'

   (b) Feminine singular; e.g., muʔaddaba

   (c) Plural; e.g., muʔaddabiin.

*** *** ***

PASSIVE PARTICIPLES : PRECEDED BY kaan

Like other nouns and adjectives, passive participles may be preceded by a form of the marker kaan. The meaning of a construction consisting of the marker and a following passive participle is obtained by combining the meanings of the two constituents (for the various meanings expressed through use of the marker, see : "Verbs : The Tense/Aspect Marker kaan") :

ʕali muʔaddab.	'Ali is polite.'
ʕali kaan muʔaddab.	'Ali was polite.'
ʕali biykuun muʔaddab filfaṣl.	'Ali is polite in class.'
ʕali miš naawi ykuun muʔaddab maʕaahum.	'Ali does not intend to be polite with them.'

*** *** ***

PASSIVE PARTICIPLES : SYNTACTIC USAGE

1. When they denote the basic designation (see : "Passive Participles : Meaning"), passive participles usually occur in adjectival slots.

rameet fingaan maksuur fizzibaala.	'I threw a broken cup in the garbage can.'
rameet ilfingaan ilmaksuur fizzibaala.	'I threw the broken cup in the garbage can.'

Adjectival passive participles agree with the modified noun in number, gender, and definiteness (see : "Adjectives : Adjectival Use of Participles").

Passive participles with the basic designation also occur in nominal slots :

ilmuʔaddab aḥsan min ʔaliil ilʔadab.	'A polite person is to be preferred over an impolite one.'

Notice however that, when used nominally, a passive participle with the basic designation is a contraction of an attributive construction; thus ilmuʔaddab in the above sentence stands for iššaxṣ ilmuʔaddab 'a polite person'.

A passive participle may be derived from a verb whose action is transmitted to a recipient by means of a preposition (see : "Passive Participles : Derivation"). When such is the case, the participle is invariable in form and always co-occurs with the preposition in question; contrasts in number and gender are indicated by pronominal suffixes attached to the preposition.

ilmaɦkama ɦakamit ʕala ssitt bilʔiʕdaam.	'The court sentenced the woman to death.'
issitt di maɦkuum ʕaleeha bilʔiʕdaam.	'This woman is sentenced to death.'
sitt maɦkuum ʕaleeha	'a sentenced woman'
issitt ilmaɦkuum ʕaleeha	'the sentenced woman'
sitteen maɦkuum ʕaleehum	'two sentenced women'
issitteen ilmaɦkuum ʕaleehum	'the two sentenced women'
ṛaagil maɦkuum ʕaleeh	'a sentenced man'
iṛṛaagil ilmaɦkuum ʕaleeh	'the sentenced man'
riggaala maɦkuum ʕaleehum	'sentenced men'
irriggaala lmaɦkuum ʕaleehum	'the sentenced men'

In the examples below, the participle is inflected although it is followed by a preposition; this is because in the source strings the preposition is not a means of transmitting the action of the verb to a recipient.

innaas yiʕṛafu ssayyid muxtaaṛ fi maṣṛ.	'People know Mr. Mukhtar in in Egypt.'

issayyid muxtaaṛ maʕṛuuf fi maṣṛ.	'Mr. Mukhtar is well known in Egypt.'
iṛṛaagil ilmaʕṛuuf fi maṣṛ	'the man who is well known in Egypt'
issitt ilmaʕṛuufa fmaṣṛ	'the lady who is well known in Egypt'
iṛṛagleen/issitteen ilmaʕṛufiin fi maṣṛ	'the two men/women who are well known in Egypt'

2. When used with a semantic extension, a passive participle usually occurs in nominal slots :

ilmaʔmuuṛ margiʕš.	'The commissioner has not returned.'
ʔabilna lmaʔmuuṛ.	'We met the commissioner.'
saʔalt ʕan ilmaʔmuuṛ.	'I asked about the commissioner.'
maʔmuuṛ ilmanṭiʔa miš miwaafiʔ.	'The district commissioner does not agree.'
ħaḍritak ṣadiiʔ ilmaʔmuuṛ ?	'Are you the commissioner's friend ?'

***   ***   ***

PATTERN WITH ROOTS

Root is a term used in Arabic grammar for the consonant core of a word in Egyptian Arabic. It does not occur in isolation, but in any of various word patterns. All derivatives of the root (k-t-b), for example, have to do with "writing". The basic meaning of the root is modified by the various patterns with which it occurs. Patterns, then, are vowels (sometimes accompanied by certain non-root consonants) added to the root to form a word, e.g.,

k-t-b	-a-a-	--->	katab	'he wrote'
k-t-b	ma--a-	--->	maktab	'office; desk'
k-t-b	--aa-i-	--->	kaatib	'writer'

Thus, /k/, /t/ and /b/ of /katab/ are the three radicals that constitute the k-t-b root, whose meaning has to do primarily with writing. /-a-a-/ is the vocalic pattern which forms the perfect (past tense) form /katab/ 'he wrote'.

Consider :

	/kaatib/	'writer'
	/maktab/	'office, desk'
	/maktaba/	'library; bookshop'

The above are some of the derivatives of the root k-t-b, all achieved by different vocalic patterns or consonantal-vocalic patterns; i.e., /-aa-i-/ in /kaatib/ and /ma--a-/ in /maktab/ and /ma--a-a/ in /maktaba/. Since the three radicals that constitute the root k-t-b are all consonants, we will call it a Sound Triconsonantal Root.

*** *** ***

HARYNGEAL

A place of articulation consisting of the root of the tongue and pharynx forming a stricture / ɦ, ʕ /.

*** *** ***

HARYNX

The pharynx is the throat, one of the resonance cavities.

*** *** ***

PHONEME

The minimal unit of sound which distinguishes two words otherwise identical in a language; e.g., English "till" and "dill" differ in only one phoneme. Likewise Egyptian Arabic /taab/ 'he repented' and /daab/ 'it melted' differ in one phoneme. Such words are referred to as a Minimal Pair. A phoneme may have positionally conditioned allophones (q.v.).

*** *** ***

PHRASE VERSUS SENTENCE

(a) n (indef) + adj (indef) = Indefinite Phrase

/walad kibiir/ 'a big boy'

(b) n (def) + adj (def) = Definite Phrase

/ilwalad ilkibiir/ 'the big boy'

(c) n (def) + adj (indef) = Sentence

/ilwalad kibiir/ 'the boy is big'

Example (c) above is known as an Equational Sentence. It consists of a definite subject and an indefinite predicate. It can be made interrogative by the use of rising intonation.

*** *** ***

PLURAL

A look at :	kitaab - kutub	'book'
	walad - awlaad	'boy'
	gumla - gumal	'sentence'
	kilma - kalimaat	'word'

shows that plurals of nouns are unpredictable and must be learned for each noun separately. Such plurals are referred to as broken plurals. This term is in contrast with the regular predictable plurals which are termed sound plurals. Examples of the sound plurals are :

/fallaaħ/	'farmer' (m)	/fallaħiin/	'farmers' (m)

(Thus the suffix /-iin/ is the marker of sound masculine plural.)

/fallaaħa/	'farmer' (f)	/fallaħaat/	'farmers' (f)

(Thus the suffix /-aat/ is the marker of sound feminine plural.)

With human plural nouns, adjectives agree in number :

/awlaad kubaaṛ/	'big boys'
/banaat kubaaṛ/	'big girls'

However, with non-human plural nouns, either plural adjectives or feminine singular adjectives may be used :

/kutub kubaaṛ/	'big books'
/kutub kibiira/	'big books'

The latter form is sometimes applied even to modify human nouns by some speakers of EA, e.g. :

	/awlaad kutaaṛ/	'many boys'
	/awlaad kitiira/	'many boys'
and	/banaat kutaaṛ/	'many girls'
	/banaat kitiira/	'many girls'

*** *** ***

POSSESSION

Pronominal Suffixes in Combination with Nouns

The paradigm is listed here as :

vocalic set	-i	my
	-ak	your (m)
	-ik	your (f)
	-u	his

consonantal set	-ha	her
	-na	our
	-kum	your (p)
	-hum	their

Notice :

a) With nouns like /kitaab/ 'book' changes resulting from suffixation are expected before the consonantal set, e.g. :

/kitaabi/ 'my book' but /kitabkum/ 'your (p) book'

(EA does not permit the sequence VVCC in a word.)

b) Also, nouns ending in -iC# will show changes before the vocalic set, e.g. :

/waagib/ 'homework' but /wagbi/ 'my homework'

(elision of /i/ of -iC# ; see : Vowels : Elision)

c) Feminine and plural nouns ending in -a# will always be in their construct state before pronominal endings, e.g. :

/gazma/	'shoe'
/gazmiti/	'my shoe'
/gazmitha/	'her shoe'

<u>/ʕand/ 'to have'; 'with'; 'in one's possession'; 'at one's place'; French chez</u>

Egyptian Arabic does not have a verb that corresponds to English 'to have' as in 'I have a book.' EA expresses this by the particle /ʕand/ which means 'at', 'to have', 'in one's possession', 'with' or <u>chez</u>.

/ʕand/ can be followed by a noun or a pronominal suffix. Notice the forms of the pronominal suffixes with /ʕand/, particularly with the second set which has an <u>extra vowel</u> :

ʕand	i	I have (<u>or</u> 'with me' <u>or</u> 'at my place')
ʕand	ak	you (m) have
ʕand	ik	you (f) have
ʕand	u	he has
ʕand	aha	she has
ʕand	ina	we have
ʕand	ukum	you (p) have
ʕand	uhum	they have

Notice that the pronominal suffixes here are the same as those suffixed to nouns, except for an extra vowel in the consonantal suffixes /-ha/, /-na/, /-kum/, /-hum/ --> /-aha/, /-ina/, /-ukum/ and /-uhum/.

(See also : Adjectival Phrase Introduced by bitaaʕ ; Construct Phrases; Vowels : Extra)

*** *** ***

PREFIX

A formative (a single phoneme or syllable) placed before a word to modify its meaning or derive a new word, e.g. :

katab 'to write' inkatab 'to be written'

*** *** ***

PREFIX OF FUTURITY

The imperfect verb forms may be preceded by /ɦa-/ ~ /ha-/, the prefix of futurity. Thus, /-yiktib/ can be preceded by /ɦa-/ :

ɦayiktib 'he will write, he is going to write'

*** *** ***

PREPOSITION

A word used with a noun or a pronoun or adverb to show the relation of the noun or pronoun or adverb to some other word in the sentence. Some Egyptian Arabic prepositions and prepositional phrases are listed here :

fi ~ f in

ʕala ~ ʕa on

(/ʕala/ has the short form /ʕa/ before the definite article, e.g., /ʕa lmaktab/ 'on the desk')

taħt	under
foo?	on; above
maʕa	with
guwwa	inside; inside of
?uddaam	in front of
waṛa	behind
ʕand	chez; to have
baṛṛa	outside (of)
?abl	before
baʕd	after
gamb ~ ganb	beside; near
min	from

(/min/ has the short form /mi/ before the definite article, e.g., /milwalad/ 'from the boy'; /missitt/ 'from the lady')

*** *** ***

PRESENTATIONAL PARTICLE

/ahó/ (ms) and /ahé/ (fs) 'here is' are here referred to as presentational particles. They agree in gender with the singular noun referred to, e.g. :

ahó ṭṭaalib innabiih	Here is the intelligent student (m).
ahé ṭṭaaliba nnabiiha	Here is the intelligent student (f).

/ahúm/ 'there are' is the plural form of /ahó/ and /ahé/.

Also note the invariable presentational particle /aadi/ 'here is/are'.

ahó (ms)	here is
ahé (fs)	here is
ahúm (p)	here are
ahó lwalad	Here is the boy.
ahé lbint	Here is the girl.
ahúm ilwilaad	Here are the boys.
ahúm ilbanaat	Here are the girls.

(See also : Adjectival Phrase Introduced by bitaaʕ; Possession)

*** *** ***

RONOMINAL SUFFIXES WITH CERTAIN PARTICLES

This section will list paradigms of pronominal suffixes in connection with the following particles : /li/ 'to, for', /bi/ 'with, by', /fi/ 'in', /ʕala/ 'on', /wayya/ 'with, in possession of' and /min/'from'.

	/li/	/fi/	/bi/	/ʕala/
1 s	liyya	fiyya	biyya	ʕalayya
2 ms	liik ~ lak	fiik	biik	ʕaleek
2 fs	liiki ~ liki	fiiki	biiki	ʕaleeki
3 ms	liih ~ luh	fiih	biih	ʕaleeh
3 fs	liiha ~ laha	fiiha	biiha	ʕaleeha
1 p	liina ~ lina	fiina	biina	ʕaleena
2 p	liikum ~ likum	fiikum	biikum	ʕaleekum
3 p	liihum ~ lihum	fiihum	biihum	ʕaleehum

	/wayya/	/min/
1 s	wayyaaya	minni
2 ms	wayyaak	minnak
2 fs	wayyaaki	minnik
3 ms	wayyaah	minnu
3 fs	wayyaaha	minnaha ~ minha
1 p	wayyaana	minnina
2 p	wayyaakum	minnukum ~ minkum
3 p	wayyaahum	minnuhum ~ minhum

*** *** ***

PRONOUN

A word used to replace a proper name or a noun, or to refer to the person, object, idea, etc., designated by a noun. The following are sets of the pronouns and pronominal suffixes of Egyptian Arabic :

a) Independent Subject Pronouns :

ana	I	iħna	we
inta	you (ms)	intu	you (p)
inti	you (fs)		
huwwa	he	humma	they
hiyya	she		

b) Pronominal Suffixes associated with nouns, particles, and prepositions ending in consonants :

kitaabi	my book
kitaabak	your (ms) book
kitaabik	your (fs) book
kitaabu	his book
kitabha	her book
kitabna	our book
kitabkum	your (p) book
kitabhum	their book

c) Direct Object pronominal endings suffixed to transitive verbs :

ḍaṛabni	he hit me
ḍaṛabak	he hit you (ms)
ḍaṛabik	he hit you (fs)
ḍaṛabu	he hit him
ḍaṛabha	he hit her
ḍaṛabna	he hit us
ḍaṛabkum	he hit you (p)
ḍaṛabhum	he hit them

d) Pronominal Suffixes added to verbs ending in /-a#/ :

warraani	he showed me
warraak	he showed you (ms)
warraaki	he showed you (fs)
warraah	he showed him
warraaha	he showed her
warraana	he showed us
warraakum	he showed you (p)
warraahum	he showed them

e) Pronominal Suffixes added to certain particles : /li/ 'to,for', /bi/ 'with,by', /fi/ 'in', /ʕala/ 'on', /wayya/ 'with, in possession of' :

liyya	to me	ʕalayya	on me
liik ~ lak	to you (ms)	ʕaleek	on you (ms)
liiki ~ liki	to you (fs)	ʕaleeki	on you (fs)
liih ~ luh	to him	ʕaleeh	on him
liiha ~ laha	to her	ʕaleeha	on her
liina ~ lina	to us	ʕaleena	on us
liikum ~ likum	to you (p)	ʕaleekum	on you (p)
liihum ~ lihum	to them	ʕaleehum	on them

*** *** ***

RONOUN : PERSONAL

The independent personal pronouns are listed here for reference :

singular		plural	
ana	I	iħna	we
inta	you (m)	intu	you
inti	you (f)		
huwwa	he	humma	they
hiyya	she		

*** *** ***

PRONOUN : RELATIVE

(See : Relative Clauses with illi)

*** *** ***

PRONOUN OF SEPARATION

Sentences where the predicate is a definite phrase are relatively few. Most definite phrases functioning as predicate must be preceded by a pronoun whose antecedent is the subject. The pronoun in question is called "the pronoun of separation" because it separates the predicate from the subject. When the predicate is a construct phrase, the occurrence of the pronoun of separation is optional.

issayyid aħmad huwwa l?ustaaz iggidiid .	'Mr. Ahmad is the new professor.'
muna hiyya lbint illi tʕawwaṛit .	'Muna is the girl who was injured.'
dool humma ttalamiiz illi kasaṛu ššibbaak .	'These are the students who broke the window.'
ʕali huwwa ṭṭawiil .	'Ali is the tall one.'
ustaazak huwwa ana .	'Your teacher is me.'
tilmizti hiyya suzaan .	'My student is Suzanne.'
ilkitaab illi ?ultilak ʕannu huwwa da .	'The book I told you about is this (one).'
suha (hiyya) tilmizti .	'Suha is my studient.'
ilmutaʕallimiin (humma) quwwit ilbalad .	'The educated people are the strength of the nation.'

*** *** ***

PRONOUN : SUFFIXES WITH AUXILIARIES

Pronominal suffixes may be added to /laazim/ 'it is necessary', /yimkin + l-/ 'it is possible', /yadoob/ 'to have just done something' and /yareet/ 'to wish'.

lazmu yidris .	'He needs to study.'
lazmak ɦaaga ?	'Do you need something?'
lazmak tidris .	'You must study.'
da miš lazimni .	'I don't need this.'
yimkinlak tiṛuuɦ dilwaʔti .	'You may go now.'
yadoobu wiṣil .	'He has just arrived.'
yaretni maṛuɦtiš .	'I wish I hadn't gone.'

*** *** ***

PRONOUN : SUFFIXES WITH VERBS

/ʔulli/ 'tell me' is the verb /ʔaal/ (Q) 'to say' in the imperative /ʔuul/ plus the preposition /-l-/'to' plus the pronominal suffix /-i/ 'me'. The pronominal suffixes associated with particles and nouns were discussed in the entry entitled 'Pronoun'.

This section lists the pronominal suffixes added as objects of verbs.

object pronoun + /ḍaṛab/ 'to hit' ; + /ɦabb/ 'to like, love'

1st person s	ḍaṛab	ni	ɦabb	i	ni
2nd person ms	ḍaṛab	ak	ɦabb		ak
2nd person fs	ḍaṛab	ik	ɦabb		ik
3rd person ms	ḍaṛab	u	ɦabb		u
3rd person fs	ḍaṛab	ha	ɦabb	a	ha
1st person p	ḍaṛab	na	ɦabb	i	na
2nd person p	ḍaṛab	kum	ɦabb	u	kum
3rd person p	ḍaṛab	hum	ɦabb	u	hum

Notice :

a) The forms are all the same, irrespective of whether they are added to verbs, particles, prepositions or nouns, except for the first person singular which is always /-ni/ after verbs.

b) Of more importance, please note that in /ɦabb/ above, the helping vowel which is almost always /-i-/ changes to /-a-/ before /-ha/ and to /-u-/ before /-kum/ and /-hum/. It may help you to remember this if you note that the helping vowel in these instances is the same as the vowel of the suffixes in /-aha/, /-ukum/, /-uhum/.

c) Another thing worth mentioning here is that the singular forms of the pronominal suffixes will show certain differences in form according to whether the verb, particle or noun to which they are added ends in a consonant or vowel.

Study the following paradigms :

	After -C	After -V
1st person s	-i / -ni (after verbs)	-ya
2nd person ms	-ak	-k
2nd person fs	-ik	-ki
3rd person ms	-u (~ -hu)	-h (~ -hu)
3rd person fs	-ha	-ha
1st person p	-na	-na
2nd person p	-kum	-kum
3rd person p	-hum	-hum

Examples :

kitaab	'book'	kitaabi	'my book'
wara?a	'a piece of paper'	wara?ti	'my paper' (CS of f used)
ḍaṛab	'he hit'	ḍaṛabni	'he hit me'
ɦabb	'he liked'	ɦabbini	'he liked me'
ax	'brother'	axuuya	'my brother'
waṛa	'behind'	waṛaaya	'behind me'

Examples of the occurrence of the variant form /-hu/ in the 3rd person ms

katabu	'he wrote it (m)'
katabulha ~ katabhulha	'he wrote it (m) to her
makatabulhaaš	'he did not write it (m) to her'

*** *** ***

- *Q* -

QAAF

(See : Glottal Stop)

*** *** ***

QUADRILITERAL (= QUADRIRADICAL) VERB

A verb (q.v.) having four radicals (q.v.) or constituent elements, e.g., /targim/ 'to translate', /zalzil/ 'to shake' (reduplicative verb, q.v.).

*** *** ***

QUESTIONS : ALTERNATIVE QUESTIONS

An alternative question presents two or more choices which presumably include the answer.

iggaww fmaṣṛ ɦaṛṛ walla bard ? 'Is the weather in Egypt hot or cold?

In EA, alternative questions are characterized by the presence of /walla/ 'or' (notice that the word for 'or' in EA <u>statements</u> is usually /aw/). While the English word 'or' occurs only once in a given alternative question, the EA word /walla/ occurs between each pair of choices :

tištayal maʕaaya walla maʕaaha walla maʕa ḥseen ? 'Would you like to work with me, with her or with Hussein ?

EA has two intonation patterns for alternative questions : one that ends with a rising pitch, and another that ends with a falling pitch. Of these, the former is considered the more courteous.

tiḥibb nuʔʕud filmuntazah walla nirgaʕ ilbeet ?
'Would you like us to stay in the park or to go home? '

tiḥibb nuʔʕud filmuntazah walla nirgaʕ ilbeet ?
'Would you like us to stay in the park or to go home?'

*** *** ***

QUESTIONS : INFORMATION QUESTIONS

An information question solicits new information as an answer (in contrast with yes-or-no questions which solicit "Yes" or "No", and in contrast with alternative questions which presumably contain the answer). The set of question words used here excludes walla 'or' and hal.

The intonation patterns associated with information questions are represented below. The first is considered more courteous than the second :

ʔaṛeet ilkitaab da leeh ? 'Why did you read this book?'

ʔaṛeet ilkitaab da leeh ? 'Why did you read this book?'

Notice that the second intonation pattern is used frequently with English information questions. The first pattern is used in English to convey reassurance or protest :

I won't hurt you!

That's not what I meant!

With respect to grammatical structure, a statement is changed to an information question by substituting the appropriate question word for a given constituent. We shall call the expression to be replaced "the questioned constituent". In the following example, the questioned constituent is the adverbial baʕd iḍḍuhṛ 'in the afternoon'.

ħayirgaʕ baʕd iḍḍuhṛ --> 'He will return in the afternoon.'
ħayirgaʕ imta ? 'When will he return?'

The question word usually occupies the slot previously occupied by the questioned constituent. In many cases, however, the question word may be transposed to sentence-initial position :

ħayirgaʕ imta ? --> imta ħayirgaʕ ? 'When will he return?'

Transposition is rather rare in the following situations :

1. When the questioned constituent is related by strong cohesion to an adjacent constituent, e.g., when the questioned constituent is the second term of a construct phrase or the object of a preposition. If it does occur in this situation, transposition must involve two constituents: the question word, and the closely related constituent. In the following examples, the questioned constituents are underlined, and relatively rare constructions are identified by an asterisk :

maħmuud ṣaaħib ilwaziir --> 'Mahmoud is the minister's friend.'
maħmuud ṣaaħib miin ? --> 'Whose friend is Mahmoud?'
*ṣaaħib miin maħmuud ? 'Whose friend is Mahmoud?'

ilkitaab maʕa samiira --> 'The book is with Samira.'
ilkitaab maʕa miin ? --> 'With whom is the book?'
*maʕa miin ilkitaab ? 'With whom is the book?'

2. When the questioned constituent is the direct or the indirect object of a verb. Thus šaafu rṛaagil 'They saw the man' yields šaafu miin ? 'Whom did they see?' but rarely *miin šaafu ?. Likewise, fahhimit ʕali ddars 'She helped Ali to understand the lesson' commonly yields fahhimit miin iddars ? 'Whom did she help to understand the lesson?' but rarely *miin fahhimit iddars ?. Notice that miin irṛaagil illi šafuu ? 'Who is the man that they saw?' involves no transposition. It is derived from a sentence whose subject is the questioned constituent :

huwwa ṛṛaagil illi šafuuh --> 'He is the man that they saw.'

miin iṛṛaagil illi šafuuh ? 'Who is the man that they saw?'

Listed below are the most common of the question words which occur in information questions. The list includes glosses and relevent comments and examples.

1. eeh 'what?' : Replaces a non-human noun.

katabit kitaab -->	'She wrote a book.'
katabit eeh ?	'What did she write?'
ʔaṛa maqaala -->	'He read an article.'
ʔaṛa eeh ?	'What did he read?'
fiih kitabeen ʕa ṭṭaṛabeeza -->	'There are two books on the table.'
fiih eeh ʕa ṭṭaṛabeeza ?	'What is there on the table?'
ištaru lkutub -->	'They bought the books.'
ištaru eeh ?	'What did they buy?'

2. miin 'who?' : Replaces a human noun.

ʕali filbeet -->	'Ali is at home.'
miin filbeet ?	'Who is at home?'
ʔablit samiira -->	'She met Samira.'
ʔablit miin ?	'Whom did she meet?'
ziʕil min ilwaladeen -->	'He was angry with the two boys.'
ziʕil min miin ?	'Whom was he angry with?'
di kutub ilbinteen -->	'These are the two girls' books.'
di kutub miin ?	'Whose books are these?'
dool awlaadi -->	'These are my sons.'
dool miin ?	'Who are these (people)?'
idduktooṛ wabbax ilmumaṛṛiḍaat -->	'The doctor scolded the nurses.'
idduktooṛ wabbax miin ?	'Whom did the doctor scold?'

3. anhu, anhi and anhum 'which?' : These three forms replace definite adjectival constituents. The first is selected when the modified noun is masculine singular, the second when the modified noun is feminine singular (or non-human plural) and the third when the

modified noun is either dual or plural.

ɦayiʔṛa lkitaab iggidiid -->	'He will read the new book.'
ɦayiʔṛa lkitaab anhu ?	'Which book will he read?'
ɦayʔaabil iṛṛaagil ilʔamṙikaani -->	'He will meet with the American man.'
ɦayʔaabil iṛṛaagil anhu ?	'Which man will he meet with?'
ilmaqaala tnašarit figgariida ssuʕudiyya -->	'The article was published in the Saudi newspaper.'
ilmaqaala tnašarit figgariida anhi ?	'Which newspaper was the article published in?'
ṛaaɦ iddukkaan maʕa lbint illi wiššaha mdawwaṛ -->	'He went to the shop with the round-faced girl.
ṛaaɦ iddukkaan maʕa lbint anhi ?	'Which girl did he go to the store with?'
ilʔustaaz ʕaayiz ilkutub ilʔadiima -->	'The professor wants the old books.'
ilʔustaaz ʕaayiz ilkutub anhi ?	'Which books does the professor want?'
ɦayaaxud ilkitabeen dool -->	'He will take these two books.'
ɦayaaxud ilkitabeen anhum ?	'Which two books will he take?'
ɦayʔaabil ilmuwaẓẓafteen iggudaad -->	'He will meet with the two new employees.'
ɦayʔaabil ilmuwaẓẓafteen anhum ?	'Which two employees will he meet with?'
itʕaṛṛafit ʕala ṛragleen ilʕiraʔiyyiin -->	'She got acquainted with the two Iraqi men.'
itʕaṛṛafit ʕala ṛragleen anhum ?	'Which two men did she get acquainted with?'
ɦayitkallim maʕa lmuwaẓẓafiin illi fmaktabak -->	'He will talk to the employees (m) who are in your office.'
ɦayitkallim maʕa lmuwaẓẓafiin anhum ?	'Which employees will he talk to?'
biyitkallim ʕan ilbanaat illi fṣaffu -->	'He is talking about the girls who are in his class.'
biyitkallim ʕan ilbanaat anhum ?	'Which girls is he talking about?'

A construction consisting of a noun and one of the postnominal question words anhu, anhi and anhum may be replaced by a construction in which the question word is pre-nominal. Thus the following constructions are equivalent:

(a) ilmadrasa anhi ? 'which school?'

(b) anhi madrasa ? 'which school?'

It must be stressed, however, that the two constructions under discussion differ in two important respects:

(a) While the modified noun in construction (a) is definite, the modified noun in construction (b) is indefinite.

ilbint anhi ? 'which girl?'

anhi bint ? 'which girl?'

(b) While the question word in construction (a) shows contrast for both number and gender, the question word in construction (b) shows contrast for neither. The prenominal slot of construction (b) is usually occupied by anhi; anhu is interchangeable with anhi, and anhum does not usually occur.

anhi/anhu walad ? 'which boy?'

anhi/anhu bint ? 'which girl?'

anhi/anhu riggaala ? 'which men?'

anhi/anhu sittaat ? 'which women?'

4. imta 'When?': Replaces an adverbial of time.

ɦaysaafir bukra --> 'He will leave tomorrow.'

ɦaysaafir imta ? 'When will he leave?'

ɦayirgaʕ lamma yitxarrag miggamʕa --> 'He will return when he graduates from the university.'

ɦayirgaʕ imta ? 'When will he return?'

5. feen 'Where?': Replaces an adverbial of place.

kaanit sakna hina --> 'She used to live here.'

kaanit sakna feen ? 'Where did she used to live?'

itʔablu fiššaariʕ --> 'They met in the street.'

itʔablu feen ? 'Where did they meet?'

laʔathum makaan ma sabithum --> 'She found them where she had left

laʔathum feen ? 'Where did she find them?'

6. mineen 'from where?': Replaces a prepositional phrase consisting of min 'from' and a following expression of place.

amaal min maṣr -->	'Amal is from Egypt.'
amaal mineen ?	'Where is Amal from?'
ištara lkutub di middukkaan illi ṣaħbu šaami -->	'He bought these books from the shop whose owner is a Syrian.'
ištara lkutub di mineen ?	'From where did he buy these books?'

7. izzaay 'how?': Replaces an adverbial of manner.

biyimši bisurʕa -->	'He walks fast.'
biyimši zzaay ?	'How does he walk?'

8. lee ~ leeh 'Why?': Replaces an adverbial of purpose or cause.

raaħit faransa ʕašaan tidris iṭṭibb -->	'She went to France in order to study medicine.'
raaħit faransa lee ?	'Why did she go to France?'
biyikrahha ʕašaan bitikrahu -->	'He hates her because she hates him.'
biyikrahha lee ?	'Why does he hate her?'

9. išmiʕna: Replaces an adverbial of cause or purpose to indicate that, in the source sentence, the modified constituent is contrasted with or opposed to another constituent:

ʕali biyzurna ʕašaan biyħibbina, laakin amaal miš bitzurna -->	'Ali visits us because he likes us, but Amal does not visit us.'
išmiʕna ʕali biyzurna ?	'How come Ali visits us?'

In the source sentence of the above example, the expressions which are opposed to each other are (a) the modified constituent ʕali biyzurna 'Ali visits us', and (b) the constituent amaal miš bitzurna 'Amal does not visit us.' Notice that the second of these is deleted by the transformation which derives the question from the statement, but the context indicates what has been deleted.

10. kaam 'how many': Replaces a numeral and is followed by a singular indefinite noun.

ʕandu talat kutub -->	'He has three books.'
ʕandu kaam kitaab ?	'How many books does he have?'

In addition to the above, two interrogative expressions occur frequently in EA: maal, and maal wi maal. An attempt to postulate underlying constituents would complicate the presentation unnecessarily. We shall therefore be content with delineating their meanings and commenting on their co-occurrence relationships. Notice that in all contexts maal is followed by a noun or a pronoun.

11. maal (= ma + ɨ-) has three common meanings:

(a) It means 'why?' when followed by a subject and a predicate.

maalu saakit kida ?	'Why is he so quiet?'
maal samiira bitzaʕʕaʔ ?	'Why is Samira yelling?'

(b) It denotes inquiry about relation or interest if preceded by the subject of the sentence and followed by a pronominal suffix which refers to the subject. (ma + ɨ- + pronominal suffix)

inta maalak ?	'What's your business?'
ʕali maalu biik ?	'What has Ali got to do with you?

(c) It is translatable by 'what's the matter with . . . ?' in most of the remaining contexts.

maalak ?	'What's the matter with you?'
maal fariida ?	'What's the matter with Farida?'

12. maal wi maal usually inquires about relation or interest. Each occurrence of maal in the expression is followed by a noun or a pronominal suffix.

maal ʕali wmaalak ?	'What has Ali got to do with you?
maalu wmaal fariida ?	'What has he got to do with Farid
malha wmaali ?	'What has she got to do with me?'

*** *** ***

QUESTIONS: TAGS

English has a set of sentences, called "tag questions", each of which comprises a statement and a following interrogative "tag". In the following examples, tags are underlined :

He's a pilot, isn't he?

He'll go, won't he?

You can't go, can you?'

EA employs tags of which the most common are listed and illustrated below:

1. miš kida ? 'Isn't that so?'

inta ṭaalib. miš kida ? 'You're a student, aren't you?' (literally: 'You're a student, isn't that so?)

2. walla eeh ? 'or what (is the fact)?'

inta ṭaalib. walla eeh ? 'You're a student, aren't you?' (literally: 'You're a student, or what are you?')

3. walla laʔ ? 'Or isn't it so?'

inta ṭaalib. walla laʔ ? 'You're a student, aren't you?' (literally: 'You're a student, or isn't it so?')

4. walla ana ɣalṭaan ? 'Or am I mistaken?'

inta ṭaalib. walla ana ɣalṭaan ? 'You're a student, or are you?' (literally: 'You're a student, or am I mistaken?')

Notice that each of the last three tags begins with the word walla 'or'. Note the following:

1. While English tags are preceded by a sustained pitch (represented in the script by a comma), EA tags are usually preceded by a falling pitch (represented in the script by a period).

2. English tags may end in a rising or a falling pitch (the difference in pitch being parallel to a difference in meaning). EA tags, on the other hand, usually end in a rising pitch.

3. Both the subject and the verb of a given English tag are determined by the preceding statement:

He can go, can't he?

You have a book, haven't you?

On the other hand, the EA tags listed above are largely interchangeable :

inta ṭaalib. miš kida ? / walla eeh ? / walla laʔ ? / walla ana ɣalṭaan ?	'You're a student, aren't you?'

4. In regard to negation, an English tag may be similar to or different from the preceding statement (with a distinct meaning in each case) :

You're going to fire me, aren't you?
You're going to fire me, are you?

No such relationship exists between an Arabic tag and the preceding statement.

*** *** ***

QUESTIONS : YES-OR-NO QUESTIONS

A yes-or-no question is one which solicits "Yes" or "No" as an answer. The following is an example :

ilħaala lʔigtimaʕiyya tħassinit ?	'Has the social situation improved

Two important facts must be noted:

1. The structure of a yes-or-no question is usually identical to that of the corresponding statement. Of the following pair, the first sentence is a statement and the second is a question :

iggamʕa di mašhuura	'This university is famous.'
iggamʕa di mašhuura ?	'Is this university famous?'

Under the influence of Standard Arabic, educated Egyptians--when speaking in semi-formal situations--may place the particle hal at the beginning of a yes-or-no question. Thus a professor lecturing in EA may ask the following question rhetorically :

hal min ilmaʕʔuul inn umma liiha lʔadab irṛafiiʕ da tikuun bidaaʔiyya ?	'Is it reasonable to assume that a nation with such exquisite literature is primitive?'

The word hal has no lexical equivalent in English. It means 'What follows is a yes-or-no question.'

2. An English yes-or-no question may end in a rising or a falling pitch. In the following examples, a line is used to represent the pitch pattern :

Are you from France?

Are you from France?

An Arabic yes-or-no question, on the other hand, always ends in a rising pitch. This is hardly surprising since EA yes-or-no questions are usually identical to the corresponding statements in grammatical structure.

The following forms are common responses to EA yes-or-no questions :

aywa.	'Yes.'
aa.	'Yes.' (very casual)
naʕam.	'Yes.' (formal)
ay naʕam.	'Yes.' (very formal)
ṭabʕan.	'Of course!'
akiid.	'Certainly!'
qaṭʕan.	'Definitely!'
biduun šakk or bila šakk.	'Without a doubt!'
ʔummaáḷ.	'Of course! What did you think?'
laʔ.	'No.'
abadan.	'Not at all!'
mustaħiil.	'Impossible!'

*** *** ***

- R-

RADICALS : TYPES

A "radical" is a root consonant; e.g., the root ktb consists of the radicals /k/, /t/ and /b/.

There are two types of radicals : sound and weak. A sound radical is one which always has a consonantal realization. In contrast, a weak radical is one which does not always have a consonantal realization.

Two consonants constitute weak radicals : /w/ and /y/. Thus the last radical of the root dʕw is realized as /w/ in daʕwa 'invitation', but as zero in ḍaʕa 'to invite'. Again, the middle radical of the root ɣyb is realized as /y/ in ɣiyaab 'absence', but as vowel length in ɣaab 'to be absent'.

Consonants other than /w/ and /y/ constitute sound radicals.

*** *** ***

REDUPLICATIVE VERB

A quadriliteral verb (q.v.) in which the last two radicals (consonants) are a repetition of the first two, e.g., zalzil 'to shake'.

*** *** ***

RELATIVE ADJECTIVE

(See : Nisba Adjectives)

*** *** ***

RELATIVE CLAUSES WITH illi

A typical relative clause construction contains three elements :

a) an antecedent

b) the invariable relative pronoun /illi/

c) a clause

Examples :

	(a)	(b)	(c)
šuft	ilwilaad	illi	gaabu lgawabaat.
	(a)	(b)	(c)
I saw	the boys	who	(they) brought the letters.

Note that the relative clause by itself is a complete sentence, i.e., it can stand by itself without the relative pronoun : gaabu lgawabaat 'they brought the letters'. /u/, the inflection of the verb gaabu, is the formal reference to the antecedent ilwilaad 'the boys'.

In the sentence :

da lgawaab illi gabuuh imbaariḥ. 'This is the letter which they brought yesterday.'

the object of the verb gabuuh 'they brought it' refers to the antecedent.

In the sentence :

da lwalad illi ktaabu ḍaaʕ. 'This is the boy whose (his) book got lost.'

the suffixed pronoun on kitaab is the reference.

In the sentence :

feen ilkitaab illi ʔultilak ʕaleeh ? 'Where is the book which I talked to you about (it) ?

the reference is through the preposition and its object ʕaleeh 'about it'. Note that the above examples have definite antecedents. If the antecedent is indefinite, there is no relative pronoun in the construction.

Compare :

šuft ilwilaad illi gaabu lgawabaat. 'I saw the boys who brought the letters.'

and :

šuft wlaad gaabu gawabaat. 'I saw (some) boys who had brought (some) letters.'

Note the relative constructions in the following examples :

a) iṛṛaagil da lli byišṛab šaay almaani.

'This man who is drinking tea is German.'

b) ilwalad da lli ʔaaʕid ganb ilbint ismu saami.

'This boy who is sitting next to the girl is named Sami (his name is Sami)

c) issitt illi min faṛansa safrit imbaariḥ.

'The lady who is from France left (traveled) yesterday.'

d) ilwalad illi hnaak da ṣaḥbi.

'That boy (who is) over there is my friend.'

e) illi faat maat. (Proverb)

'That which is done is done.' (Lit. : 'That which has passed has died.'

f) feen illi ʔultilak ʕaleeh ?

'Where is that which I talked to you about (it)?'

g) ilwalad illi smu saami ṣaḥbi.

'The boy whose name is Sami is my friend.'

h) iṛṛaagil illi šuftu imbaariḥ saafir innahaṛda.

'The man whom you saw yesterday left (traveled) today.

i) ilwalad huwwa lli naam.

'It's the <u>boy</u> who slept.'

(See also : Adjective : Relative Clauses)

*** *** ***

RELATIVE PRONOUN : <u>illi</u>

(See : Adjective : Relative Clauses; Relative Clauses with <u>illi</u>)

*** *** ***

RESONANCE CAVITIES

There are three major resonance cavities : the mouth, which is known as the oral cavity; the nose or nasal cavity; and the throat or pharynx. Their main function in speech is to serve as resonators.

*** *** ***

ROOT

A term used for the core of a word in Arabic and in other Afro-Asiatic languages. Most Egyptian Arabic words consist of a triconsonantal (c.f. also triradical or triliteral (q.v.)) root. Biradical (also biliteral) roots are less frequent and consist of two consonants. Roots with four consonants (quadriliteral or quadriradical) occur in Egyptian Arabic, but rarely. A root occurs with patterns (q.v.). A pattern can be vocalic and/or consonantal. The root normally has a certain meaning attached to it. The basic meaning of the root is modified by the pattern. Compare the following words :

katab	'to write'
kitaab	'book'
maktaba	'library'
kaatib	'writer'

The words in question share a set of consonants (/k/, /t/ and /b/) which invariably occur in the same order. Furthermore, those words share a semantic element : all of them have to do with writing (katab designates the act of writing ; kitaab a volume made up of written or printed pages; maktaba a place where written or printed volumes are kept; and kaatib one who writes). It is reasonable to assume that the shared meaning belongs to the shared form. In other words, it is reasonable to assume that ktb is a discrete, minimum meaningful entity.

Entities like ktb are called "roots", and the constituent consonants of a root are called "radicals". Listed below are some more roots :

drs (occurring in daras 'to study', dars 'lesson', madrasa 'school, diraasi 'scholastic', etc.)

ʕrf (occurring in ʕirif 'to know', maʕrifa 'knowledge', etc.)

xdm (occurring in xadam 'to serve', xaddaam 'servant', xidma 'service', etc.)

zʕl (occurring in ziʕil 'to get angry', zaʕl 'anger', zaʕlaan 'angry', etc.)

skn (occurring in sakan 'to dwell', maskin 'abode', iskaan 'housing', sukkaan 'resident, etc.)

As illustrated above, some EA roots consist of three radicals, others consist of four, and still others consist of five. The first group is the largest, and the third is the smallest.

*** *** ***

- S -

SCRIPT

(1) <u>Key to Literary Arabic graphic symbols and corresponding Egyptian Arabic symbols :</u>

Literary Arabic	Egyptian	Literary Arabic	Egyptian
أ	?	ط	ṭ
آ	?aa	ظ	ẓ or ḍ
ا	aa	ع	ʕ
ـَ	a	غ	ɣ
ـِ	i	ف	f
ـُ	u	ف	(v in foreign words
ـً	an (finally)	ق	? or q
ـٍ	in "	ك	k
ـٌ	un "	ل	l or ḷ
ى	aa	م	m
ب	b	ن	n
ب	p (in foreign words)	ه	h
ت	t	و	w
ث	t or s	ـُو	u, uu, oo
ج	g	ي	y
ج	ž (in foreign words)	ـِي	i, ii, ee
ح	ḥ	ـَي	ay, ee
خ	x	ه	a or h
د	d	ة	-t or -it or -a
ذ	d or z		

Literary Arabic	Egyptian		Literary Arabic	Egyptian
ر	r	ṛ	ّ (shadda)	doubling of consonant
ز	z		ْ (sukuun)	absence of a vowel after a consonant
س	s			
ش	š			
ص	ṣ			
ض	ḍ			

(2) Numerals

Examples of numerals and numerical uses :

(a) ١ ٢ ٣ ٤ ٥ ٦ ٧ ٨ ٩ ١٠

1 2 3 4 5 6 7 8 9 10

(b) ٥٤ ١٦ ٣٩ ٤٨ ٧٥

54 16 39 48 75

(c) ٧٨٪ ٣/٤ ١/٥ ١١٢ ١/٣ ٤٢

78% 3/4 1/5 112 1/3 42

(d) ١٩٧٥ ١٩٧٦ ٢٣٤ ٧٥٣ ١٩١٤

1975 1976 234 753 1914

*** *** ***

SEMITIC

A family of languages constituting a branch of the Afro-Asiatic language stock. It includes Akkadian, Arabic, Ethiopic, Aramaic, Hebrew and Ugaritic, which share certain common characteristics, e.g., a root (q.v.) and pattern (q.v.) structure, a set of derived verb forms, a set of back consonants / q, x, ɣ, ɦ, ʕ /, a set of emphatic consonants (q.v.) / ṭ, ḍ, ṣ, ð̣ /, a tense formed by prefixation and another by suffixation, grammatical gender, feminine formative /-t/, two-way plural noun formation : sound plural (q.v.) and broken plural (q.v.).

The adjective "Semitic" was brought into use by A. L. Schlözer in 1781 on the basis of Genesis X and XI. Before Schlözer, the Semitic languages were referred to as "Oriental languages".

*** *** ***

SEMI-VOWEL

A vowel-like sound which functions as a consonant : / w, y /. Also called "glide".

*** *** ***

SENTENCE: EQUATIONAL

(See : Phrase Versus Sentence)

*** *** ***

SENTENCE STRUCTURE

The structure of EA sentences is presented below in outline form. It must be emphasized that only the major patterns are dealt with, and that the treatment is not exhaustive.

A sentence consists of a nucleus and optional adjuncts.

I. A nucleus consists of an optional pre-verb, a subject and a predicate. Pre-verbs are usually modals. In the following sentences, pre-verbs are underlined :

labudd ʕali yirgaʕ ʔabl lmaɣrib	'Ali must return before sunset.'
yimkin ʕali biyħibb samiira	'Maybe Ali loves Samira.'

It is usually possible for the pre-verb and the subject to exchange places :

ʕali labudd yirgaʕ ʔabl lmaɣrib	'Ali must return before sunset.'
ʕali yimkin biyħibb samiira	'Maybe Ali loves Samira.'

II. The subject may be a "minimum subject" or an "expanded subject". The predicate may be a "minimum predicate or an "expanded predicate".

A. A minimum subject is a noun or a noun replacer. The most common noun replacers are :

1. Personal pronouns, e.g., huwwa, 'he'; hiyya 'she'; inta 'you (ms)'; inti 'you (fs)', etc.

2. fulaan 'so and so (ms)' and fulaana 'so and so (fs)'.
3. The indefinite forms waaɦid 'someone (m)' and waɦda 'someone (f)

In the following sentences, minimum subjects are underlined :

zeenab mumaṛṛiḍa.	'Zeinab is a nurse.'
ilmudiir ʕandu gtimaaʕ baʕd saaʕa.	'The director has a meeting in an hour.'
ana min maṣṛ.	'I am from Egypt.'
baʔaalik usbuuʕ ʔaṛfaani bikkalaam ilfaariɣ da : fulaan ṛaaɦ, wi flaana rigʕit. wiɦna malna ?	'For a week you have been making me sick with this nonsense : so and so went, so and so returned! What business is that of ours?'
fiih waaɦid biyisʔal ʕannak.	'There's someone asking for you.'

B. An expanded subject usually consists of a noun phrase. A noun phrase may be any of the following structures :

Determiner + Noun
Noun + Adjectival
Determiner + Noun + Adjectival

Determiners include quantifiers such as aktaṛ, aɣlab, muʕzam (all translatable by 'most'), gamiiʕ, kull (both translatable by 'all' and baʕd 'some'. An adjectival expression may be a demonstrative, an adjective, a prepositional phrase or a clause. A noun construct may be considered a sub-class of Noun + Adjectival since the second member of a noun construct qualifies the first (notice that kitaab ʕali 'Ali's book' is equivalent to ilkitaab illi l-ʕali 'the book which belongs to Ali').

In the following examples, expanded subjects are underlined :

aktaṛ talamziti min maṣṛ .	'Most of my students are from Egyp
ilkitaab da byibɦas ilwaḍʕ issiyaasi fissudaan .	'This book discusses the political situation in the Sudan.'
ilʕaṛabiyya zzarʔa btaʕti.	'The blue car is mine.'
iṭṭaṛabeeza lli fmaktabi ʔadiima.	'The table in my office is old.'

ʕaṛabiyyiti tsaaʕ xamas tinfaaṛ.	'My car is big enough for five people.'
il?ustaaz illi biydarrisni ttariix maṣṛi.	'The professor who teaches me history is Egyptian.'

C. A minimum predicate may be a noun, an adjective, a verb, an adverb or a prepositional phrase. The verb may co-occur with at least one closely associated element. A closely associated element may be a direct object, an indirect object or a preposition which forms with the verb a close-knit expression. In other words, a minimum predicate may be any of the structures generated by the folllowing notation (constituents which occur within parentheses are optional; those which occur within braces are mutually exclusive) :

Verb (Direct Object) ({Preposition + Object / Indirect Object})

In the following examples, minimum predicates are underlined :

ʕali tilmiiz.	'Ali is a student.'
fariida gamiila .	'Farida is pretty.'
ɦasan biyistaɦamma .	'Hasan is taking a bath.'
ʕali daras iddars .	'Ali studied the lesson.'
salma bitmuut fil?ays kriim .	'Salma loves ice cream.'
axuuya ṭamminha ʕala bintaha .	'My brother reassured her in regard to her daughter.'
il?ustaaz fahhim fariid iddars .	'The professor explained the lesson to Farid.'
ilfaṛaɦ bukṛa .	'The wedding is tomorrow.'
illigtimaaʕ baʕd ilɣada .	'The meeting is (going to be held) after lunch.'

D. Expanded predicates correspond to minimum predicates :

1. Corresponding to the minimum predicate which consists of a noun is an expanded predicate which consists of a noun phrase. In the following sentence, the predicate is a noun phrase :

ittadxiin ʕaada muḍiṛṛa . 'Smoking is a harmful habit.'

2. Corresponding to the minimum predicate which consists of an adjective is an expanded predicate which consists of an adjective and an expression of degree. Degree is usually expressed by :

   (a) An adverb, e.g., ʔawi, giddan, xaalis, all translatable by 'very'.

   (b) A stressed verbal noun whose root is the same as that of the adjective and which is followed by a rising terminal pitch.

   (c) A phrase consisting of the preposition li- 'to', the noun daraga 'degree, extent', and a modifier.

   In the following examples, the predicate contains an expression of degree :

iggamʕa di kbiira ʔawi.	'This university is very large.'
ilmudarrisa gamiila gamáal.	'The teacher (f) is so pretty.'
ilmudarrisa gamiila ldaraga tgannin.	'The teacher (f) is incredibly beautiful.'

3. Corresponding to the minimum predicate which consists of an adjective is an expanded predicate which consists of a comparative construction. The comparative construction may be modified by an expression of degree such as biktiir 'by far'. In the following examples, the predicate is a comparative construction :

axuuya aʔwa minni.	'My brother is stronger than I.'
axuuya aʔwa minni biktiir.	'My brother is much stronger than
samya aštar tilmiiza.	'Samya is the smartest student.'

4. Corresponding to the minimum predicate which consists of a verb (with or without closely-related elements) is an expanded predicate which consists of a verbal sequence. In the following example, the predicate is a verbal sequence :

uxti tħibb tiigi tidris ingliizi.	'My sister would like to come to study English.'

5. Corresponding to the minimum predicate which consists of a verb (with or without closely-related elements) is an expanded predicate consisting of a verb or a verbal sequence and a following adverbial. The adverbials here are : Type, Degree, Benefactive, Instrument, Source, Destination and Manner (less frequent adverbials, such as Accompaniment, occur). In the following examples, the predicate contains an adverbial :

ʕali tʔallim ʔalam faẓiiʕ.	'Ali suffered horrible pain.'
ilʔustaaz ziʕil giddan.	'The professor became very angry.'
ħilmi štara ktaab lisaami.	'Hilmi bought a book for Sami.'
iṛṛaagil ʔatal miṛaatu bisikkiina .	'The man killed his wife with a knife.'
ilxubaṛa lʔamrikaan rigʕu min maṣṛ.	'The American experts returned from Egypt.'
iggamʕa baʕatit ustazeen lilʕiraaʔ.	'The university sent two professors to Iraq.'
ittalamza rigʕu bsurʕa.	'The students returned fast.'

The adverbials in question may co-occur. It would be unusual, however, to find more than three in any one sentence. Co-occurring adverbials are usually in the following order if they have the same structure : Type, Degree, Benefactive, Instrument, Source, Destination, Manner.

išširka naʔalit ilʕizaal liʕali billoori min ilqaahiṛa lʔaṣwaan.	'The company transported the furniture for Ali by truck from Cairo to Aswan.'

When two adjacent adverbials have the same structure, their positions may be reversed to indicate relative emphasis (the adverbial to be emphasized is placed ahead of the other). In addition, the positions may be reversed for the same purpose when one adverbial is a word and the other is a phrase.

salma štarit kitaab liʕali milmaktaba .	'Salma bought a book for Ali from the bookshop.'
salma štarit kitaab milmaktaba liʕali.	'Salma bought a book from the bookshop for Ali.'

il?ustaaz rigiʕ min masr ʕayyaan .	'The professor returned from Egypt in poor health.'
il?ustaaz rigiʕ ʕayyaan min masr .	'The professor returned, in poor health, from Egypt.'

An adverbial consisting of a clause usually follows one which consists of a word or a phrase.

il?ustaaz rigiʕ min masr wħaltu ssiħħiyya mutadahwira .	'The professor returned from Egypt in poor health.'

The adverbials in question differ from adjuncts in that the latter may introduce the sentence.

(a) A type adverbial is typically a noun phrase consisting of a) a verbal noun whose root is the same as that of the modified verb, and b) an adjectival expression. In the following examples, the type adverbial is underlined :

ʕali naam noom ʕamii? .	'Ali slept soundly (literally: Ali slept a sound slee
ʕali ʕaaš ʕiišit rafahiyya .	'Ali lived a life of luxury.'

Adverbials other than those of type are typically prepositional phrases.

(b) A degree adverbial is often a prepositional phrase introduced by lidaraga 'to an extent', or lidaragit inn 'to the extent that' :

ilmasriyyiin yixtilfu ʕan il?amrikaan lidaraga kibiira .	'Egyptians differ from Americans to a great extent.'
issinaaʕa lyabaniyya itħassinit lidaragit inn amriika btistawrid ilʕarabiyyaat milyabaan .	'Japanese industry has progressed to the extent that America imports cars from Japan.'

A degree adverbial may consist of the prepositional phrase lilħaddin ma ~ ila ħaddin ma 'to a certain extent' or the prepositional phrase lidaragatin ma ila daragatin ma 'to a certain extent'.

iṣṣinaaʕa tʔaddimit fi maṣr lidaragatin ma / ila daragatin ma / lihaddin ma / ila haddin ma .	'Industry has progressed in Egypt to a certain extent.'

Certain adverbs may be used to express degree. The most common of these are ʔawi, giddan, xaaliṣ and kitiir (all translatable by 'very, very much, a great deal'), taʔriiban 'nearly', and šiwayya 'a little, somewhat' :

ilʔustaaz ziʕil ʔawi .	'The professor was very angry.'
maṣr itʔaddimit ʔawi .	'Egypt has progressed a great deal.'

(c) A benefactive adverbial is usually a prepositional phrase introduced by the preposition li- 'for'. If the object of the preposition is a pronoun, the prepositional phrase may be suffixed to the verb.

suzaan ištarit hidiyya liʕali .	'Suzanne bought a gift for Ali'
suzaan ištarit hidiyya liih.~ suzaan ištaritlu hdiyya .	'Suzanne bought a gift for him.'

When the preposition li- is not suffixed, its vowel is lengthened before a pronominal object : liih 'for him', liiha 'for her', liihum 'for them', liik 'for you (ms)', liiki 'for you (fs), liikum 'for you (p)', liina 'for us'. The form liyya 'for me' is an exception.

When suffixed to a verb, the preposition li- assumes the form -l-. Sometimes a sequence of more than two consonants results from adding to the verb a prepositional phrase consisting of -l- and a pronominal ending. In such cases, a vowel is inserted between the second and the third consonants. That vowel is /u/ before -hum or -kum, /a/ before -ha, and /i/ otherwise.

ištara + -l- + -na = ištaralna 'he bought for us'
ištarit + -l- + -hum = ištaritluhum 'she bought for them'
ištarit + -l- + -kum = ištaritlukum 'she bought for you (p)'
ištarit + -l- + -ha = ištaritlaha 'she bought for her'
ištarit + -l- + -na = ištaritlina 'she bought for us'
ʕadd + -l- + -i = ʕaddili 'he counted for me'
ʕadd + -l- + -hum = ʕaddilhum 'he counted for them'
ʕadd + -l- + -kum = ʕaddilkum 'he counted for you (p)'
ʕadd + -l- + -ha = ʕaddilha 'he counted for her'
ʕadd + -l- + -na = ʕaddilna 'he counted for us'

A prepositional phrase with li- may be an indirect object of the preceding verb or a benefactive adverbial. In sentence (i) below, the underlined phrase is an indirect object; in sentence (ii), a benefactive adverbial :

(i) ʕallimt iddars lfariid . 'I taught the lesson to Farid.'
(ii) ištareet hidiyya lfariid . 'I bought a gift for Farid.'

Notice, however, that the first sentence may occur without li- (in which case fariid occurs before iddars). Such a possibility does not exist for the second sentence. Notice also that fariid can become the subject if sentence (i) is made passive, but not if sentence (ii) is made passive.

ʕallimt fariid iddars . 'I taught the lesson to Farid.'
but not
*ištareet fariid hidiyya

fariid itʕallim iddars . 'The lesson was taught to Farid.'
but not
*fariid itšara hdiyya

(d) An adverbial of instrument is usually a prepositional

phrase introduced by the preposition bi- 'by, with'. Less frequently, the phrase is introduced by biwasṭit 'by means of' or ʕan ṭariiʔ 'through, by way of'.

iṛṛaagil da ʔatal miṛaatu bisikkiina.	'This man killed his wife with a knife.'
išširka btunʔul ilbatṛool biwasṭit issufun .	'The company transports oil by means of ships.'
ilħukuuma ħaẓẓarit iššaʕb ʕan ṭariiʔ ilʔizaaʕa.	'The government warned the people through (use of) the radio.'

(e) An adverbial of source is usually a prepositional phrase introduced by min 'from'.

uxti štarit ilhidiyya milmaħall da .	'My sister bought the gift from this shop.'

(f) An adverbial of destination is usually a prepositional phrase introduced by li- 'to' :

ibni byimši milbeet lilmadrasa kull yoom .	'My son walks from home to school every day.'

If the adverbial of destination slot is immediately after one of certain verbs, the preposition is usually (though not necessarily) deleted. The verbs in question include ṛaaħ 'to go', ga 'to come', rigiʕ 'to return', ṭiliʕ 'to ascend, to go up', saafir 'to travel' :

ʕali ṛaaħ (l)ilmadrasa .	'Ali went to school.'
ʕali ṛaaħ maʕa saami (l)ilmadrasa .	'Ali went with Sami to school.'

(g) A manner adverbial is often a prepositional phrase introduced by the preposition bi- 'with' :

fariida btizʕal bisurʕa .	'Farida gets upset easily (literally: 'with speed')'

A manner adverbial may also be a word or a clause :

ilmanduub ṭiliʕ milligtimaaʕ <u>ɣaḍbaan</u>.	'The delegate left the meeting angry.'
matzaʕʕaʔš <u>kida</u>.	'Don't shout this way.'
ilmanduub xaṛag milligtimaaʕ <u>wi huwwa biysibb wyilʕan</u>.	'The delegate left the meeting swearing and cursing.'

6. The predicate may be a clause consisting of a subject and a predicate :

a) ʕali <u>abuuh naggaaṛ</u>.	'Ali's father is a carpenter (literally: 'Ali his father is a carpenter.').'
b) maṣṛ <u>iqtiṣadha tʔaddim</u>.	'Egypt's economy has progressed (literally: 'Egypt its economy has progressed.').'
c) layla <u>axuuha rigiʕ min aṣwaan biṭṭayyaaṛa</u>.	'Leila's brother returned from Aswan by plane (literally: 'Leila her brother returned from Aswan by plane.').'

Sentences such as the above are derived from structurally simpler sentences. Thus sentence (a) is derived from <u>abu ʕali naggaaṛ</u> 'Ali's father is a carpenter.'. Likewise, sentence (b) is derived from <u>iqtiṣaad maṣṛ itʔaddim</u> 'Egypt's economy has progressed.' Notice that the derivation is accomplished by (a) transposing a noun from sentence-medial position, and (b) supplying a pronoun to occupy the position previously occupied by the transposed noun. Notice too that the supplied pronoun refers to the transposed noun and agrees with it.

III. An adjunct is a constituent which can occur before or after the nucleus and which modifies the entire nucleus. In the following examples, the adjunct is underlined. The nucleus is the rest of the sentence :

innaas mašɣuliin <u>hina</u>.	'People are busy here.'

hina nnaas mašɣuliin .	'Here people are busy.'
ɦargaʕ maṣṛ lamma tintihi ssana ddiṛasiyya .	'I will return to Egypt when the school year ends.'
lamma tintihi ssana ddiṛasiyya ɦargaʕ maṣṛ .	'When the school year ends, I will return to Egypt.'

IV. Adjuncts include expressions of place, time, condition, purpose and reason. In regard to structure, an adjunct may be a word, a phrase, or a clause. In the following sentences, the adjuncts are underlined :

hinaak ilfuluus ahamm min ilmabaadiʔ .	'Over there, money is more important than principle.'
bukra ɦanzuuṛ ilmatɦaf .	'Tomorrow we will visit the museum.'
iza lmašṛuuʕ da fašal ɦanixsaṛ fuluus kitiir .	'If this project fails, we will lose a lot of money.'
ilɦukuuma banit ilmaṣaaniʕ litaɦsiin ilwaḍʕ liqtiṣaadi .	'The government built factories to improve the economic situation.'
baṛuuɦ maṣṛ kull ṣeef ʕašaan ʕilti hinaak .	'I go to Egypt every summer because my family is there.'

When two or more adjuncts co-occur, they are usually in the following order if they have the same structure (i.e., if all are words, phrases, or clauses) : Place, Time, Condition, Purpose, Reason.

ilɦaala liqtiṣaadiyya wiɦša flubnaan filwaʔt ilɦaali bsabab ilɦaṛb ilʔahliyya .	'The economic situation is bad in Lebanon at the present time because of the civil war.'

When two adjacent adjuncts have the same structure, their positions may be reversed to indicate relative emphasis (the adjunct to be emphasized is placed ahead of the other) :

ilɦaala liqtiṣaadiyya wiɦša flubnaan filwaʔt ilɦaali .	'The economic situation is bad in Lebanon at the present time.'
ilɦaala liqtiṣaadiyya wiɦša filwaʔt ilɦaali flubnaan .	'The economic situation is bad at the present time in Lebanon.'

If different in structure, co-occurrent adjuncts are arranged in accordance with the following rule : a word precedes a phrase, and a phrase precedes a clause.

ħaṛakit ilmuṛuuṛ ħatkuun wiħša <u>bukṛa</u> <u>bsabab ilmuẓahṛa</u>.	'The traffic will be bad tomorrow because of the strike.'
ħaṛakit ilmuṛuuṛ ħatkuun wiħša <u>bsabab ilmuẓahṛa</u> <u>lamma nirgaʕ</u> <u>milmadrasa</u>.	The traffic will be bad, because of the strike, when we return from school.'

V. Discussed under the appropriate headings are the transformations which change sentences from statements to questions or commands, from active to passive, from affirmative to negative, and from complete to elliptic. Also discussed in detail under the appropriate headings are the processes of embedding and conjoining.

*** *** ***

SEPARATION : PRONOUN OF

(See : Pronoun of Separation)

*** *** ***

SEQUENCE OF VERBS

In the sentence <u>kunt baħaawil azaakir ʕaṛabi</u> 'I was trying to study Arabic', there is a sequence of three verbs. This is not unusual for Egyptian Arabic. Examples :

tiħibb tišrab ʔahwa mʕaaya ?	'Would you like to drink coffee with
tiħibb tṛuuħ nišuuf haani ?	'Would you like to go and see Hani?'
ħayṛuuħ yidxul yinaam.	'He will go enter in order to sleep.'
ṛuuħ naam !	'Go and sleep!'
yaḷḷa nṛuuħ nišṛab ʔahwa.	'Let's go and drink coffee.'
yaḷḷa ṛuuħ naam !	'Go and sleep.'

*** *** ***

HORTENING OF VOWELS

(See : Vowels : Contraction; Vowels : Shortening of Long Vowels)

*** *** ***

HORT VOWELS

(See : Vowels)

*** *** ***

LOT

The position that a word (or phrase) occupies in a frame or pattern; the significant position or positions which a word (or phrase) occupies with respect to other elements in a sequence.

		Adjective	Noun	
English	a	big	boy	
EA		walad	kibiir	'a big boy'

Note in the above examples the Adjective and Noun slots. In the English the adjective slot precedes the noun slot whereas in EA the noun slot precedes the adjective slot.

*** *** ***

TEM

A stem is a root (q.v.) in combination with a pattern (q.v.), to which inflections (q.v.) are added.

*** *** ***

STOP

Refers to consonants characterized by a complete closure of the air passage, thus blocking the air stream momentarily, e.g., closing of both lips in production of /b/. EA stops are /p, b, t, ṭ, d, ḍ, k, g, q, ʔ/.

*** *** ***

STRESS

Each EA word has one primary (i.e., relatively more prominent) stress. The domain of primary stress is almost totally predictable in terms of syllable structure.

Primary stress is most frequently on the penult (i.e., pre-final syllable), e.g., yiktíbu 'they write', madrása 'school'. However, in certain cases, primary stress occurs on the ultima (i.e., the final syllable and in other cases it occurs on the antepenult (i.e., the third syllable from the end).

The ultima is stressed if (a) it contains a long vowel or if (b) it ends in two consonants, e.g., katabúu 'they wrote it', katábt 'I wrote'. The antepenult is stressed if the last three syllables have the structure CVCVCV(C), e.g., šábaka 'a net', kátabit 'she wrote', inkásarit 'it broke', muxtálifa 'different (fs)'.

Contrary to the above rules, primary stress is on the penult if the structure CVCVCV(C) constitutes a feminine singular perfect-tense verb whose final V(C) is a pronoun suffix, e.g., ramítu 'she threw it away'. Again, primary stress is usually on the penult if the structure CVCVCV(C) constitutes a broken plural form with identical high vowels in the first two syllables, e.g., sibíta 'baskets', numúra 'tigers'.

Note : The long vowel of the word-final syllable CVV(C) is shortened when its pronunciation in close association with a following word would result in _VVCC. In this context, shortening does not alter the placement of primary stress :

banáa	'he built it'
baná mbaariɦ	'he built it yesterday'

maríiḍ	'sick'
maríḍ xaaliṣ	'very sick'

*** *** ***

UFFIX

A formative (a single phoneme, syllable or syllables) added at the end of a word to modify its meaning or derive a new word, e.g. :

walad	'boy'	waladeen	'two boys'
katab	'to write'	katabna	'we wrote'

(See also : Pronoun : Suffixes with Auxiliaries; Pronoun : Suffixes with Particles; Pronoun : Personal; Possession)

*** *** ***

;UFFIX : /-a/ -- CHANGE IN FORM TO /-it/

A feminine noun ending in /-a/ has a special form for the construct state : the /-a/ drops and /-it/ is added.

madiina	'city'	madiinit ṭanṭa	'the city of Tanta'

*** *** ***

;YLLABLES

a) In EA syllables have the following structures :
CV, CVC, CVV, CVVC#, CVCC#
(C = consonant; V = vowel; -# = final)

b) Syllables do not begin with vowels; they always begin with C (?V, CV).

c) The sequence /VVCC/ does not occur within a single word; thus long vowels are only followed by a single consonant in a word.

d) Syllables with the structures /CVVC#/ or /CVCC#/ occur only stressed.

e) Thus, we might summarize as follows :
- Every syllable begins with /C/.

- Every syllable has /V/ or /VV/.
- Syllables may be open or closed (an open syllable is a syllable that ends in a vowel; a closed syllable is a syllable that ends in a consonant).
- No closed syllable has the structure /VVCC/, but rather /CVVC#/ or /CVCC#/.

*** *** ***

- T -

TAP

Refers to the articulatory process by which the tip of the tongue makes a single rapid contact against the alveolar ridge producing a consonant : /r, ṛ/.

*** *** ***

TENSENESS

A tense (also fortis) consonant in general is produced with more force that its lax (also lenis) counterpart. Tense here refers to two indentical consonants with no intervening vowel pronounced with stronger articulation and greater tension on the muscles of the articulator and, usually, aspiration. Lax refers to a single consonant pronounced with lesser muscle tension and weaker, laxer articulation.

A tense consonant (also known as gemminate) has precisely twice the duration of a single (lax) consonant, e.g. :

katab	'to write'
kattib	'to cause to write'

*** *** ***

TRILITERAL ROOTS : TYPES

A triliteral root is one which consists of three radicals. There are two types of such roots : sound and weak.

A sound root is one which consists entirely of sound radicals (e.g., drs, ktb, ʕrf, dxl). A weak root is one which does not consist entirely of sound radicals (See : Radicals : Types).

Weak roots fall into three subtypes : the assimilated, the hollow and the defective :

1. An assimilated root is one whose first radical is weak, e.g., wṣl. In verbs of Measure VIII, the initial weak radical is totally assimilated to the following /t/. Thus wṣl combines with iFtaʕaL to produce iṭṭaṣal rather than the expected *iwṭaṣal. This assimilation gives the root its name.

2. A hollow root is one whose medial radical is weak, e.g., nwm, γyb.

3. A defective root is one whose final radical is weak, e.g., dʕw, rmy.

*** *** ***

- U -

UNIT NOUNS

(See : Collective Nouns)

*** *** ***

UVULAR

The uvula is the small appendage that hangs down from the very edge of the velum. Uvular refers to a place of articulation consisting of the tongue dorsum and the uvula : /q/.

*** *** ***

- V -

VELAR

A place of articulation consisting of the tongue dorsum and the back of the palate : /k, g/.

*** *** ***

VELUM

The area behind the hard palate, also called the soft palate.

*** *** ***

VERB : AGREEMENT WITH THE SUBJECT

Verbs agree with the subject in number, gender and person. Perfect forms are marked for such agreement by suffixes only; some imperfect forms are marked by prefixes only, while others are marked by both prefixes and suffixes.

The set of affixes marking agreement with various subjects is the same for verbs of all types; however, the addition of those affixes requires certain changes in some stems.

(a) The following forms result from adding the agreement affixes to the sound stems katab 'to write' (perfect form) and yiktib (imperfect form). The affixes are set off by hyphens.

	Perfect	Imperfect
(huwwa)	katab	yi-ktib
(hiyya)	katab-it	ti-ktib
(humma)	katab-u	yi-ktib-u
(inta)	katab-t	ti-ktib
(inti)	katab-ti	ti-ktib-i
(intu)	katab-tu	ti-ktib-u
(ana)	katab-t	a-ktib
(iħna)	katab-na	ni-ktib

Most of the imperfect forms listed above contain /i/ in the prefix. If the second syllable of the imperfect form contains /u/ or /uu/, the /i/ is interchangeable with /u/, e.g., yixrug yuxrug 'to exit', yiruuħ yuruuħ 'to go'.

(b) Lest a cluster of three consonants result, /ee/ is inserted between the last radical of a doubled perfect stem and a suffix which begins with or consists of a consonant. The following forms result from adding the agreement affixes to ʕadd 'to count' (perfect form) and yiʕidd (imperfect form). (ʕadd is a doubled stem.)

	Perfect	Imperfect
(huwwa)	ʕadd	yi-ʕidd
(hiyya)	ʕadd-it	ti-ʕidd
(humma)	ʕadd-u	yi-ʕidd-u
(inta)	ʕaddee-t	ti-ʕidd
(inti)	ʕaddee-ti	ti-ʕidd-i
(intu)	ʕaddee-tu	ti-ʕidd-u
(ana)	ʕaddee-t	a-ʕidd
(iħna)	ʕaddee-na	ni-ʕidd

The long vowel /ee/ is also inserted between the last radical of a Measure IX perfect stem and a suffix which begins with or consists of a consonant. The following forms result from adding the agreement affixes to *iswadd* 'to turn black' (perfect form) and *yiswadd* (imperfect form).

	Perfect	Imperfect
(huwwa)	iswadd	yi-swadd
(hiyya)	iswadd-it	ti-swadd
(humma)	iswadd-u	yi-swadd-u
(inta)	iswaddee-t	ti-swadd
(inti)	iswaddee-ti	ti-swadd-i
(intu)	iswaddee-tu	ti-swadd-u
(ana)	iswaddee-t	a-swadd
(iħna)	iswaddee-na	ni-swadd

(c) Upon the addition of a suffix which begins with or consists of a consonant, the long vowel of *FaaL* is replaced by a short vowel (in EA, a long vowel does not normally occur before two consonants). The short vowel in question is /u/ if the imperfect stem has /uu/; otherwise the short vowel is /i/.

The following forms result from adding the agreement affixes to *ṛaaħ* 'to go' (perfect form) and *yiṛuuħ* (imperfect form).

	Perfect	Imperfect
huwwa	ṛaaħ	yi-ṛuuħ
hiyya	ṛaaħ-it	ti-ṛuuħ
humma	ṛaaħ-u	yi-ṛuuħ-u
inta	ṛuħ-t	ti-ṛuuħ
inti	ṛuħ-ti	ti-ṛuuħ-i
intu	ṛuħ-tu	ti-ṛuuħ-u

	Perfect	Imperfect
(ana)	ṛuɦ-t	a-ṛuuɦ
(iɦna)	ṛuɦ-na	ni-ṛuuɦ

The following forms result from adding the agreement affixes to <u>gaab</u> 'to bring' (perfect form) and <u>yigiib</u> (imperfect form).

	Perfect	Imperfect
(huwwa)	gaab	yi-giib
(hiyya)	gaab-it	ti-giib
(humma)	gaab-u	yi-giib-u
(inta)	gib-t	ti-giib
(inti)	gib-ti	ti-giib-i
(intu)	gib-tu	ti-giib-u
(ana)	gib-t	a-giib
(iɦna)	gib-na	ni-giib

The following forms result from adding the aggreement affixes to <u>naam</u> 'to sleep' (perfect form) and <u>yinaam</u> (imperfect form).

	Perfect	Imperfect
(huwwa)	naam	yi-naam
(hiyya)	naam-it	ti-naam
(humma)	naam-u	yi-naam-u
(inta)	nim-t	ti-naam
(inti)	nim-ti	ti-naam-i
(intu)	nim-tu	ti-naam-u
(ana)	nim-t	a-naam
(iɦna)	nim-na	ni-naam

The vowel replacement rule given above is restricted to Measure I of hollow verbs; elsewhere, a long vowel is replaced by its short counterpart before two consonants. The following forms result from adding the agreement suffixes to azaal 'to remove' and istagaab 'to respond' :

(huwwa)	azaal	istagaab
(hiyya)	azaal-it	istagaab-it
(humma)	azaal-u	istagaab-u
(inta)	azal-t	istagab-t
(inti)	azal-ti	istagab-ti
(intu)	azal-tu	istagab-tu
(ana)	azal-t	istagab-t
(iɦna)	azal-na	istagab-na

(d) Upon the addition of a suffix beginning with or consisting of a vowel, the final vowel of a defective stem is deleted; upon the addition of a suffix beginning with or consisting of a consonant, the final vowel of a defective stem is replaced by /ee/.

The following forms result from adding the agreement affixes to bana 'to build' (perfect form) and yibni (imperfect form).

	Perfect	Imperfect
(huwwa)	bana	yi-bni
(hiyya)	ban-it	ti-bni
(humma)	ban-u	yi-bn-u
(inta)	banee-t	ti-bni
(inti)	banee-ti	ti-bn-i
(intu)	banee-tu	ti-bn-u
(ana)	banee-t	a-bni
(iɦna)	banee-na	ni-bni

The following forms result from adding the agreement affixes to nisi 'to forget' (perfect form) and yinsa (imperfect form).

	Perfect	Imperfect
(huwwa)	nisi	yi-nsa
(hiyya)	nis-it	ti-nsa
(humma)	nis-u	yi-ns-u
(inta)	nisee-t	ti-nsa
(inti)	nisee-ti	ti-ns-i
(intu)	nisee-tu	ti-ns-u
(ana)	nisee-t	a-nsa
(iɦna)	nisee-na	ni-nsa

If the final vowel of the perfect defective is /i/, it may be replaced by /y/ (rather than being deleted) before a suffix which begins with or consists of a vowel. Before a suffix which begins with or consists of a consonant, the /i/ in question may be lengthened (rather than being replaced by /ee/) :

(huwwa)	nisi
(hiyya)	nisy-it
(humma)	nisy-u
(inta)	nisii-t
(inti)	nisii-ti
(intu)	nisii-tu
(ana)	nisii-t
(iɦna)	nisii-na

The addition of agreement affixes to quadriliteral verbs involves no new principles.

The following forms result from adding the agreement affixes to daɦṛag 'to roll' (perfect form) and yidaɦṛag(imperfect form).

	Perfect	Imperfect
(huwwa)	daɦṛag	yi-daɦṛag
(hiyya)	daɦṛag-it	ti-daɦṛag
(humma)	daɦṛag-u	yi-daɦṛag-u
(inta)	daɦṛag-t	ti-daɦṛag
(inti)	daɦṛag-ti	ti-daɦṛag-i
(intu)	daɦṛag-tu	ti-daɦṛag-u
(ana)	daɦṛag-t	a-daɦṛag
(iɦna)	daɦṛag-na	ni-daɦṛag

The following forms result from adding the agreement affixes to iṭma?ann 'to be reassured' (perfect form) and yiṭma?inn (imperfect form).

	Perfect	Imperfect
(huwwa)	iṭma?ann	yi-ṭma?inn
(hiyya)	iṭma?ann-it	ti-ṭma?inn
(humma)	iṭma?ann-u	yi-ṭma?inn-u
(inta)	iṭma?annee-t	ti-ṭma?inn
(inti)	iṭma?annee-ti	ti-ṭma?inn-i
(intu)	iṭma?annee-tu	ti-ṭma?inn-u
(ana)	iṭma?annee-t	a-ṭma?inn
(iɦna)	iṭma?annee-na	ni-ṭma?inn

The following forms result from adding the agreement affixes to itbahdil 'to be treated contemptuously' (perfect form) and yitbahdil (imperfect form).

	Perfect	Imperfect
(huwwa)	itbahdil	yi-tbahdil
(hiyya)	itbahdil-it	ti-tbahdil
(humma)	itbahdil-u	ti-tbahdil
(inta)	itbahdil-t	ti-tbahdil
(inti)	itbahdil-ti	ti-tbahdil-i
(intu)	itbahdil-tu	ti-tbahdil-u
(ana)	itbahdil-t	a-tbahdil
(iɦna)	itbahdil-na	ni-tbahdil

*** *** ***

VERB : ASPECT

The prefixes ɦa- ~ -ha and bi- are added to imperfect verb forms to indicate aspect.

The prefix ɦa- designates the future :

ɦayirgaʕ bukṛa. 'He will return tomorrow.'

With certain verbs (mainly stative verbs and verbs which indicate change or fixation of location), bi- indicates habitual or repetitive occurence :

biyifham biṣʕuuba. 'He comprehends with difficulty.'
biyṛuuɦ maṣṛ fiṣṣeef. 'He goes to Egypt in the summer.'
biyuskun maʕaana lamma yizuuṛ masr. 'He stays with us when he visits Egypt.'

With all other verbs, bi- may designate either continuity or repetitiveness ("continuity" being viewed as the feature of an action or an event in progress) :

uxti btidris dilwaʔti. 'My sister is studying now.'
uxti btidris billeel. 'My sister studies at night.'

Stative verbs should not be confused with verbs that indicate change of state. The latter designate a perceptible process leading from one state to another, while the former designate a state without focussing on a process. The following examples may help in differentiating stative verbs from verbs which indicate change of state :

1. Stative : biyɣiib 'he is (usually) absent', biyiɦḍar 'he is (usually) present', biyiʕraf 'he (usually) knows'.

2. Change of state : biyitɦaggar 'it (m) is getting/gets petrified', biyitgammid 'it (m) is solidifying/solidifies', biyiɦlaww 'he is getting/ gets to be good-looking', biyduub 'it (m) is dissolving/dissolves', biyinṣihir 'it (m) is melting/usually melts'.

With verbs that indicate change of state, bi- denotes either continuity or repetitiveness.

In most cases, the absence of an aspect prefix on an imperfect verb form indicates possibility as opposed to fact (see : Verbs : Subjunctive) :

laazim yiigi.	'He must come.'
tiigi maʕaana ?	'Would you like to come with us?'

There are, however, a few contexts where absence of the aspect prefix does not indicate possibility; for example, the underlined verb in the following sentence has no aspect prefix due to a process of deletion which is motivated by redundancy :

ɦanɦaarib wi ɦanintiṣir. --> 'We will fight and we will win.'
ɦanɦaarib wi nintiṣir.

*** *** ***

VERB : AUXILIARIES

A "verbal sequence" consists of two or more verbs occurring in immediate succession. According to this definition, the first of the following expressions is a verbal sequence, but the second is not (since the two verbs are separated by a pronominal suffix) :

(1) ɦayxaaf yitkallim. 'He will be afraid to talk.'

(2) šuftu byiktib. 'I saw him writing.'

In a verbal sequence the last verb is called the main verb, and the rest are called auxiliaries. A verbal sequence may include as many as six verbs :

kaan yiɦibb yibtidi yṛuuɦ yitʕallim yiʔṛa. 'He would have liked to start going to learn how to read.'

As may be expected, verbal sequences as long as the one above rarely occur; it is still true, however, that such sequences are possible.

Verbal sequences in EA are characterized by two syntactic features.

(1) The main verb may be replaced by any other verb. On the other hand, each of the auxiliaries is replaceable by a limited number of verbs.

(2) The auxiliaries occur in a fixed order; thus while the first sequence below is grammatical, the second is not :

yitmanna yṛuuɦ yidris 'He would love to go to study.'
*yiṛuuɦ yitmanna yidris

The following chart includes some auxiliaries which are common in Egyptian Arabic. The auxiliaries are listed as classes, and the classes are arranged according to relative position. The verb kaan is excluded from the chart since it requires special considerations.

I	II	III	IV	Main Verb
yitfaḍḍal 'prefers'	yibtidi 'begins'	yiigi 'comes'	yitʕallim 'learns	yiktib 'to write'
yinwi 'intends'	yifḍal 'keeps on'	yinzil 'goes down'	yitʕawwid 'gets accustomed'	etc.
yiṛḍa 'is willing'	yinsa 'forgets'	yiṭlaʕ 'goes up'		
yitmanna 'wishes'	yitgaṛṛaʔ 'dares'	yiṛawwaɦ 'goes home'		
yiʔbal 'agrees'	yiɦaawil 'tries'	yiṛuuɦ 'goes'		
yiɦibb 'likes, wants'	yiʕṛaf 'knows'	yiʔuum 'gets up'		
yixaaf 'fears'		yudxul 'enters'		
yiɣwa 'likes'		yixṛug 'goes out'		
yiʔṣud 'means, intends'				

Any one or combination of the above auxiliary classes may be deleted from the verbal sequence :

yifaḍḍal yibtidi yitʕallim yiktib.	'He would prefer to start learning how to write.'
yifaḍḍal yitʕallim yiktib.	'He would prefer to learn how to write.'
ḥayitʕallim yiktib.	'He will learn how to write.'

Each member of a given class may co-occur (in a verbal sequence) with some member of every other class. However, it would be incorrect to assume that members can be selected at random from various classes and strung together into a verbal sequence (semantic, rather than formal, restrictions preclude this possibility).

Three classes of auxiliaries are worthy of special notice : those are Class I, Class II, and Class III :

1. Class I auxiliaries have two distinctive characteristics :

(a) The subject of a Class I auxiliary may differ from the subject of the main verb. In contrast, the subject of a Class II, Class III or Class IV auxiliary is always the same as the subject of the main verb.

yiḥibb yibtidi yidris.	'He would like to start studying.'
aḥibb yibtidi yidris.	'I would like him to start studyin

(b) Class I auxiliaries usually express wish, desire, fear, intention, preference, etc.

(c) When they occur without an aspect prefix, Class I auxiliaries usually imply some provision or condition; thus this usage corresponds to the English conditional "would".

biyḥibb yzuṛna.	'He likes visiting us.'
yiḥibb yzuṛna.	'He would like to visit us (if possible, if given a choice, etc

2. Class II auxiliaries usually indicate progress (or lack of progress) in the direction of an action.

3. Class III auxiliaries have three distinctive characteristics :

(a) A Class III auxiliary, if it begins a verb sequence, and a following verb may both be perfect, imperfect or imperative. Additionally, the Class III verb may be perfect and followed by an imperfect verb. A third verb in the sequence is always imperfect.

ṛaaɦ daras.	'He went and studied.'
biyṛuuɦ yidris.	'He goes to study.'
ṛuuɦ idris.	'Go and study.'
ṛaaɦ yidris.	'He went to study.'
ṛaaɦ yitʕallim yiʔṛa.	'He went and learned how to read.'
biyṛuuɦ yitʕallim yiʔṛa.	'He goes to learn how to read.'
ṛuuɦ itʕallim tiʔṛa.	'Go and learn how to read.'
ṛaaɦ yitʕallim yiʔṛa.	'He went to learn how to read.'

The situation is different in a verbal sequence whose first constituent is not a Class III auxiliary ; in such a sequence, only the first verb may be perfect or imperative; every other verb in the sequence must be imperfect.

xaaf yiṛuuɦ yiʔabilha.	'He was afraid to go to meet her.'
biyxaaf yiṛuuɦ yiʔabilha.	'He is (usually) afraid to go to meet her.'
xaaf tiṛuuɦ tiʔabilha.	'Be afraid to go to meet her.'

(b) A Class III auxiliary which introduces a verbal sequence may be followed by a conjunction.

ṭiliʕ istaɦamma or ṭiliʕ wistaɦamma.	'He went up and took a bath.'
iṭlaʕ istaɦamma or iṭlaʕ wistaɦamma.	'Go up and take a bath.'
ṭiliʕ yistaɦamma or ṭiliʕ ʕašaan yistaɦamma.	'He went up to take a bath.'
ɦayiṭlaʕ yistaɦamma or ɦayiṭlaʕ ʕašaan yistaɦamma.	'He will go up to take a bath.'

Notice that the optional conjunction is usually ʕašaan 'in order to' when the second verb is imperfect, otherwise, the optional conjunction is usually wi 'and'.

(c) Auxiliaries of Class III are mostly forms which designate motion. Some of these auxiliaries, expecially yi?uum, may co-occur with other auxiliaries of the same class.

yiħibb y?uum yuxrug yišimm ilhawa.	'He would like to get up and go out to get some fresh air.'

Aspect prefixes can be attached only to the first form of a verbal sequence. Absence of those prefixes designates the subjunctive.

ħayxaaf yiruuħ yi?aabil ilmudiir ?	'Will he be afraid to go to meet the director ?'
yixaaf yiruuħ yi?aabil ilmudiir ?	'Do you suppose he would be afraid to go to meet the director?'

The form kaan 'was' (imperfect : yikuun) may, under certain conditions, precede any of the verbal sequences described above to mark tense, aspect, or the subjunctive (see Verbs : The Marker kaan) :

biyruuħ yi?abilha.	'He goes to see her.'
kaan biyruuħ yi?abilha.	'He used to go to see her.'
yikuun biyruuħ yi?abilha ?	'Could it be that he goes to see her.'

Notes :

1. Verbal sequences are derived (through an optional transformation) from source strings where the verb forms do not follow each other in immediate succession. The following statements hold true in those strings :

(a) Class I, Class II and Class IV auxiliaries are usually followed by an expression consisting of a nominalizer and a following subject :

yifaddal innu yibtidi . . .
yiħaawil innu yiigi . . .
yitʕallim innu yiktib . . .

(b) Class III auxiliaries are usually followed by a conjunction :

yiigi ʕašaan yitʕallim . . .
raaħ w-itʕallim . . .

In the underlying string, as in the derived one, only an initial imperfect form has the option of occurring with an aspect prefix.

2. In a given verbal sequence, the first verb may be replaced by the active participle; this fact accounts for the following sentences :

ʕali ʔaaṣid yiṛuuḥ yištaɣal.	'Ali intends to go to work.'
ʕali miš ʕaarif yibsiṭ ilmudiir.	'Ali does not know how to please the director.'
ʕali ṛaayiḥ yizuṛhum.	'Ali is on his way to visit them.'
ʕali mitʕawwid yiṣḥa badri.	'Ali is accustomed to waking up early.'

*** *** ***

VERB : BARE FORM

A "bare form" is an imperfect verb occurring with no aspect prefix, e.g., yidris (in contrast with biyidris and ḥayidris).

The bare form usually indicates subjunctive meaning and results from deleting a redundant aspect prefix. In the following sentence, nintiṣir is bare as a result of deleting the redundant prefix ḥa-, the absence of ḥa- here does not denote subjunctive meaning :

ḥanḥaarib wi nintiṣir.	'We will fight and win.'

** * ** * ** *

VERB : CITATION FORM

Verb stems in EA take affixes which indicate agreement with the subject. Consequently, the verb form differs with different subjects :

(huwwa) daras	'he studied'
(hiyya) darasit	'she studied'
(inta) darast	'you (ms) studied'
etc.	
(huwwa) b-yidris	'he is studying'

(hiyya) b-tidris 'she is studying'
(inta) b-tidris 'you (ms) are studying'
etc.

For the sake of convenience, the perfect huwwa (third person ms) form is used as the "citation" form of the verb (i.e., the dictionary form. Thus daras may be translated as 'to study' although a literal translation would be 'he studied.' Notice that the perfect huwwa form is a natural choice in two senses : it is shorter than the other perfect forms, and it yields those forms through the addition of certain suffixes.

*** *** ***

VERB : CLASSIFICATION BY ROOT TYPE

Verbs are divisible into two large groups : the triliteral and the quadriliteral, the former being those with three radicals (e.g., katab 'to write', daras 'to study', simiʕ 'to hear') and the latter being those with four radicals (e.g., daɦraq 'to roll (something)' targim 'to translate', dardiš 'to chat').

Triliteral verbs are either sound or weak. A sound verb is one which has a sound root (e.g., ṭalab 'to request', daxal 'to enter', šakar 'to thank') and a weak verb is one which has a weak root (q.v.).

Weak verbs fall into three types : the assimilated, the hollow, and the defective. The three types are defined as follows :

(1) Assimilated verbs are those whose initial radical is weak, e.g., wiṣil 'to arrive' (root wṣl).

(2) Hollow verbs are those whose middle radical is weak, e.g., naam 'to sleep' (root nwm), ɣaab 'to be absent' (root ɣyb).

(3) Defective verbs are those whose final radical is weak, e.g., daʕa 'to invite (root dʕw), rama 'to throw' (root rmy), nisi 'to forget' (root nsy).

For convenience of reference, these classes are tabulated below :

I. Triliteral
   A. Sound
   B. Weak
      1. Assimilated
      2. Hollow
      3. Defective
      4. Doubled
II. Quadriliteral

*** *** ***

VERB : kaan

The verbal form kaan (imperfect : yikuun) functions as carrier of a tense, an aspect, or a mood distinction which would otherwise have no carrier :

1. Equational sequences such as ʕali taʕbaan 'Ali is tired' designate contemporaneity. To such sentences may be added the constituent "Perfect" (to express past time), bi- (to express recurrence), or ɦa- (to express futurity) :

(a) ʕali + Perfect + taʕbaan

(b) ʕali + bi- + taʕbaan

(c) ʕali + ɦa- + taʕbaan

Since "Perfect", bi- and ɦa- must be carried by a verbal form, yikuun is added to the above sentences :

(a) ʕali + Perfect + yikuun + taʕbaan

(b) ʕali + bi- + yikuun + taʕbaan

(c) ʕali + ɦa- + yikuun + taʕbaan

In sentence (a) the sequence Perfect + yikuun produces kaan; in sentence (b), the sequence bi- + yikuun produces biykuun; and in sentence (c), the sequence ɦa- + yikuun produces ɦaykuun. The three sentences therefor assume the following forms :

ʕali kaan taʕbaan.	'Ali was tired.'
ʕali biykuun taʕbaan filmasa.	'Ali is usually tired in the evening.'
ʕali ɦaykuun taʕbaan.	'Ali will be tired.'

2. The sentence ʕali daras 'Ali studied' designates a completed event, and the sentence ʕali byidris 'Ali is studying' designates an event in progress. Futurity may be superimposed on both sentences by the addition of /ɦa-/.

(a) ʕali + ɦa- + daras lamma niwṣal. — 'Ali will have studied shen we arrive.'

(b) ʕali + ɦa- + biyidris lamma niwṣal. — 'Ali will be studying when we arrive.'

In sentence (a), the verb daras must retain its perfect form because the desired meaning includes completion. Thus ɦa- cannot combine with the following verb to produce ɦayidris. In sentence (b), the verb must retain bi- because progression is part of the desired meaning. Thus, here again, ɦa- cannot combine with the following verb to produce ɦayidris. To provide a carrier for ɦa- in both sentences, yikuun is added :

ʕali ɦaykuun daras lamma niwṣal. — 'Ali will have studied when we arrive.'

ʕali ɦaykuun biyidris lamma niwṣal. — 'Ali will be studying when we arrive.'

3. The sentence ɣiliṭ wi ṛaaɦ ilmustašfa ? 'Did he mistakenly go to the hospital?' asks about a completed event (hence the use of perfect verbs). A subjunctive meaning can be superimposed on the sentence (for example, the sentence may be changed to mean 'Could it be that he mistakenly went to the hospital?'); this would require the addition of an imperfect form without an aspect prefix. The required form is yikuun

yikuun ɣiliṭ wi ṛaaɦ ilmustašfa ? — 'Could it be that he mistakenly went to the hospital?'

The same process accounts for the occurrence of yikuun in the following sentences :

yikuun biyɦibbaha ? — 'Could it be that he loves her?'

yikuun ɦayṛuuɦ maʕaaha ? — 'Could it be that he will go with her?'

Like all other verbal forms, kaan and yikuun agree with the subject in number, gender and person :

(huwwa)	kaan biyidris.	'He was studying.'
(hiyya)	kaanit bitidris.	'She was studying.'
(ana)	kunt badris.	'I was studying.'
etc.		
(huwwa)	ɦaykuun biyidris.	'He will be studying.'
(hiyya)	ɦatkuun bitidris.	'She will be studying.'
(ana)	ɦakuun badris.	'I will be studying.'
etc.		
(huwwa)	kaan ɦayirḍa n?ablu.	'He was going to let us see him.'
(hiyya)	kaanit ɦatirḍa n?abilha.	'She was going to let us see her.'
(inta)	kunt ɦatirḍa n?ablak.	'You (ms) were going to let us see you.'

*** *** ***

VERB MEASURES : MEANINGS OF DERIVED VERBAL MEASURES

The contrasts in form between derived and primary verbs are paralleled by fairly consistent contrasts in meaning. Before specifying the meanings in question, we must emphasize two facts :

1. The meanings ascribed to a given derived measure hold true in a large number of cases where a source verb exists. They hold true less frequently when a source verb does not exist. For example, reciprocity is usually expressed by Measure III of triliteral verbs; yet of the two Measure III verbs kaatib 'to correspond with' and saafir 'to travel', only the first has associative meaning. Significantly, kaatib has a source verb (katab 'to write') while saafir does not.
2. There is no root which combines with every verbal measure. For this reason, the student may end up with a non-existent word if he yields to the temptation of combining a root he knows with a certain measure to express a certain meaning. The meanings listed below are given to help students guess and learn the designation of a new verb, rather than to

facilitate the forecasting of unattested verbs.

The meanings most commonly expressed by the derived measures of triliter verbs are the following :

1. Measure II is most often used to express the following two designations :

(a) Causation, i.e., causing an action (usually the one specified by the corresponding Measure I verb). Examples xaaf 'to be afraid': xawwif 'to frighten', dafaʕ 'to pay: daffaʕ 'to make (someone) pay', ɣayyar 'to change (something)'. Closely related to this meaning is the designation of helping (or enabling) someone to perform an action, e.g., šaal 'to carry': šayyil 'to help (someone) carry', rikib 'to ride': rakkib 'to give (someone) a ride'.

(b) Acquisition of a state or a characteristic. Examples : sawwis 'to decay (bones)', ʕaffin 'to rot', warram 'to swell', dawwid 'to become wormy', nattin 'to stink'. Measure II verbs with this designation do not usually have corresponding source verbs; in most cases, however, such verbs have corresponding nouns; e.g., suus 'decay (of bones)', ʕufuuna 'rottenness', waram 'swelling', duud 'worms', nataana 'stench', etc.

Other meanings expressed by Measure II are :

(c) Intensification of some action (usually that specified by the source verb). Examples : kasar 'to break': kassar 'to smash', ʔatal 'to kill' ʔattil 'to slaughter'.

(d) Estimation, i.e., deeming or regarding. Examples : kidib 'to lie' kaddib 'to accuse of lying'.

Because causation is their most frequent meaning, Measure II verbs are typically transitive when the source verbs are intransitive and ditransitive when the source verbs are transitive.

ʕali xarag.	'Ali went out.'
ahmad xarrag ʕali.	'Ahmad let Ali out.'
fariid akal irruzz.	'Farid ate the rice.'
ʔakkalt fariid irruzz.	'I fed Farid the rice.'

2. The most frequent meaning associated with Measure III is associativ Measure III technically means 'to engage someone in a reciprocal activity

Examples : katab 'to write': kaatib 'to correspond with', liʕib 'to play: laaʕib 'to play with', naaʔiš 'to discuss with', šaawir 'to confer with'.

Measure III verbs which express reciprocity are usually transitive :

kat ibtuhum. 'I corresponded with them.'

In some cases where the Measure III verb has associative meaning, the source verb can express the same meaning through co-occurrence with a preposition :

ʕali laaʕib ibni. 'Ali played with my son.'

ʕali liʕib maʕa bni. 'Ali played with my son.'

3. Measure IV often expresses causation. Examples : zahar 'to appear': azhar 'to show', saar 'to rebel': asaar 'to agitate', awgad 'to bring about'. Measure IV verbs which express causation are typically transitive :

asaar iššaʕb. 'He agitated the people.'

In expressing causation, Measure II is used more commonly than Measure IV (and seems to be supplanting it in EA). Use of Measure IV to express causation is indicative of education and acquaintance with Standard Arabic.

4. Measure V has three common usages :

(a) It may add reflexivity to the meaning of the source verb (i.e., the Measure II verb). For example, the Measure II verb ʕallim means 'to teach', and the Measure V verb itʕallim means 'to learn (i.e., to obtain learning on one's own or with the help of another)'. Measure V verbs which indicate reflexivity usually have animate subjects.

(b) It may indicate the acquisition of a state or a characteristic. Examples : itħaggar 'to become petrified', itkabbar 'to be pompous'. Here corresponding source verbs rarely exist, but corresponding nouns and adjectives often do (e.g., ħagar 'a stone', kibiir 'big').

(c) It may indicate the passive of the source verb. Examples : saxxan 'to heat (something)': itsaxxan 'to be heated', gammaʕ 'to gather together': itgammaʕ 'to be gathered together'.

A Measure V verb is usually intransitive unless the source verb is ditransitive (in which case the Measure V verb takes one object) :

salma tkabbaṛit.	'Salma became pompous.'
ilkutub di tgammaʕit fi xamsiin sana.	'These books were collected over a period of fifty years.'
ʕallimt wdaad ʕaṛabi.	'I taught Widad Arabic.'
widaad itʕallimit ʕaṛabi.	'Widad learned Arabic.'

It might be mentioned in passing that the prefix it- is consistently associated with intransitivity and passivity. Thus (, in addition to Measure V) the Measures itFaaʕiL, itFaʕaL and itFaʕL$\overset{a}{i}$L express passivity as well as intransitivity. This fact will be reiterated below.

5. Measure VI is commonly associated with three meanings :

(a) Reciprocity. Examples : kaatib 'to correspond with (someone)': itkaatib 'to correspond with each other', baaɦis 'to confer with (someone)': itbaaɦis 'to confer together'. A Measure VI verb which expresses reciprocity is usually derived from a Measure III verb which also expresses reciprocity; when such is the case, the two verbs differ in regard to the constructions where they occur :

(i) The Measure III verb is usually transitive, while the Measure VI verb is usually intransitive; this is because the object of the former usually becomes part of a compound phrase which functions as subject of the latter :

fariid raasil ʕali.	'Farid corresponded with Ali.'
fariid wiʕali traslu.	'Farid and Ali corresponded with each other.'

(ii) The Measure III verb is not restricted in regard to taking a singular subject. In contrast, the Measure VI verb usually has a dual or a plural subject :

fariid kaatib ʕali.	'Farid corresponded with Ali.'
ittalamza tkatbu.	'The students corresponded with each other.'

As seen from the above examples, the Measure VI verb is often translatabl by an expression including 'with each other' or 'together'.

(iii) When it has a singular subject, the Measure VI verb is usually followed by a preposition :

fariid itkaatib maʕa ʕali.	'Farid corresponded with Ali.'

In addition to the syntactic differences specified above, Measures III and VI differ semantically. While Measure III indicates that the subject of the verb initiates the action, Measure VI indicates equal participation by the parties involved.

(b) Feigning. Examples : itmaawit 'to feign death', itnaawim 'to pretend to be asleep'.

(c) The passive of Measure III. The following is an example :

saʕidna fariid.	'We helped Farid.'
fariid itsaaʕid.	'Farid was helped.'

As illustrated by the above examples, Measure VI verbs are typically intransitive.

6. Measure VII is commonly used in two contexts : to express "yielding" and reflexivity. The two usages are explained below.

(a) Yielding is a common meaning expressed by Measure VII. Arabic verbs which express yielding are sometimes translatable by intransitive English verbs (e.g., ilbaab infataḥ 'the door opened', ilfingaan inkasar 'the cup broke'). Other times they are translatable by the English passive construction, which tends to obscure a distinction in EA. Compare the following sentences :

ilbaab infataḥ fagʔah.	'The door opened suddenly.'
maʕṛafš miin fataḥ ilbaab. illi aʕṛafu inn ilbaab itfataḥ (~ infataḥ)	'I do not know who opened the door; what I do know is that the door was opened.'

In both sentences it is true that someone or something opened the door, and that the agent is unknown; the difference is that the first sentence highlights what the recipient (the door) did: it yielded to the action of an agent. Thus the difference between the construction with inFaʕaL ~ itFaʕaL and the passive construction may be represented as follows :

inFaʕaL construction	Passive construction
Agent is unknown.	Agent is unknown.
Action of the recipient is highlighted.	Existence of an agent is highlighted.

The measure inFaʕaL is indicative of education and acquaintance with Standard Arabic. Many Egyptians (especially those not so influenced by Standard Arabic) usually use itFaʕaL (rather than inFaʕaL) to express yielding; even educated Egyptians, when speaking informally, often use itFaʕaL to express yielding. As has already been mentioned, the measure itFaʕaL often expresses passivity; therefore the context may be the only means of deciding whether a given verb of the Measure itFaʕaL indicates passivity or yielding.

(b) Reflexivity is a meaning expressed by a few Measure VII verbs. Examples : ṣaṛaf 'to dismiss': inṣaṛaf 'to dismiss oneself = to depart', saħab 'to withdraw (someone)': insaħab 'to withdraw oneself.' Measure VII verbs which express reflexivity typically have animate subjects and are not usually replaceable by verbs of the measure itFaʕaL.

Measure VII is typically intransitive as can be seen from the following examples :

ilfingaan inkasaṛ.	'The cup broke.'
ilbeet inhadam.	'The house fell down.'
ilmandubiin inṣaṛafu.	'The delegates left.'

7. Measure VIII expresses a variety of meanings each of which is designated by a handful of verbs. The relatively frequent meanings are reflexivity and reciprocity.

(a) Reflexive Measure VIII verbs are typically intransitive and have animate subjects. Examples : gamaʕ 'to bring together': igtamaʕ 'to come together', naʔal 'to move or transfer (soemone)': intaʔal '(for someone) to move'.

ilʔustaaz gamaʕ ittalamza.	'The professor gathered the student
ittalamza gtamaʕu.	'The students gathered.'
ilmudiir naʔal ilmuwaẓẓaf limadiina bʕiida.	'The director moved the employee to a distant city.'

ilmuwazzaf intaʔal limadiina bʕiida.	'The employee moved to a distant city.'

(b) Reciprocal verbs of Measure VIII usually have two or more agents. If it has only agent a Measure VIII verb takes a preposition :

samiira ʔasamit ilgibna.	'Samira divided the cheese.'
samiira wfariid iʔtasamu lgibna.	'Samira and Farid divided the cheese between them.'
ilbanaat iʔtasamu lgibna.	'The girls divided the cheese among them.
samiira ʔtasamit ilgibna maʕa fariid.	'Samira divided the cheese with Farid.'

8. Measure IX usually indicates color; it means 'to become or to turn a certain color.' Examples : iħmarr 'to become red', ixdarr 'to become green', iṣfarr 'to become yellow', ibyaḍḍ 'to become white', iswadd 'to become black', izraʔʔ 'to become blue'. Verbs of this type are intransitive :

ittiffaaħ iħmarr.	'The apples turned red.'

9. Measure X has several meanings of which the most frequent are the following :

(a) Estimation. Examples : istaħla 'to consider (something) sweet or pleasant', istamsax 'to consider (something) distasteful', istaẓraf 'to consider (someone) nice', istaʕbat 'to consider (someone) stupid.'

(b) Seeking to bring about an event (usually that which is designated by the source verb). Examples : ɣafar 'to forgive': istaɣfar 'to seek forgiveness', fihim 'to understand': istafhim 'to inquire'.

istaɣfar rabbu.	'He asked forgiveness of his Lord.'
istafhimna ʕan miʕaad ligtimaaʕ.	'We inquired about the time of the meeting.'

(c) Causative - middle (cause something to happen for one's own benefit). Examples : istaxdim 'to use (something), to employ (someone)', istaʕmil 'to use (something)'. This meaning is closely related to the one described in (b) above. For example, istaxdim is derived from xadam; the source verb means 'to serve', and the derived verb means 'to seek service from (something)'.

10. The Measure itFaʕaL frequently designates the following :

(a) Yielding. Verbs in this category are typically intransitive :

ilbaab itfataħ.	'The door opened.'
ilbeet ithadam.	'The house fell down.'

As has already been pointed out, a given root may combine either with inFaʕaL or with itFaʕaL to express yielding; thus inkasar 'to break' is equivalent in meaning to itkasar. The difference between inFaʕaL and itFaʕaL, when both express yielding, is as follows :

(i) The former measure indicates that the speaker is educated and acquainted with Standard Arabic.

(ii) The former measure includes certain verbs to which no corresponding verbs of the latter measure exist, e.g., inʕaʔad '(for a meeting) to convene'. Most of the verbs in question are borrowings from Standard Arabic.

(b) The passive of Measure I. Examples :

talamziti fihmu ddars.	'My students understood the lesson.
iddars itfaham.	'The lesson was understood.'

Passive verbs of the measure itFaʕaL are typically intransitive :

ilħukuuma saganit ilgawasiis.	'The government put the spies in ja
ilgawasiis itsaganu.	'The spies were put in jail.'

11. Some verbs of the Measure istaFaʕʕaL indicate intensification, e.g., istamanna 'to yearn for (something)' :

fariida btistamanna kilma minnu.	'Farida yearns for a word from him.

The itFaʕaL and istaFaʕʕaL forms do not exist in Standard Arabic.

12. Of the quadriliterals only Measure II verbs are consistently associated with particular meanings. Measure II expresses the meanings which are usually designated by the prefix it-.

(a) It may express reflexivity :

fariid daħṛag ilħagaṛ.	'Farid rolled the stone.'
fariid iddaħṛag ʕa lħašiiš.	'Farid rolled on the grass.'

(b) It may express yielding :

za??eet ilħagar faddaħrag. 'I pushed the stone and it rolled.'

(c) It may express the passive of the source verb :

targimt ilmaqaala mbaariħ. 'I translated the article yesterday.'

ilmaqaala ttargimit imbaariħ. 'The article was translated yesterday.'

*** *** ***

VERB MEASURES : PRIMARY AND DERIVED

Some measures of EA verbs are derived from other measures. For example, Measure VI (itFaaʕiL) is formed by adding the prefix it- to Measure III (FaaʕiL). In the following table, the derived measures are listed on the right; for each derived measure, the source is given on the left :

Source	Derived
Triliteral:	
I	II, III, IV, VII, VIII, X, itFaʕaL
II	V
III	VI
X + II	istaFaʕʕaL
Quadriliteral:	
I	II, IV

For convenience of reference, triliterals of Measures II - X are called "derived triliterals". For the same reason, quadriliterals of Measure II and Measure IV are called "derived quadriliterals".

*** *** ***

VERB : QUADRILITERALS CLASSIFIED BY STEM MEASURE

Listed below are the measures of quadriliteral verbs; the perfect form precedes the imperfect, with a colon separating the two forms. Notice that EA does not have the form iFʕanLaL which exists in Standard Arabic as Measure III.

(1) Measure I of the quadriliteral is FaʕLiL : yiFaʕLiL, or FaʕLaL : yiFaʕLaL. The difference in the stem vowel is usually predictable in terms of the adjacent consonants : in general, /a/ occurs next to gutterals and emphatics, while /i/ occurs next to other consonants. Some examples are :

margaħ 'to swing (someone)': yimargaħ
farʔaʕ 'to pop, to burst': yifarʔaʕ
daħrag 'to roll (something)': yidaħrag
gargar 'to drag': yigargar
baħtar 'to scatter': yibaħtar
galgil 'to reverberate': yigalgil
bahdil 'to treat contemptuously': yibahdil
ʕarbid 'to be boisterous': yiʕarbid

(2) Measure II of quadriliteral verbs is itFaʕLiL : yitFaʕLiL or itFaʕLaL : yitFaʕLaL. The difference between the stem vowels is determined by the environment : /a/ occurs next to gutturals and emphatics, while /i/ occurs elsewhere. They are intransitive or passive. Examples :

itmargaħ 'to swing (intransitive)': yitmargaħ
itdaħrag 'to roll (intransitive)': yitdaħrag
itgargar 'to be dragged': yitgargar
itbaħtar 'to be scattered': yitbaħtar
itbalbil 'to be confused': yitbalbil

(3) Measure IV of the quadriliteral is iFʕaLaLL : yiFʕaLiLL. Some examples are :

iṭmaʔann 'to be reassured': yiṭmaʔinn
iqšaʕarr 'to shudder': yiqšaʕirr

*** *** ***

VERB : SUBJUNCTIVE

The subjunctive denotes a possibility (as opposed to a fact). Compare, for example, the underlined verbs in the following sentences :

biyṛuuħ maṣr kull ṣeef.	'He goes to Egypt every summer.'
ʕaawiz yiṛuuħ maṣr kull ṣeef.	'He wants to go to Egypt every summer.'

The underlined verb in the first sentence indicates a fact : the subject--as a matter of fact--does go to Egypt every summer. On the other hand, the underlined verb in the second sentence indicates a possibility which may or may not materialize.

Specifically, a subjunctive construction denotes possibility, probability, wish, hope, desire, intent, fear, expectation, preference, choice, acceptance, attempt, command, exhortation, permission, duty, obligation, necessity, ability, etc. All of these fall within the range of possibility (as opposed to fact), and will therefore be called subjunctival submeanings.

The general concept of possibility (as opposed to fact) is marked by the absence of the aspect prefix; the particular subjunctival submeaning (obligation, necessity, wish, desire, etc.) is usually specified lexically by a form which precedes the "bare" imperfect (e.g., a modal or a participle) :

labudd yidris.	'He must study.'
laazim yidris.	'He must study.'
naawi yidris.	'He intends to study.'

A form which specifies the subjunctival submeaning may be deleted when the context makes its presence redundant :

(a) tigiili lbeet ?	'Can you come to my house?'
(b) aagi mta ? (= tiħibb aagi mta ?)	'When would you like me to come?'

Subjunctive meaning cannot be expressed by lexical specification alone; absence of the aspect prefix is necessary. Thus both of the following sentences contain the form labudd 'must', but only the first expresses subjunctive meaning :

labudd yṛuuħ.	'He must go.'
labudd biyṛuuħ.	'It must be a fact that he goes.'

Clearly, yiṛuuħ in the first sentence expresses a possible event--one that may or may not occur. On the other hand, biyṛuuħ in the second sentence expresses a fact rather than a possibility : the sentence means 'It is my conclusion that he goes'. This is equivalent to saying that the first sentence has a verb which expresses possibility and a modal which specifies the type of possibility, while the second sentence has a verb which expresses a fact and an adverb which says something about that fact. The same difference distinguishes the following two sentences :

yimkin yiṛuuħu.	'They might go.'
yimkin biyṛuuħu.	'Perhaps they go.'

The second sentence may be paraphrased by 'The fact that they go is not certain.'

Sometimes the distinction signalled by the subjunctive is very subtle; compare, for example, the following sentences :

yimkin yiṛuuħ.	'He might go.'
yimkin ħayṛuuħ.	'It is possible that he will go.'

The two sentences are very similar in meaning; nevertheless, the absence of an aspect prefix from the first sentence and the presence of such a prefix in the second results in a subtle distinction : while the first sentence straightforwardly asserts a possibility, the second states a fact and (by means of an adverb) assigns a degree of probability to that fact. The degree of probability may be shifted to the other end of the scale by changing the adverb :

qaṭʕan ħayṛuuħ.	'He most certainly will go.'

Note :

It was stated above that the subjunctival submeaning is usually expressed lexically by a form which precedes the bare imperfect. There are, however a few verbs whose imperfect occurs without an aspect prefix to express both possibility (as opposed to fact) and the subjunctival submeaning.

The verbs in question are those which we have called Class I auxiliaries (see Verbs : Auxiliaries), and the subjunctival submeaning expressed is usually some kind of provision or condition.

lamʕi yḥibb yṛuuḥ.	'Lam'i would like to go (if he can, if given a choice, etc.).'
faxri yiṛḍa yṛuuḥ.	'Faxri would agree to go (if asked to do so, etc.).'

The majority of Class I auxiliaries can be used to produce contrasts like the following :

mamduuh ḥayḥibb yṛuuḥ.	'Mamduh will want to go.'
mamduuh biyḥibb yṛuuḥ.	'Mamduh usually wants to go.'
mamduuh ḥaabib yiṛuuḥ.	'Mamduh is desirous of going.'
mamduuh yiḥibb yṛuuḥ.	'Mamduh would like to go.'

*** *** ***

VERB : TENSE

EA verbs show two tenses : the perfect and the imperfect.

The perfect most frequently designates the following :

1. An event which was completed prior to the moment of speaking :

min yumeen šuftaha hina.	'Two days ago I saw her here.'

2. An event which took place at some past time but whose results linger on :

fihimt.	'I have understood.'
maṣr it?addimit xaaliṣ.	'Egypt has progressed a great deal.'

3. An event which is considered completed immediately upon the act of speaking or by the very act. Verbs which designate this meaning are often translatable by an expression including herewith or hereby.

a-- uskut.	'Shut up!'
b-- sikitt.	'Fine, I'm shutting up!'

a-- biʕhaali. 'Sell it to me.'

b-- biʕtahaalak. 'I hereby sell it to you.'

The imperfect form usually occurs with one of the aspect prefixes bi- or ɦa- ~ ha-. For the meanings of bi- and ɦa-, (see : Verb : Aspect). Absence of an aspect prefix usually designates subjunctive meaning (see: Verb : The Subjunctive).

Perfect verbs are characterized by the fact that they take suffixes but not prefixes. In contrast, imperfect verbs are characterized by the fact that some forms have prefixes only while others have prefixes as well as suffixes. In the following examples, the stem is underlined :

	Perfect	Imperfect
(hiyya)	katabit	tiktib
(iɦna)	katabna	niktib
(inti)	katabti	tiktibi
(intu)	katabtu	tiktibu
	etc.	etc.

*** *** ***

VERB : TRILITERALS CLASSIFIED BY STEM MEASURE

The table below shows the measures of triliteral verbs. For each measure, the perfect and imperfect forms are given, with examples in parentheses. Notice that :

1. The Roman numeral assigned to a given measure is the one which designates the corresponding measure in Modern Standard Arabic. The last two measures are left unnumbered since they do not exist in Modern Standard Arabic.

2. The measures of assimilated verbs are identical to those of sound verbs. For this reason, assimilated verbs do not occur in the table as a distinct category (but see Note 3 below the table).

3. The word or in the table indicates unpredictability. The sign ~ indicates free variation.

	Sound		Doubled	
	Perfect	Imperfect	Perfect	Imperfect
I	FaʕaL or FiʕiL (katab 'to write' ʕirif 'to know')	a yiFʕiL (see Note u 6 for examples)	Faʕʕ (ʕadd 'to count', maṛṛ 'to pass')	yiFiʕʕ (yiʕidd) or yiFuʕʕ (yimuṛṛ)
II	FaʕʕaL (ħaṣṣan 'to fortify') FaʕʕiL (darris 'to teach')	yiFaʕʕiL (yiħaṣṣan) yiFaʕʕiL (yidarris)	Faʕʕaʕ (kaṛṛar 'to repeat') Faʕʕiʕ (sabbib 'to cause')	yiFaʕʕaʕ (yikaṛṛaṛ) yiFaʕʕiʕ (yisabbib)
III	FaaʕiL (kaatib 'to correspond with')	yiFaaʕiL (yikaatib)		
IV	aFʕaL (aʕdam 'to execute')	yiFʕiL (yiʕdim)	aFaʕʕ (aʕadd 'to prepare (some-thing)')	yiFiʕʕ (yiʕidd)
V	itFaʕʕaL (itħaṣṣan 'to be fortified') itFaʕʕiL (itʕazzib 'to suffer')	yitFaʕʕaL (yitħaṣṣan) yitFaʕʕiL (yitʕazzib)	itFaʕʕaʕ (itkaṛṛaṛ 'to be repeated') itFaʕʕiʕ (itbaddid 'to be dispersed')	yitFaʕʕaʕ (yitkaṛṛaṛ) yitFaʕʕiʕ (yitbaddid)
VI	itFaaʕiL (itkaatib 'to correspond with each other')	yitFaaʕiL (yitkaatib)		
VIIA	inFaʕaL (insaħab 'to withdraw')*	yinFiʕiL (yinsiħib)	inFaʕʕ (inšaʔʔ 'to split')	yinFaʕʕ (yinšaʔʔ)
VIII	iFtaʕaL (ištaṛak) 'to participate')	yiFtiʕiL (yištiṛik)	iFtaʕʕ (iħtadd 'to become angry')	yiFtaʕʕ (yiħtadd)
IX	iFʕaLL (iħmaṛṛ 'to turn red')	yiFʕaLL (yiħmaṛṛ)		
X	istaFʕaL (istaʕbaṭ 'to act stupid') istaFʕiL (istaʕmil 'to use')**	yistaFʕaL (yistaʕbaṭ) yistaFʕiL (yistaʕmil)	istaFaʕʕ (istaʕadd 'to get ready')	yistaFiʕʕ (yistaʕidd)
* VIIB	itFaʕaL (itnaʔal 'to be transferred')	yitFiʕiL (yitniʔil)	itFaʕʕ (itgann 'to 'to become insane')	yitFaʕʕ (yitgann)
** X + II	istaFaʕʕaL (istalaʔʔaf 'to catch (e.g., a ball)')	yistaFaʕʕaL (yistalaʔʔaf)	istaFaʕʕaʕ (istaħammam 'to bathe')	yistaFaʕʕaʕ (yistaħammam)

Hollow		Defective	
Perfect	Imperfect	Perfect	Imperfect
FaaL (raaħ 'to go', naam 'to sleep', gaab 'to bring')	yiFuuL (yiruuħ) yiFaaL (yinaam) yiFiiL (yigiib)	FaʕA (raga 'to implore', daʕa 'to invite', bana 'to build, saʕa 'to attempt') or Fiʕi (nisi 'to forget', giri 'to run')	yiFʕu (yirgu), yiFʕi (yidʕi, yibni), or yiFʕa (yisʕa) yiFʕa (yinsa) or yiFʕi (yigri)
FaʕʕaL (ʕawwar 'to injure', bayyad 'to paint') FaʕʕiL (kawwin 'to form', ʕayyin 'to appoint')	yiFaʕʕaL (yiʕawwar, yibayyad) yiFaʕʕiL (yikawwin, yiʕayyin)	Faʕʕa (rabba 'to rear, bring up')	yiFaʕʕi (yirabbi)
FaaʕiL (ħaawil 'to try', ʕaayin 'to inspect')	yiFaaʕiL (yiħaawil, yiʕaayin)	Faaʕa (naada 'to call to')	yiFaaʕi (yinaadi)
aFaaL (azaal 'to remove')	yiFiiL (yiziil)	aFʕa (aɣra 'to entice')	yiFʕi (yiɣri)
itFaʕʕaL (ittawwar 'to evolve', itħayyar 'to be puzzled') itFaʕʕiL (itʕawwid 'to become accustomed', itʕayyin 'to be appointed')	yitFaʕʕaL (yittawwar, yitħayyar) yitFaʕʕiL (yitʕawwid, yitʕayyin)	itFaʕʕa (itmanna 'to wish')	yitFaʕʕa (yitmanna)
itFaaʕiL (itʕaawin 'to co-operate', itħaayil 'to plead')	yitFaaʕiL (yitʕaawin yitħaayil)	itFaaʕa (itfaada 'to avoid')	yitFaaʕa (yitfaada)
inFaaL (insaab 'to flow')	yinFaaL (yinsaab)	inFaʕa (inmaħa 'to vanish')	yinFiʕi (yinmiħi)
iFtaaL (iħtaag 'to be in need')	yiFtaaL (yiħtaag)	iFtaʕa (intaha 'to end')	yiFtiʕi (yintihi)
iFʕaLL (iswadd 'to turn black', ibyadd 'to turn white')	yiFʕaLL (yiswadd, yibyadd)	iFʕaLL (iħlaww 'to become good-looking')	yiFʕaLL (yiħlaww)
istaFaaL (istagaab 'to respond)	yistaFiiL (yistagiib)	istaFʕa (istaɣla 'to consider something expensive')	yistaFʕi (yistaɣli yistaFʕa yistaɣla)
itFaaL (itbaaʕ 'to be sold')	yitFaaL (yitbaaʕ)	itFaʕa (itʕama 'to become blind')	yitFiʕi (yitʕimi)
istaFaʕʕaL (istarayyaħ 'to rest')	yistaFaʕʕaL (yistarayyaħ)	istaFaʕʕa(istaɣamma 'to blindfold oneself', istaragga 'to implore', istaxabba 'to hide')	yistaFaʕʕa (yistaɣamma, yistaragga, yistaxabba)

The following notes are applicable to the above table :

1. Hollow verbs of Measure II are the same in shape as the sound counterparts; so are hollow verbs of Measure III, Measure V, Measure VI, Measure IX, and the last measure. Hollow verbs of other measures are not the same in shape as the sound counterparts.

2. As the muṭaawiʕ ("yielding" form) of FaʕaL (see : Verb Measures : Meaning), inFaʕaL is interchangeable with itFaʕaL. The following qualifications restrict this statement :

(a) inFaʕaL is more common than itFaʕaL in the speech of educated Egyptians. Thus an educated Egyptian is likely to say ilbaab infataɦ 'the door opened' rather than ilbaab itfataɦ (although both forms are possible).

(b) For some verbs, the form inFaʕaL exists without the alternative possibility of itFaʕaL (most of those verbs are borrowings from Modern Standard Arabic); for example, the form for 'to be impetuous' is indafaʕ but not *itdafaʕ.

3. The first radical of assimilated verbs is totally assimilated to the /t/ of iFtaʕaL. Thus Measure VIII from the root wṣl is ittaṣal rather than *iwtaṣal; from wfʔ, ittafaʔ rather than *iwtafaʔ; and from wzn, ittazan rather than *iwtazan. In contrast, the first radical of assimilated verbs is not assimilated to the /t/ of itFaʕaL, e.g., itwaṣal, itwazan.

4. In the case of most measures, the perfect and the imperfect forms have the same vowel pattern; for example, FaʕʕiL and yiFaʕʕiL share the vowel pattern a-i.

5. Some derived measures* have two perfect-tense forms : one whose stem vowel is /a/, and another whose stem vowel is /i/; for example, the perfect of Measure II is either FaʕʕaL of FaʕʕiL. The difference between the two forms is usually predictable from the environment : the stem vowel is /a/ if it is adjacent to one of certain segments, and /i/ otherwise. The segments in question are (a) the back consonants /ʔ/, /h/, /ɦ/, /ʕ/, /x/, /ɣ/, and (b) the emphatic consonants /ṣ/, /ẓ/, /ṭ/, /ḍ/, /ṛ/. Examples are wabbax 'to scold', waḍḍaɦ 'to clarify', lammaʕ 'to polish', naḍḍaf 'to clean', kassil 'to be lazy', ʕayyin 'to appoint'.

---

* Except for the first, all of the measures listed in the chart are "derive

6. In the imperfect tense, Measure I of sound triliterals is $\text{yiF}ʕ\overset{a}{\underset{u}{\text{i}}}\text{L}$ (i.e., yiFʕiL, yiFʕaL, or yiFʕuL). It is impossible, given a sound perfect-tense form of the measure FaʕaL, to predict with certainty the imperfect form. Nevertheless, the following rules facilitate prediction in a large number of instances :

(a) The stem vowel is /a/ next to a guttural (i.e., /ʔ/, /h/, /ɦ/, and /ʕ/); e.g., yisʔal 'he asks', yinhab 'he plunders', yismaɦ 'he allows', yilʕan 'he curses'. Notice, however, that the stem vowel is not usually /a/ next to a glottal stop which corresponds to /q/ in the Modern Standard Arabic pronunciation of the verb; e.g., yirʔud 'to lie down' (Standard : /yarqud/).

(b) The stem vowel is /u/ next to a back consonant which is not a guttural or next to an emphatic consonant, provided that the other adjacent consonant is not a guttural. The consonants in question are /q/, /k/, /g/, /x/, /ɣ/ and the emphatic consonants are /ṣ/, /ẓ/, /ṭ/, /ḍ/, and /ṛ/. Examples are : yiṣqul 'to burnish', yiskun 'to dwell', yisgud 'to bow down', yidxul 'to enter', yizɣud 'to nudge', yiɦṣud 'to reap', yinẓur 'to look, yišṭub 'to cancel', yirfuḍ 'to refuse', yiɦfuṛ 'to dig'. The stem vowel is usually /u/ if it is adjacent to a glottal stop which corresponds to a /q/ in the Standard pronunciation; e.g., yirʔud 'to lie down ' (Standard /yarqud/), yisʔub 'to pierce' (Standard : /yaθqub/).

(c) Otherwise, the stem vowel is /i/; e.g., yiʕbid 'to worship', yixdim 'to serve', yinsif 'to blow up (something)'.

7. The imperfect of FiʕiL is usually yiFʕaL; e.g., ʕilim 'to know': yiʕlam, rikib 'to ride': yirkab, ṭiwil 'to become tall': yiṭwal. Some exceptions are ʕimil 'to do': yiʕmil, libis 'to wear': yilbis, nizil 'to descend': yinzil.

8. Given a perfect form of the measure FaaL, it is impossible to forecast the imperfect form.

Notice that for Measure I of hollow verbs there are three imperfect shapes (yiFuuL, yiFiiL, and yiFaaL) but only one perfect shape (FaaL). The student is therefore advised to learn the imperfect form of each Measure I hollow verb, and from it to obtain the perfect counterpart. The alternative to this procedure is to learn both the perfect and the imperfect as items.

9. In the case of Measure I defective verbs, the imperfect forms are not totally predictable from the prefect forms. Of the imperfect forms listed, yiFʕu and yiFʕi are relatively rare :

(a) The form yiFʕu pertains to a few--but not to all-verbs whose last radical is /w/ :

Perfect	Imperfect
raga 'to implore' (root: rgw)	yirgu
sama 'to be eminent' (root: smw)	yismu
daʕa 'to invite' (root: dʕw)	yidʕi
šaka 'to complain about' (root: škw)	yiški

(b) yiFʕi is the imperfect of Fiʕi in a few instances; in most cases, the imperfect of Fiʕi is yiFʕa :

Perfect	Imperfect
giri 'to run'	yigri
nisi 'to forget'	yinsa
liʔi 'to find'	yilʔa
riḍi 'to be satisfied'	yirḍa

10. When the second syllable of the imperfect contains /u/ or /uu/, the prefix is yi- ~ yu-; e.g., yixrug ~ yuxrug 'to go out', yiħuṭṭ ~ yuħuṭṭ 'to put', yiruuħ ~ yuruuħ 'to go'.

11. The /n/ of Measure VII is usually replaced by /m/ before the labial consonants /b/, /f/, and /m/ :

imbaaʕ 'to be sold'	yimbaaʕ
imfagar 'to explode'	yimfigir
immaħa 'to vanish'	yimmiħi

12. Each triliteral measure has more than one shape; in other words, a measure is a class of shapes. For example, Measure IV embraces the shapes aFʕaL (sound), aFaʕʕ (doubled), aFaaL (hollow), and aFʕa (defective). The differences between these shapes are predictable in terms of general phonological rules which hold true throughout the language (e.g., /awa/ → /aa/). Through the application of the rules in question, the sound shape yields the other shapes (e.g., FawaL and FayaL become FaaL). For this reason, the sound shape stands for the measure as a whole, and the other shapes are considered variants.

*** *** ***

VERBAL NOUNS : DEFINITENESS

An Arabic noun is indefinite when its meaning is ambiguous (i.e., when it is likely to elicit the question "Which one?"). It is definite when its meaning is not ambiguous (i.e., when it does not normally elicit the question "Which one?").

Abstract verbal nouns (see Verbal Nouns : Meaning) have unambiguous designations, and for that reason they are definite in form. Consider, for example, the underlined verbal nouns in the following sentences :

1. <u>ilʕilm</u> aħsan min <u>iggahl</u>. 'Education is better than ignorance.'
2. <u>fahm</u> ilmuškila di ṣaʕb. 'Understanding this problem is difficult.'

One who hears sentence 1 would not normally ask "Which education?" or "Which ignorance?" because reference is to education and ignorance in general. Likewise, one who hears sentence 2 is not likely to ask "Which understanding?" In other words, <u>ilʕilm</u>, <u>iggahl</u>, and <u>fahm</u> (as used in the above sentences) are definite in meaning. For this reason, they have definite forms. <u>Notice that the English equivalents are not preceded by the. This fact often misleads students who try to fashion Arabic expressions after English ones</u>.

The statement that abstract verbal nouns are definite in form means that such verbal nouns occur (a) with the definite article or (b) as the first term of a construct phrase :

<u>ittadriis</u> ṣaʕb. 'Teaching is difficult.'
<u>tadriis illuɣa lʔingliiziyya</u> ṣaʕb. 'Teaching English is difficult.'

Concrete (i.e., not abstract) verbal nouns may be definite or indefinite in form :

ʔaṛeena <u>ttaʔriir</u>. 'We read the report.'
ʔaṛeena <u>taʔriir</u>. 'We read a report.'

*** *** ***

VERBAL NOUNS : DERIVATION

Listed below are the verbal nouns of the various triliteral verb forms. In each case, the verb form precedes the verbal noun, with a colon separating the two. Examples are given in parentheses.

	Sound	Doubled
I	FaʕaL, FiʕiL: (1) Transitive: FaʕL (akal 'to eat': akl, darab 'to beat': darb) etc. (2) Intransitive: (a) FuʕaaL, FaʕiiL, especially from verbs denoting sound (ṣarax 'to scream': ṣuraax, nabaħ 'to bark': nubaaħ; zaʔar 'to roar': zaʔiir, ṣahal 'to neigh': ṣahiil) (b) FuʕuuL (daxal 'to enter': duxuul, xarag 'to exit': xuruug, rikib 'to ride': rukuub, ṭiliʕ 'to ascend': ṭuluuʕ, nizil 'to descend': nuzuul, wiʔif 'to stand': wuʔuuf)	Faʕʕ: (1) Faʕʕ (ʕadd 'to count': ʕadd, sadd 'to block': sadd, radd 'to answer': radd, lamm 'to gather': lamm) (2) Less commonly Fuʕʕ, Fiʕʕ (ħabb 'to love': ħubb, wadd 'to desire': widd)
II	Faʕʕ$^{i}_{a}$L: taFʕiiL (ħaṣṣan 'to fortify': taħṣiin, darris 'to teach': tadriis)	Faʕʕ$^{i}_{a}$ʕ: taFʕiiʕ (karrar 'to repeat': takriir, sabbib 'to cause': tasbiib)
III	FaaʕiL: (1) muFaʕLa (ʔaabil 'to meet': muʔabla, ʕaamil 'to treat': muʕamla) (2) Infrequently, as an alternate of muFaʕLa, FiʕaaL (ʔaatil 'to fight with': ʔitaal, gaadil 'to argue with': gidaal)	
IV	aFʕaL: iFʕaaL (aʕdam 'to execute': iʕdam)	aFaʕʕ: iFʕaaʕ (aʕadd 'to prepare (something)': iʕdaad, aqarr 'to admit': iqraar)
V	itFaʕʕ$^{i}_{a}$L: taFaʕʕuL (itħaṣṣan 'to be fortified': taħaṣṣun, itsallim 'to receive': tasallum)	itFaʕʕ$^{i}_{a}$ʕ: taFaʕʕuʕ (itkarrar 'to be repeated': takarrur, itbaddid 'to be dispersed': tabaddud)
VI	itFaaʕiL: taFaaʕuL (itkaatib 'to correspond with each other': takaatub)	
VII	inFaʕaL: inFiʕaaL (insaħab 'to withdraw': insiħaab)	inFaʕʕ: inFiʕaaʕ (inšaʔʔ 'to split': inšiʔaaʔ)
VIII	iFtaʕaL: iFtiʕaaL (ištarak 'to participate': ištiraak)	iFtaʕʕ : iFtiʕaaʕ (iħtadd 'to become angry': iħtidaad)
IX	iFʕaLL: iFʕiLaaL (iħmarr 'to turn red': iħmiraar)	
X	istaFʕaL: istiFʕaaL (istaʕbaṭ 'to act stupid': istiʕbaaṭ)	istaFaʕʕ: istiFʕaaʕ (istaʕadd 'to get ready': istiʕdaad)

	Hollow	Defective
I	FaaL: (1) When medial radical is /w/: FooL (maat 'to die': moot, naam 'to sleep': noom) etc. (2) When medial radical is /y/: FeeL (maal 'to be inclined': meel, baaʕ 'to sell': beeʕ) etc.	Faʕa: Faʕy (ʔala 'to boil (something)': ʔaly, ṭawa 'to fold': ṭawy, rama 'to throw away': ramy, saʕa 'to attempt': saʕy, bara 'to sharpen': bary) etc. Fiʕi: Faʕayaan (giri 'to run': garayaan, ʕimi 'to become blind': ʕamayaan, nisi 'to forget': nasayaan)
II	Faʕʕ$^{i}_{a}$L: taFʕiiL (ʕawwar 'to injure': taʕwiir, bayyad 'to paint': tabyiid, kawwin 'to form': takwiin, ʕayyin 'to appoint': taʕyiin)	Faʕʕa: taFʕiya (rabba 'to rear': tarbiya, samma 'to name': tasmiya)
III	FaaʕiL: (1) muFaʕLa (ħaawil 'to try': muħawla, ʕaayin 'to inspect': muʕayna) (2) Infrequently, as an alternative of muFaʕLa, FiʕaaL (gaawir 'to live next door to': giwaar)	Faaʕa: muFaʕaat (daawa 'to administer medical treatment to': mudawaat, saawa 'to treat equally': musawaat)
IV	aFaaL: iFaaLa (azaal 'to remove': izaala, aʕaad 'to repeat': iʕaada)	aFʕa: iFʕaaʔ (aɣra 'to entice': iɣraaʔ, anha 'to end (something)': inhaaʔ)
V	itFaʕʕ$^{i}_{a}$L: taFaʕʕuL (itṭawwar 'to evolve': taṭawwur, itʕawwid 'to be accustomed': taʕawwud, itħayyin 'to take advantage of an opportunity': taħayyun)	itFaʕʕa: taFaʕʕi (itmanna 'to wish': tamanni)
VI	itFaaʕiL: taFaaʕuL (itʕaawin 'to cooperate': taʕaawun, itħaayil 'to plead': taħaayul)	itFaaʕa: taFaaʕi (itfaada 'to avoid': tafaadi)
VII	inFaaL: inFiyaaL (insaab 'to flow': insiyaab)	inFaʕa: inFiʕaaʔ (inmaħa 'to vanish': inmiħaaʔ)
VIII	iFtaaL: iFtiyaaL (iħtaag 'to be in need': iħtiyaag)	iFtaʕa: iFtiʕaaʔ (intaha 'to end': intihaaʔ)
IX	iFʕaLL: iFʕiLaaL (iswadd 'to turn black': iswidaad, ibyadd 'to turn white': ibyidaad)	
X	istaFaaL: istaFaaLa (istagaab 'to respond': istigaaba, istafaad 'to benefit': istibaada)	istaFʕa: istiFaaʔ (istaɣla 'to consider something expensive': istiɣlaaʔ, istawla 'to take over; to seize': istiwlaaʔ)

The following notes pertain to the above chart :

1. Measure I verbs, especially the sound, have unpredictable verbal nouns. The student is therefore advised to learn the verbal noun for each Measure I verb as an item.

2. Measure II verbs (especially when designating causation or intensification) usually take the verbal nouns specified for them in the chart. A few, however, take unpredictable shapes of which the most common is FaʕaaL. Examples : darris 'to teach': tadriis, ɦaddid 'to specify': taɦdiid, ṭawwaṛ 'to develop, to advance (something)': taṭwiir, ṛabba 'to rear': tarbiya, kassaṛ 'to smash': taksiir, ʔattil 'to slaughter': taʔtiil, but kallim 'to talk to (someone)': kalaam.

Some derived verbs (especially those of Measure II which denote causation and those which are associated with Standard Arabic) take the verbal nouns specified in the chart as well as the verbal nouns of the source verbs (when such source verbs exist). Derived verbs with no corresponding source verbs take the verbal nouns specified in the chart.

The specific implications of these general statements are as follows :

(a) Verbs of the measure istaFaʕʕaL take the verbal nouns of the corresponding Measure X verbs (which explains why the measure istaFaʕʕaL is excluded from the chart). Thus istarayyaɦ 'to rest' takes the verbal noun of istaṛaaɦ 'to rest', namely, istiraaɦa. Some verbs of the measure istaFaʕʕaL have no source verbs of Measure X; notwithstanding this fact, such verbs take the verbal nouns which would be taken by Measure X verbs (e.g., istaɦammam 'to take a bath': istiɦmaam).

(b) Derived verbs with it- usually take the verbal nouns of the source verbs :

(i) Verbs of the measure itFaʕaL almost always take the verbal nouns of the corresponding source verbs (which explains the exclusion of itFaʕaL from the chart). Examples : itkatab 'to be written': kitaaba, itʕadd 'to be counted': ʕadd, itšaal 'to be carried': šeel, itbara 'to be sharpened': bary.

(ii) Verbs of Measure V usually take the verbal nouns of the corresponding Measure II verbs. Some Measure V verbs take the verbal nouns specified for them in the chart. These usually take, in addition, the verbal nouns of the corresponding Measure I and Measure II verbs (if such Measure I and Measure II verbs exist.). Examples : itʕallim 'to learn': taʕliim, itħaddid 'to be specified': taħdiid, itʕawwid 'to be accustomed': taʕwiid, itrabba 'to be reared': tarbiya, itmarrad 'to rebel': tamarrud, itraddad 'to hesitate': taraddud, itʕazzib 'to suffer': taʕazzub or taʕziib or ʕazaab, itɣayyar 'to change (intransitive)': taɣayyur or taɣyiir, itkallim 'to speak': takallum or kalaam.

(iii) Verbs of Measure VI usually take the verbal nouns of Measure III. Some Measure VI verbs take the verbal nouns specified for them in the chart; these verbs usually take, in addition, the verbal nouns of the corresponding Measure III verbs (if such Measure III verbs exist). Examples : it?aabil 'to meet each other': mu?abla, itbaara 'to compete with each other': mubaraat, itʕaamil 'to deal with each other': muʕamla, itdaawa 'to receive medical treatment': mudawaat, itnaazil 'to relinquish': tanaazul, itraakum 'to pile up': taraakum, itmaada 'to go to extremes': tamaadi, itbaadil 'to exchange with each other': tabaadul or mubadla.

(c) Other derived verbs usually take the verbal nouns specified for them in the chart; they may also take the verbal nouns of the corresponding source verbs (when such source verbs exost). Examples : ħaakim 'to try (in court)': muħakma, raasil 'to correspond with': murasla, ħaasib 'to call (someone) to account': muħasba or ħisaab, gaalis 'to sit with (someone)': mugalsa or guluus, arɣam 'to force': irɣaam, adrak 'to realize': idraak, anzar 'to threaten': inzaar, askan 'to allocate living quarters to (someone)': iskaan, axrag 'to let out': ixraag or xuruug, inṣaraf 'to depart': inṣiraaf, inʕa?ad '(for a meeting) to be held': inʕi?aad or ʕa?d, inkasar 'to break (intransitive)': inkisaar or kasr, infataħ 'to open (intransitive)': infitaaħ or fatħ, intaha 'to end (intransitive)': intihaa? or nihaaya.

The verbal nouns of quadriliteral verbs are as follows :

(1) From Measure I verbs, the verbal noun is FaʕLaLa; e.g., targim 'to translate': targama, daħrag 'to roll (something)': daħraga, margaħ 'to swing (someone)': margaħa.

(2) Measure II verbs take the verbal nouns of the corresponding source (i.e., Measure I) verbs; e.g., iddaħrag 'to roll (intransitive)': daħraga,

ittargim 'to be translated': targama, itmargaɦ 'to swing (intransitive)': margaɦa.

(3) From Measure IV verbs, the verbal noun is iFʕiLLaaL (where the two medial L's stand for different consonants); e.g., iṭmaʔann 'to be re-assured': iṭmiʔnaan, iqšaʕaṛṛ 'to shudder': iqšiʕraaṛ.

*** *** ***

VERBAL NOUNS : DERIVING THE "NOUN OF QUALITY"

The ending -iyya is added to certain nouns--many of which are verbal nouns--to produce the form known as "the noun of quality". The noun of quality expresses the designation of the source noun as a general concept, a doctrine, a quality, or a totality; the noun of quality is therefore similar to English nouns which end in -ism or -ity. In the examples below, the source noun precedes the colon :

šuyuuʕ	'spread'	:	šuyuʕiyya	'communism'
ištiṛaak	'participation'	:	ištiṛakiyya	'socialism'
wuguud	'existence'	:	wugudiyya	'existentialism'
insaan	'human being'	:	insaniyya	'humanity'
ilmasiiɦ	'Christ'	:	masiɦiyya	'Christianity'

Not all nouns can yield the noun of quality, and no general rule delineates the nouns which can. The student must therefore learn the nouns of quality as items.

Singular nouns of quality are feminine.

*** *** ***

VERBAL NOUNS : DERIVING THE NOUN OF SINGLE OCCURRENCE

Certain nouns designate an event which has taken place once. An exampl is the underlined word in the following sentence :

simiʕt ṣaṛxa waṛaaya. 'I heard a scream behind me.'

Such nouns are formed by adding the feminine suffix -a to verbal nouns. It must be emphasized that not every verbal noun can yield a noun of single occurrence, and that no infallible rule can be given to determine which verbal nouns yield the noun of single occurrence. The following are helpful--though not fool-proof--guidelines :

1. Most nouns of single occurrence are derived from the verbal nouns FaʕL and taFʕiiL. Examples : ramya 'a throw', taxriima 'a shortcut', taʕwiira 'an injury'.

2. Verbal nouns other than FaʕL and taFʕiiL rarely yield the noun of single occurrence.

Some nouns of single occurrence have acquired a semantic extension in addition to the basic designation. Thus akla is not only 'an act of eating' but also 'a meal'; likewise, ḍaṛba is not only 'an act of striking' but also 'a plague'.

All nouns designating a single occurrence form the plural by the addition of -aat. The dual is formed by the addition of -een :

Singular	Plural	Dual
ramya 'a throw'	ramyaat	ramyiteen
akla 'a meal'	aklaat	akliteen
taxriima 'a shortcut'	taxrimaat	taxrimteen

*** *** ***

VERBAL NOUNS : GENDER OF THE SINGULAR FORM

A singular verbal noun (whether abstract or concrete) is usually masculine unless it ends in -a. Thus of the following forms, the ones on the left are masculine and the ones on the right are feminine :

ʕarḍ 'an offer'	diṛaasa 'an academic discipline'
ʕamal 'a task'	kitaaba 'a writing'
taṣṛiiħ 'a permit'	mu?abla 'an interview'
intiqaad 'a criticism'	istigaaba 'a response'
ḍarb 'beating'	ibaada 'exterminating'

*** *** ***

VERBAL NOUNS : MEANING

A verbal noun names the action designated by the corresponding verb. For example, the verbal noun d̤iraasa 'studying' names the action which is designated by the verb daras 'to study'. Similarly, the verbal noun akl 'eating' names the action which is designated by the verb akal 'to eat'.

The meaning of a verbal noun can be either abstract or concrete, as is evident from conparing the underlined words in the following sentences :

(1) ilkitaab da miš kuwayyis. 'This book is not good.'

(2) il?akl ?abl innoom mubaašaṛatan muḍirr. 'Eating immediately before sleeping is harmful.'

The noun ilkitaab denotes a discrete object with one unit of lexical meaning; for this reason, (a) it can be counted, and (b) it is equally capable of being definite or indefinite. In this sense, ilkitaab is concrete. That countability is a distinctive characteristic of concrete nouns is self-evident; what may not be self-evident is the fact that unrestricted freedom to occur as either definite or indefinite is also a distinctive characteristic of concrete nouns. A noun is indefinite if it is ambiguous (i.e., if it is likely to elicit the question "Which one?") and definite if it is unambiguous (i.e., if it is not likely to elicit the question "Which one?"). It is about concrete entities that we normally ask the question "Which one?" and it is therefore the nouns designating such entities that may be either definite or indefinite. (For further comments on the meaning of definiteness, see : Definite Article : Meaning).

The verbal noun il?akl has a generic meaning ('eating in general') rather than a discrete referent, and for that reason (a) it cannot be counted, and (b) it is usually definite. In this sense il?akl and verbal nouns like it are abstract.

The abstract meaning discussed above constitutes the "basic" designation of verbal nouns. In addition to that meaning, some verbal nouns have acquired concrete meanings; for example, diṛaasa can be used with abstract meaning, 'studying', but it can also be used with the concrete meaning 'a discipline'; again, ʕamal can be used with the abstract meaning 'working', but it also can be used with the concrete meaning 'a job.'

Verbal nouns differ from verbs in that the latter designate tense and aspect while the former do not; this fact is evident from the difference in meaning between the following sentences :

libs ilfustaan da ʕeeb.	'Wearing this dress is shameful.'
innik bitilbisi lfustaan da ʕeeb.	'The fact that you wear this dress is shameful.'
innik ḥatilbisi lfustaan da ʕeeb.	'The fact that you will wear this dress is shameful.'
innik libisti lfustaan da ʕeeb.	'The fact that you wore this dress is shameful.'

*** *** ***

VERBAL NOUNS : NUMBER

Abstract verbal nouns are not countable : they are considered grammatically singular, and they can be made neither dual nor plural. Concrete verbal nouns, on the other hand, have singular, dual and plural forms. In the first sentence below, the underlined word is an abstract verbal noun; in the other four, the underlined words are concrete verbal nouns :

ittaʕliim fiṣṣiɣar zayy innaʔš ʕa lḥagaṛ.	'Training (a person) in (his) childhood is similar to engraving on stone.' (i.e., one never forgets what he learns as a child.)
kaanu biynaadu b-taʕliim ɣariib.	'They preached a strange doctrine.'
kaanu biynaadu b-taʕlimeen miš taʕliim waaḥid.	'They preached two doctrines, not one.'
kaanu biynaadu b-talat taʕaḷiim.	'They preached three doctrines.'
ittaʕaliim illi biynaadu biiha ɣariiba.	'The doctrines they preach are strange.'

Concrete verbal nouns of Measure I triliterals are divisible into two groups :

1. Those which have sound plurals; most of the singular verbal nouns in this group are feminine forms ending in -a :

Singular		Plural
kitaaba	'a writing'	kitabaat
diṛaasa	'an academic discipline'	diṛasaat

2. Those which have broken plurals; the broken plurals in question cannot be predicted with certainty and must therefore be learned as items It is to be noted, however, that the plural of Faʕ L is often Fuʕ uuL and that the plural of FaʕaL is often aFʕaaL :

Singular		Plural
faṛḍ	'an assumption'	fuṛuuḍ
ʕaṛḍ	'an offer'	ʕuṛuuḍ
ʕamal	'a task, a job'	aʕmaal

The concrete verbal nouns of derived triliterals are usually formed by adding the sound feminine plural suffix -aat to the singular form :

Singular		Plural
taṣṛiiɦ	'a permit'	taṣriɦaat
taʕbiir	'an expression	taʕbiṛaat
taʕriif	'a definition'	taʕrifaat
muʔabla	'an interview'	muʔablaat
ɦiwaaṛ	'a discourse'	ɦiwaṛaat
iqṛaaṛ	'an admission'	iqṛaṛaat
iɣṛaaʔ	'an incitement'	iɣṛaʔaat
tamanni	'a wish'	tamanniyyaat
taṭawwuṛ	'a development'	taṭawwuṛaat
tanaaquḍ	'a contradiction'	tanaquḍaat
infigaaṛ	'an explosion'	infigaṛaat
intiqaad	'a criticism'	intiqadaat
iʕtiṛaaf	'a confession'	iʕtiṛafaat

istiʕmaal	'a usage'	istiʕmalaat
istigaaba	'a response'	istigabaat

In addition to the sound plural in -aat, many (though not all) verbal nouns of Measure II triliterals have the broken plural taFaʕiiL :

Singular		Plural	
taṣṛiiɦ	'a permit'	taṣṛiɦaat	taṣaṛiiɦ
taʕbiir	'an expression'	taʕbiṛaat	taʕabiir
taʕriif	'a definition'	taʕrifaat	taʕariif

The plural in -aat and the plural taFaʕiiL are usually interchangeable; sometimes, however, they occur with different designations : thus taʕaliim means 'doctrines, teachings' while taʕliimaat means 'instructions'. Some verbal nouns take one plural but not the other; for example, the plural of tanbiih 'admonition' is tanbihaat but not *tanabiih.

The dual is formed by adding the suffix -een to the singular form :

Singular		Dual
faṛḍ	'an assumption'	faṛḍeen
ʕamal	'a task, a job'	ʕamaleen
kitaaba	'a writing'	kitabteen
diṛaasa	'an academic discipline'	diṛasteen
taṣṛiiɦ	'a permit	taṣṛiɦeen
istiʕmaal	'a usage'	istiʕmaleen
targama	'a translation'	targamteen
etc.		

Concrete verbal nouns from quadriliteral verbs are rare, and of the ones that do occur FaʕLaLa is the most common. The plural of FaʕLaLa is FaʕaaLiL; e.g., targama 'a translation' : taraagim.

*** *** ***

VERBAL NOUNS : SYNTACTIC USAGE

Verbal nouns occur in the slots where other nouns occur; thus a verbal noun may be used as subject of an equational sentence, subject of a verb, object of a verb, object of a preposition, predicate of an equational sentence, the first or second term of a construct phrase, etc.

ilʕamal miš ʕeeb.	'Work is not shameful.'
ittaʕliim yihazzib il?axlaa?.	'Education refines one's character.
ana miš faahim ittaʕbiir da.	'I do not understand this expressic
tiʕibt min lintiẓaaṛ .	'I am tired of waiting.'
ilwiħda ʕibaada.	'Solitude is a form of worship.'
kutr ittikṛaaṛ yiʕallim ilħumaaṛ.	'Much repetition teaches (even) a donkey.'

Verbal Noun as the First Term of a Construct Phrase

A verbal noun may occur as the first term of a construct phrase. In this context, the second member may be the subject or the object of the source sentence. Consider the following :

1. su?uuṭ fariid fillimtiħaan zaʕʕalni. — 'Farid's failing the test upset me.
2. šuṛb ilxamṛa ħaṛaam. — 'Drinking wine is unlawful.'

In sentence 1., the underlined expression is derived from a sentence whose subject is fariid :

fariid sa?aṭ fillimtiħaan. — 'Farid failed the text.'

In sentence 1 , then, the verbal noun su?uuṭ 'failure' is in construct with the subject of the source sentence.

In sentence 2 , the underlined expression is derived from a sentence whose direct object is ilxamṛa :

innaas biyišṛabu lxamṛa. — 'People drink wine.'

In sentence 2 , then, the verbal noun šuṛb 'drinking' is in construct with the direct object of the source sentence.

The source sentence determines not only the construct phrase but also whether certain elements must co-occur with that phrase :

1. If the source sentence contains no direct object, the verbal noun is in construct with the subject :

ʕali nigiḥ. — 'Ali succeeded.'

nagaaḥ ʕali fa̧ŗraḥni. — 'Ali's success pleased me.'

2. If the source sentence contains a single direct object, the transformation is one of the following :

(a) Either the subject or the object is omitted; the constituent which is not omitted becomes the second term of the construct phrase.

(i) fariida b-tiḥtirim ʕali. — 'Farida respects Ali.'

(ii) iḥtiŗaam fariida miš mustaɣŗab. — 'Farida's respect is not surprising.'

(iii) iḥtiŗaam ʕali miš mustaɣŗab. — 'Respecting Ali is not surprising.'

Notice that the construct phrase of (ii) omits the object of the source sentence : iḥtiŗaam fariida 'Farida's respect' does not indicate the recipient of respect; also notice that the construct phrase of (iii) omits the subject of the source sentence : iḥtiŗaam ʕali 'respecting Ali' does not indicate who respects Ali.

It is clear from comparing (ii) and (iii) that phrases like iḥtiŗaam fariida and iḥtiŗaam ʕali would be ambiguous in the absence of the source sentence. When such phrases occur, the context must be relied on to resolve the ambiguity.

(b) Neither the subject nor the object is omitted. The subject becomes the second member of the construct phrase, and the object is optionally preceded by the preposition li- :

samiir akal iggibna. — 'Samir ate the cheese.'

akl samiir iggibna mazaʕʕalniiš. — 'Samir's eating the cheese did not upset me.'

akl samiir liggibna mazaʕʕalniiš. — 'Samir's eating of the cheese did not upset me.'

3. If the source sentence contains two objects, the transformation is one of the following:

(a) No omission takes place. The verbal noun is placed in construct with the subject. The preposition li- is prefixed to the indirect object, and this prepositional phrase is placed after the direct object.

fariid ʕallim ittalamiiz illuɣa lʕaṛabiyya.	'Farid taught the students the Arabic langauge.'
taʕliim fariid illuɣa lʕaṛabiyya littalamiiz ɦaaga masimiʕtiš ʕanha abadan.	'Farid's teaching the Arabic language to the students is something I never heard about.'

(b) Omission is applied to the subject, the direct object, the indirect object, or any two of these :

(i) If only the subject is omitted, the verbal noun enters into construct either with the direct object or with the indirect object. In the first case, the preposition li- is prefixed to the indirect object. In the second case, li- is not used at all.

ʕali ʕallim ittalamiiz illuɣa lʕaṛabiyya.	'Ali taught the students the Arabic language.'
taʕliim illuɣa lʕaṛabiyya littalamiiz šeeʔ kuwayyis.	'Teaching the Arabic language to the students is a good thing.'
taʕliim ittalamiiz illuɣa lʕaṛabiyya šeeʔ kuwayyis.	'Teaching the students the Arabic language is a good thing.'

(ii) if the subject is retained and only one object is omitted, the verbal noun is placed in construct with the subject. The preposition li- optionally added to the retained object (addition being the norm).

ʕali ʕallim ittalamiiz illuɣa lʕaṛabiyya.	'Ali taught the students the Arabic language.'
taʕliim ʕali (li-) lluɣa lʕaṛabiyya šeeʔ gamiil.	'Ali's teaching the Arabic language is a good thing.'
taʕliim ʕali (li-) ttalamiiz šeeʔ gamiil.	'Ali's teaching the students is a good thing.'

(iii) If the subject and one of the objects are omitted, the verbal noun is placed in construct with the retained object.

taʕliim illuɣa lʕaṛabiyya ṣaʕb.	'Teaching the Arabic language is difficult.'
taʕliim ittalamiiz ṣaʕb.	'Teaching the students is difficu

*** *** ***

VOCATIVE PARTICLE

A particle introducing a noun referring to the person addressed. There is one such particle in Egyptian Arabic : /ya/ ~ /a/ 'hey . . .'.

ya mɦammad	'Hey Mohammed!'
ya ɦabiibi	'Dear!'
ya ustaaz	'Mr.!'

*** *** ***

VOICING

Refers to the vibration of the vocal cords or lack thereof during the production of a sound. A voiced consonant is one which is accompanied by vibration of the vocal cords, for example, /v/ in the English word "vine". A voiceless consonant is one which is produced without any accompanying vibration of the vocal cords, for example, /f/ in the English word "fine".

The difference between voicing and voicelessness can be felt strongly if one covers one's ears with one's hands, then pronounces English "fine" and "vine", paying attention to the /f/ and /v/.

EA Voiceless Consonants	EA Voiced Counterparts
p	b
t	d
ṭ	ḍ
k	g
q	-
ʔ	-
f	v
s	z
ṣ	ẓ
š	ž
x	ɣ
ɦ	ʕ
h	-

Voiced consonants / m n l ḷ r ṛ w y /.

*** *** ***

VOWELS

A vowel is a sound produced by unobstructed air passage through the oral cavity.

To produce a vowel sound, the tongue is arched High, Mid or Low in the mouth. The arching of the tongue is either toward the Front of the palate or the Back. Thus, we describe the vowels in terms of these parameters. We can, for example, say that /i/ is a high front vowel.

The position of the lips, whether unrounded as in /i,a/ or rounded as in /u,o/ is also important in describing vowel sounds.

Vowels are voiced; that is, vowels are produced with vibration of the vocal cords.

Egyptian Arabic Vowels

	Short		Long	
	Front	Back	Front	Back
High	i	u	ii	uu
Mid	e	o	ee	oo
Low	a		aa	

Arabic vowels present few difficulties to the learner. They are similar to the English vowels. The short vowels /i,u/ are like English 'hit' and 'put'. /a/ is the vowel of 'cot' next to emphatic consonants, and somewhat like the [a] of 'fat' elsewhere. /e, o/ are not very common. /e/ is pronounced almost like the vowel of English 'bet' and /o/ almost like that of English 'soap'. When short /e,o/ occur, it is sometimes difficult for a non-native speaker to distinguish them from short /i,u/ respectively particularly in rapid speech; e.g. :

bétna	'our house'
bítna	'we spent the night'
ʔóṭṭi	'my room'
ʔúṭṭi	'my cat (m)'

Fortunately, the occurrence of short /e,o/ is not common in Egyptian Arabic.

The long vowels /ii,uu,oo,ee/ are like those in English "feet", "food", "boat" and "bait", respectively. It must be mentioned that long vowels in Arabic are not glided. A glide is a transitional sound produced when the vocal organs shift from the articulation of one sound to the articulation of another sound.

Notes on EA Vowels :

a) In EA, words or utterances never begin with a vowel, whether short or long. In all cases where a student hears what he thinks is an initial vowel, it is always /ʔ/ + vowel.

b) Short vowels occur stressed and unstressed, medially and finally.

c) Long vowels occur only stressed.

d) EA does not permit more than one long vowel in a word; in the case of two long vowels (resulting from morphological suffixation), the first vowel is shortened and stress shifts to the second; e.g. :

/šáalu/ 'they carried' + /-u/ 'it (m)' -->
/šáaluu/ --> /šalúu/ 'they carried it (m)'

*** *** ***

VOWELS : /-a/ + {/-aat/ , /-een/}

Some feminine singular nouns end in /-a/. When the sound plural suffix /-aat/ is added, the /-a/ in question is deleted. When the dual suffix /-een/ is added, the /-a/ in question is replaced by /-t/ unless a sequence of three consonants would result (in which case replacement is by /-it/) :

mudarrisa	'a teacher (f)'
mudarrisaat	'teachers (f)'
mudarristeen	'two teachers (f)'
naẓṛa	'a principal (f)'
naẓṛaat	'principals (f)'
naẓṛiteen	'two principals (f)'

*** *** ***

VOWELS : CONTRACTION

Note the difference between the masculine and feminine forms of the adjective šaaṭir, šaṭra - šaṭriin 'clever'. This difference is the result of the operation of two phonological rules in EA. The first rule states that an unstressed /i/ is elided if it precedes a consonant which is followed by a vowel which may or may not be across a word boundary (symbolize by #) or a morpheme boundary (symbolized +). Another way of stating the Vowel Elision rule is :

$$i \dashrightarrow \emptyset \;/\; \underline{\quad} \; C \; \left(\begin{Bmatrix} \# \\ + \end{Bmatrix}\right) \; V$$

This rule is applied when the feminine morpheme /-a/ is added to the masculine form of the adjective as follows :

šaaṭir + -a --> šaaṭra

A second rule must now be applied in order to produce the feminine form of the adjective as it is actually pronounced. This rule states that a long vowel is shortened if it precedes two consonants, or if it is unstressed. Another way of stating the Vowel Shortening rule is :

$$VV \dashrightarrow V \;/\; \underline{\quad} \begin{Bmatrix} CC \\ C\acute{V} \end{Bmatrix}$$

When the Vowel Shortening rule is applied to the output of the Elision rule the result is the feminine form of the adjective as it is actually pronounced :

šaaṭra --> šaṭra

Other instances of the application of these rules can be seen in the following paradigms :

/bitaaʕ/ in combination with pronominal suffixes :

bitaaʕ	i	bitaʕt	i	bituuʕ	i	my
bitaaʕ	ak	bitaʕt	ak	bituuʕ	ak	your (m)
bitaaʕ	ik	bitaʕt	ik	bituuʕ	ik	your (f)
bitaaʕ	u	bitaʕt	u	bituuʕ	u	his
bitaʕ	ha	bitaʕit	ha	bituʕ	ha	her
bitaʕ	na	bitaʕit	na	bituʕ	na	our
bitaʕ	kum	bitaʕit	kum	bituʕ	kum	your (p)
bitaʕ	hum	bitaʕit	hum	bituʕ	hum	their

Notice the elision of /i/ in /bitaaʕit/ before pronominal suffixes beginning with a vowel. Also note the instances of vowel shortening.

Conjugation of /ʕaaš/ (i) 'to live':

	Perfect	Imperfect	Imperative
huwwa	ʕaaš	biyʕiiš	
hiyya	ʕaašit	bitʕiiš	
humma	ʕaašu	biyʕiišu	
inta	ʕišt	bitʕiiš	ʕiiš
inti	ʕišti	bitʕiiši	ʕiiši
intu	ʕištu	bitʕiišu	ʕiišu
ana	ʕišt	baʕiiš	
iɦna	ʕišna	binʕiiš	

Notice that /ʕaaš-/ is the form used for the third person ms, fs and p in the perfect. /ʕiiš-/ is used with all other persons in the perfect; /ʕiiš-/ in imperfect and imperative forms. Also notice the shortening of /ii/ when a suffix beginning with a consonant is added.

When two long vowels occur in the same word as a result of suffixation, stress is shifted to the final long vowel, and then the Vowel Shortening rule is applied to the first long vowel :

ʔáalu 'they said' + -uh 'it (m)' -->
ʔaalúuh -->
ʔalúuh

*** *** ***

VOWELS : ELISION AT WORD BOUNDARIES TO AVOID VOWEL SEQUENCES

Vowel sequences do not occur in EA.* When deletion of an elidible glottal stop (q.v.) would otherwise result in a sequence of two short vowels, one at the beginning of a word and the other at the end of the preceding word, elision takes place in the manner specified below :

1. The final vowel of the first word is elided if it is /i/.
2. Otherwise, the initial vowel of the second word is elided.

/nifsi/ + /ʔaṛuuɦ/ = [nifsi] + [aṛuuɦ] = [nifs aṛuuɦ] 'I long to go.'

/maʕa/ + /ʔibni/ = [maʕa] + [ibni] = [maʕa bni] 'with my son'

When the deletion of an elidible glottal stop would otherwise result in two adjacent vowels of which one is long and the other is short, the short vowel is elided :

/šafuu/ + /ʔimbaariɦ/ = [šafuu] + [imbaariɦ] = [šafuu mbaariɦ]
'they saw him yesterday'

/šufnaa/ + /ʔimbaariɦ/ = [šufnaa] + [imbaariɦ] = [šufnaa mbaariɦ]
'we saw him yesterday'

/šuftii/ + /ʔimbaariɦ/ = [šuftii] + [imbaariɦ] = [šuftii mbaariɦ]
'you (fs) saw him yesterday'

* In this book, each of the symbols aa, ii and uu stands for a single long vowel rather than a sequence of vowels. (Other systems of transcription use ā, ī and ū to represent the long vowels of EA.)

*** *** ***

VOWELS : ELISION OF /i/ AND /u/ FROM WORD-FINAL $-C^{i}_{u}C$

If unstressed, the vowel of the word-final sequence $-C^{i}_{u}C$ is elided in two situations :

1. When the sequence is pronounced in close associaiton with a following word which begins with a vowel :

/madaaris/ + /ilɦukuuma/ = [madars ilɦukuuma] 'public schools'

2. When the sequence is followed by a prefix which begins with or con-

sists of a vowel :

/waa?if/ + /-iin/ = [wa?fiin] 'standing (p)'

/faahim/ + /-a/ = [fahma] 'understands (fs)'

The elision in question does not take place when it would result in a cluster of three consonants (such a cluster is not permissible in EA) :

/yimsik/ + /ilkitaab/ = [yimsik ilkitaab] 'he holds the book'

/yimsik/ + /-u/ = [yimsiku] 'he holds it (m)'

*** *** ***

VOWELS : ELISION OF /i/ AND /u/ FROM WORD-INITIAL $C_{u}^{i}C$-

If unstressed, the vowel of the word-initial sequence $C_{u}^{i}C$- is elided in two situations :

1. When the sequence is pronounced in close association with a preceding word which ends in a vowel :

/inta/ + /bitidris/ = [inta btidris] 'you (ms) study'

2. When the sequence is preceded by a prefix which ends in a vowel :

/ɦa-/ + /tikallimu/ = [ɦatkallimu] 'she will talk to him'

The elision in question does not take place if it would result in a cluster of three consonants (such a cluster is not permissible in EA):

/inta/ + /bitṛuuɦ/ = [inta bitṛuuɦ] 'you (ms) go'

/ɦa-/ + /tiktibu/ = [ɦatiktibu] 'she will write it (m)'

*** *** ***

VOWELS : EXTRA

Consonant clusters in EA comprise no more than two segments. When a sequence of three consonants would otherwise occur, a vowel is added between the second and the third consonants; this is true not only in the individual word, but across word boundaries as well.

1. When, in a sequence of two words, the first word ends in two consonants

and the second begins with a consonant, a vowel is added to the end of the first word; the vowel is a variant of /i/ which is usually shorter and more lax than the other variants. In the following example, the extra vowel is represented by a raised i :

/šuft/	'I saw'
/ṛaagil/	'a man'
[šuft^i ṛaagil]	'I saw a man.'

Notice the difference in pronunciation between [šuft^i ṛaagil] 'I saw a man' and [šufti ṛaagil] 'You (fs) saw a man': the final vowel of [šuft^i] is pronounced as a shorter and more lax sound than the final vowel of [šufti]. The raised i is often referred to as the helping vowel.

Since its graphic representation is totally redundant, the helping vowel is not, as a rule, indicated by the script.

2. When the addition of a suffix to a word would otherwise result in a sequence of more than two consonants, a vowel is inserted between the second and the third consonants. The vowel in question is /u/ before /-hum/ 'them' and /-kum/ 'you (p)', /a/ before /-ha/ 'her', and /i/ otherwise. This extra vowel is stressed if required by the stress rules. Illustrations :

/kalb/	'dog'	/gibt/	'I brought'
[kalbúhum]	'their dog'	[gibtúhum]	'I brought them'
[kalbúkum]	'your (p) dog'	[gibtúkum]	'I brought you (p)'
[kalbáha]	'her dog'	[gibtáha]	'I brought her'
[kalbína]	'our dog'	[gibtílu]	'I brought (something) for h

/kalt/	'I ate'	/ʕadd/	'he counted'
[ma-kalti-š]	'I did not eat'	[ma-ʕaddi-š]	'he did not count'

Statement 2. above has the following exception : when a suffix which begins with or consists of a consonant and which marks agreement with the subject is added to a doubled verb stem, /ee/ is inserted before the suffix :

/sabb/	'he cursed'
/sabbeet/	'I cursed'
/sabbeena/	'we cursed'

*** *** ***

VOWELS : LENGTHENING OF SHORT VOWELS

The final vowel of a form is lengthened when that form receives a suffix beginning with or consisting of a consonant :

istanna	'he waited'
istannaani	'he waited for me'
fi	'in'
fiik	'in you'
maʕna	'meaning'
maʕnaaha	'its meaning'
daʕa	'he invited'
madaʕaaš	'he did not invite'

The major exceptions to this rule are listed below :

1. Feminine singular nouns ending in /a/ when they enter into construct with a pronominal suffix. In this context, the /a/ is replaced by /-it/.

madrasa	'school'
madrasit-na	'our school'

2. The preposition ʕala 'on' when combined with any pronominal suffix :

ʕalay-ya	'on me'
ʕalee-na	'on us'
ʕalee-k	'on you (ms)'
ʕalee-ki	'on you (fs)'
ʕalee-kum	'on you (p)'
ʕalee-h	'on him'
ʕalee-ha	'on her'
ʕalee-hum	'on them'

3. Prepositions ending in /i/ when combined with the pronominal suffix -ya 'me'; e.g., the prepositions fi 'in', bi- 'by means of', and li- 'for' are combined with -ya in the following manner :

fiy-ya
biy-ya
liy-ya

4. Verb forms ending in /i/ or /a/ when combined with an agreement suffix. In this context, a verb-final /i/ is either lengthened or replaced by /ee/, while a verb-final /a/ is replaced by /ee/. The verbs nisi 'to forget' and daʕa 'to invite' may be used as examples :

(ana)	nisii-t	nisee-t	daʕee-t
(iħna)	nisii-na	nisee-na	daʕee-na
(inta)	nisii-t	nisee-t	daʕee-t
(inti)	nisii-ti	nisee-ti	daʕee-ti

*** *** ***

VOWELS : REPLACEMENT OF -a IN NOUN CONSTRUCTS

Many feminine singular nouns end in -a. When such nouns enter into construct with a following form, the final -a is replaced by -t unless a sequence of three consonants would result (in which case replacement is by -it) :

maktaba	'a library'
maktabt iggamʕa	'the university library'
maktabit gamʕitna	'our university library'
saaʕa	'a watch'
saʕti	'my watch'
saʕitna	'our watch'
saaʕit ʕali	'Ali's watch'

*** *** ***

VOWELS : SHORTENING OF LONG VOWELS

In general, a long vowel does not occur (a) before two consonants which are not separated or preceded by a break in speech, (b) prior to another long vowel in the same word, or (c) unstressed. Therefore, /ii/ and /ee/ are replaced by /i/, /uu/ and /oo/ are replaced by /u/, and /aa/ is replaced by /a/ in the following situations :

1. When the addition of a suffix would cause the long vowel in question to occur before a cluster of two consonants :

/yigiib/	'he brings'
[yigibha]	'he brings her'
/beet/	'house'
[bitha]	'her house'
/ʕuyuun/	'eyes'
[ʕuyunhum]	'their eyes'
/fooʔ/	'above'
[fuʔna]	'above us'
/gaab/	'he brought'
[gabni]	'he brought me'

2. When two consecutive words are pronounced in close association, provided that (a) the first word ends in -VVC and the second word begins with C-, or provided that (b) the first word ends in -VV and the second word begins with CC- :

/maṛiiḍ/	'sick'
[maṛiḍ xaaliṣ]	'very sick'
/saʕteen/	'two hours'
[saʕtɪn wi nuṣṣ]	'two hours and a half'
/magnuun/	'crazy'
[magnún rasmi]	'unquestionably crazy'
/koom/	'a pile'
[kum baṣal]	'a pile of onions'
/igtimaaʕ/	'a meeting'
[igtimaʕ muhimm]	'an important meeting'
/ɦayibnii/	'he will build it'
[ɦayibnɪ fmaṣṛ]	'He will build it in Egypt.'
/riglee/	'his legs'
[riglɪ btirtiʕš̌]	'His legs are shaking.'

/ḥaṭṭuu/	'they put it'
[ḥaṭṭu fdurg]	'They put it in a drawer.'
/banaa/	'he built it'
[bana mbaariḥ]	'He built it yesterday.'

3. When an affix containing a long vowel is added, since an EA word is usually pronounced with one and only one long vowel :

/miil/	'a mile'
[mileen]	'two miles'
/beet/	'a house'
[biteen]	'two houses'
/magnuun/	'crazy (ms)'
[magnuniin]	'crazy (p)'
/koom/	'a pile'
[kumeen]	'two piles'

4. When the addition of a suffix shifts the stress away from the long vowel in question :

/ḥíila/	'a trick'
[ḥilítha]	'her trick'
/béeḍa/	'an egg'
[biḍítha]	'her egg'
/ṣúuṛa/	'a picture'
[ṣuṛítna]	'our picture'
/kóoṛa/	'a ball'
[kuṛíthum]	'their ball'
/diyáana/	'a religion'
[diyaníthum]	'their religion'

Standard Arabic has a sound system which differs in many ways from the sound system of EA. Consequently, many Standard Arabic words do not conform to the above rules. When such words are borrowed into EA, their Standard pronunciation may be altered to achieve conformity with the EA rules. Alternatively, those words may retain the Standard pronunciation

in spite of the EA rules. The first option is commonly exercised in in-
formal situations, while the second is commonly exercised in formal or
semiformal situations. The following are some examples :

Informal Pronunciation		Formal or Semiformal Pronunciation
xaṣṣa	'special (f)'	xaaṣṣa
isaʔaat	'insults'	isaaʔaat
niqabaat	'unions'	niqaabaat
isaʔíthum	'their insult'	isaaʔíthum

Since it is completely predictable, the shortening discussed above does
not have to be indicated in the script.

*** *** ***

- W -

WORD STRUCTURE

The Arab grammarians use the root /FʕL/ فعل 'to do' to describe the various noun or verb patterns (q.v.). This designation and symbolization of word structure is followed in every grammar of Classical or Modern Standard Arabic. In applying this to Egyptian Arabic it is seen that the active participle (See: Participles) of the Measure I (q.v.) verb /katab/ 'to write' which is /kaatib/ 'writer, writing' is said to be of the /FaaʕiL/ pattern. Likewise, the verbal noun (q.v.) of the Measure II (q.v.) verb /baddal/ 'to change' is /tabdiil/ 'changing' which is said to be of the /taFʕiiL/ pattern.

*** *** ***

WRITING SYSTEM

Standard Arabic is written and read from right to left. There are twenty-eight letters (or twenty-nine if we count the hamzah /•/, glottal stop) in the alphabet, of which three are used for the vowels, /a,u,i/. The unconnected letters differ in form from the connected ones which, in turn, may vary in form, depending on whether they are initial, medial or final. Arabic dialects (whether Eastern, e.g., Egyptian and Lebanese, or Western, e.g., Moroccan) may be written in this alphabet. It should be noted that the written script differs to some extent from the printed. There is a substantial difference between the Western and

Eastern handwriting which makes it somewhat difficult for some Eastern Arabs to read Western manuscripts. There used to be slight differences between the Eastern and Western printed forms, e.g., the place and number of the dots in the letters that represent /f/ and /q/, e.g.,

Written and printed Eastern Arabic have :

ف /f/ ق /q/ ;

Written and printed Western Arabic had :

ف ~ ڢ /f/ ق ~ ف /q/.

Now, however, both Eastern and Western Arabic printers use the same letter type for the printing of Modern Standard Arabic. Also, Western handwriting is tending towards a greater conformity with the Eastern style.

*** *** ***

INDEX

BIBLIOGRAPHY

Abdel-Malek, Zaki N. The Closed-List Classes of Colloquial Egyptian Arabic, The Hague: Mouton, 1972.

Abdel-Malek, Zaki N. Numerals in Colloquial Egyptian Arabic, unpub. M.A. thesis, Georgetown University, 1964.

Abdel-Massih, Ernest T. Advanced Moroccan Arabic, Center for Near Eastern and North African Studies, University of Michigan, 1974.

Abdel-Massih, Ernest T. An Introduction to Egyptian Arabic, Center for Near Eastern and North African Studies, University of Michigan, 1975.

Abdel-Massih, Ernest T. An Introduction to Moroccan Arabic, Center for Near Eastern and North African Studies, University of Michigan, 1973

Harrell, Richard S., Laila Y. Tewfik and George D. Selim. Lessons in Colloquial Egyptian Arabic, Revised Edition, Georgetown University, 1963.

Mitchell, T. F. Colloquial Arabic: The Living Language of Egypt, London, 1962.

Wise, Hilary. A Transformational Grammar of Spoken Egyptian Arabic, Oxford, 1975.

Wright, William (trans.). A Grammar of the Arabic Language, Cambridge, 1964.